HERETIC BLOOD

ALSO BY MICHAEL W. HIGGINS

CO-AUTHORED WITH DOUGLAS R. LETSON

Portraits of Canadian Catholicism

*My Father's Business: A Biography of
His Eminence G. Emmett Cardinal Carter*

The Jesuit Mystique

CO-EDITED WITH DOUGLAS R. LETSON

Women and the Church: A Sourcebook

CO-EDITED WITH DONALD GRAYSTON

Thomas Merton: Pilgrim in Process

SCRIPTS FOR THE CANADIAN BROADCASTING
CORPORATION (CBC ENTERPRISES) INCLUDE:

*Gilbert Keith Chesterton vs. George Bernard Shaw:
On Sex, Socialism and Salvation*

*On Fossils, Apes and Angels: A Reconstruction of
the Celebrated Debate on Evolution Between Thomas
Henry Huxley and Bishop Samuel ("Soapy") Wilberforce*

HERETIC BLOOD

The Spiritual Geography of Thomas Merton

Michael W. Higgins

We acknowledge for their financial support
of our publishing program the Government
of Canada through the Book Publishing
Industry Development Program (BPIDP).

Published in 1998 by Stoddart Publishing Co. Limited
34 Lesmill Road, Toronto, Canada M3B 2T6
180 Varick Street, 9th Floor, New York, New York 10014

Distributed in Canada by:
General Distribution Services Ltd.
325 Humber College Blvd., Toronto, Ontario M9W 7C3
Tel. (416) 213-1919   Fax (416) 213-1917
Email customer.service@ccmailgw.genpub.com

02 01 00 99 98   1   2   3   4   5

CANADIAN CATALOGUING IN PUBLICATION DATA

Higgins, Michael W.
Heretic blood : the spiritual geography of Thomas Merton

ISBN 0-7737-3132-6

1. Merton, Thomas, 1915–1968. 2. Trappists —
United States — Biography   I. Title.

BX4705.M542H53 1998   271'.12502   C98-931778-1

Cover design: Angel Guerra
Text imaging: ECW Type and Art, Oakville, Ontario

Printed and bound in Canada

*We gratefully acknowledge the Canada Council for the Arts and
the Ontario Arts Council for their support of our publishing program.*

Pages 305 and 306 constitute a continuation of this copyright page.

*To the memory of two friends
who died while this
book was being written:
Allan MacNeil, priest,
and Bob Daggy, scholar*

CONTENTS

Acknowledgements

This work could not have been written without the inspiration and enthusiasm of Bernie Lucht, executive producer of the Canadian Broadcasting Corporation's *Ideas* series, without the keen and critical eye of my sharpest editor, my wife Krystyna, and without the support and aggressive encouragement of my friends and colleagues J.S. Porter, Bruce Powe, Charlene Diehl-Jones, Gary Draper, Alfred Kunz, and Peter Togni. In addition, Brent Charrette, Rebecca Higgins, Becky Thompson, and Alice Carroll were of considerable help in undertaking several duties related to the writing of the book.

I wish also to acknowledge the generosity of time provided by numerous people interviewed, the generosity of spirit exhibited by the faculty and staff of St. Jerome's University, and the generosity of patience manifested by Stoddart Publishing and structural editor David Kilgour and copy editor Doris Cowan.

Some of the material incorporated in this book appeared in different form in earlier publications, principally "The Making and Remaking: The Many Masks of Thomas Merton," originally the Michael Keenan Memorial Lecture, delivered at St. Thomas More College, University of Saskatchewan, in 1988, and subsequently published in *The Canadian Catholic Review*; "Window, Tower and Circle: The Wandering Monk and the Quest for Integration," which appeared in *Thomas Merton: Pilgrim in Process*, which I wrote and edited with Donald

Grayston and was published in 1983 by Griffin House; and two articles published in *The American Benedictine Review*: "A Study of the Influence of William Blake on Thomas Merton" (1974) and "Monasticism as Rebellion: Blakean Roots of Merton's Thought" (1988). Also integrated into this text is some material used in the two CBC *Ideas* series on Thomas Merton that I researched, wrote, and narrated: *Thomas Merton: Extraordinary Man* (1978) and *Heretic Blood* (1998).

Interviews conducted for this book as primary research are listed separately and are not endnoted.

HERETIC BLOOD

Introduction

There is deeply heretic blood in me. . . .
— *Michael Field in a letter to John Gray (1906)*

DANIEL BERRIGAN, the Jesuit poet and celebrated peace activist, sat silent for several moments after I asked him what
impact the death of his friend Thomas Merton had had on him.
When he spoke, his words had a measured cadence; it was as
if by talking about it he could recreate, however fleetingly, that
time of dread. He observed simply that on December 10, 1968,
he "lost the will or the emotional capacity (a block really, in
being) to speak publicly about Tom, our friendship, any aspect
of his life." It was a time of judgement and despair.
  Many people besides Berrigan were affected by the startling
reality of Merton's death. And what a death. Having concluded
his talk on "Marxism and Monastic Perspectives," delivered
to an international gathering of male and female contemplatives in Bangkok, Thailand, Merton retired to his room,
took a shower, stepped out with wet feet onto a terrazzo floor,
moved a fan over to his pallet and as a result of its faulty
wiring, electrocuted himself. These are the bald facts; theories

abound; rumours of conspiracy are rife. Dead by his own hand? A clever assassination strategy executed by the CIA? A clumsy murder?

In all likelihood Merton's death was what it appeared to be: accidental electrocution. God's charged humour. Some of the details are fuzzy, and no autopsy was performed. His death was dramatic and puzzling. It was, as the poet and critic J.S. Porter called it:

> A frugal death: one Timex watch, in the estimation of the Bangkok police worth ten dollars. The other items — one pair dark glasses in tortoise frames, two pairs bifocal eye-glasses in plastic frames, two Cistercian leather bound breviaries, one Rosary (broken), one small icon on wood of Virgin and Child — all judged to be nil in material value.[1]

And so the life of the twentieth century's most eloquent and accessible spiritual figure came to an end, a bizarre leave-taking, full of meaning, and wildly funny. Vintage Merton!

By the time of his death, Thomas Merton, born in France, a citizen of the United States, and a monk for twenty-seven years in the Trappist Abbey of Our Lady of Gethsemani in Kentucky, had an international following of enviable proportions, a publication record of staggering range, and an influence by no means limited to the Catholic world. Merton was, and remains, a phenomenon, an utterly engaging figure, controversial, iconic, the paradigmatic monk for our century.

Since his death he has been the subject of hundreds of theses and dissertations, countless essays and reviews, and dozens of studies and biographies. His life and thought have been the subject of radio and television documentaries; songs have been composed and dances choreographed, inspired by his poetry and performed internationally; and there have been numerous learned and popular conferences and workshops on his life, work, and spirituality. In short, there is a veritable Merton industry.

Berrigan speaks of him as a "baptized Picasso," his numerous writings mere "rivulets of the Mississippi" that was his creative and spiritual genius. Scores of memoirs, tributes, and biographies have been written, all attempting the Promethean task of disclosing the essential Merton. But Merton continues to defy neat classification; he teases the scholar and the commentator by forever shifting, revising, and reconfiguring:

> I am aware of the need for constant self-revision and growth, leaving behind the renunciations of yesterday and yet in continuity with all my yesterdays. For to cling to the past is to lose one's continuity with the past, since this means clinging to what is no longer there.
>
> My ideas are always changing, always moving around one center, and I am always seeing that center from somewhere else.
>
> Hence, I will always be accused of inconsistency. But I will no longer be there to hear the accusation.[2]

He was an insatiable wanderer. Merton's many peregrinations can easily be mapped but not so easily interpreted. The reader needs the key to his spiritual geography and that key, if you like, is William Blake. Artistically, spiritually, and intellectually, Merton laboured to achieve for his own time something of that visionary imagination of Blake in which, as Peter Ackroyd puts it, "there is no birth and no death, no beginning and no end, only the perpetual pilgrimage within time towards eternity."[3] Blake was the arch-rebel, provoking the establishment of his day and defying all convention with his madly experimental art and poetry. In a letter to the Polish Nobel

laureate Czeslaw Milosz, Merton wrote of Blake, the uncompromising seer:

> we all have our game with Caesar, the Little Father who is
> no longer human and who therefore *ought* to be cheated, in
> the name of humanity. I have been reading William Blake
> again. His reply to Caesar seems like psychosis, but it is
> valid and consistent and prophetic . . .[4]

Merton's "Caesar" or "Little Father" is Blake's Nobodaddy
or Urizen, figures that embody constriction of vision, the
narrowing of the senses, and diminished humanity. Blake's
"heretic blood" courses through Merton's veins. As a poet, and
as a monk, Merton understood his task to be nothing short of
the Blakean undertaking to reintegrate shattered humanity.

Simply put: Thomas Merton is the William Blake of our
time. He was engaged in the same kind of spiritual and intellectual tasks: the critiquing of a dehumanizing culture; the
subverting of conventional modes of perception; the radical
re-visioning of human destiny; the liberating of our senses from
the shackles of constrictive reason; the commingling of the
imaginative arts.

Like Blake, Merton was a social critic, a poet, a visual artist,
an outsider, the consummate rebel. And, like Blake he was
largely misunderstood by his contemporaries, his ideas and his
art sanitized for general consumption.

We forget that Merton had "deeply heretic blood" in him.

Merton saw in Blake's tenacity of vision the validation of his
own resistance to soul-numbing conformity. He knew that
"one's song is forced at times to become scandalous and even
incomprehensible."[5] The rebellious heart, "heretic blood," is
not out of place in the makeup of a poet. But in the makeup of
a monk? And Merton was very much the monk. His monastic

life was characterized by both the tragic and the salutary, precisely because it was a life lived with ruthless honesty. Becoming a monk of the Abbey of Gethsemani did not bring an end to his restless yearnings, though his vow of stability would severely limit his physical travels for many years, and he realized quite early on that the easy confidence and comforting security that had initially attracted him to Trappist life on the eve of U.S. involvement in the Second World War would over the years give way to something far more difficult and demanding, profoundly tempered by his spiritual temerity.

In letters to Berrigan, for instance, he could and often did give blunt expression to his feelings, with no regard for the proprieties and norms that define a traditional correspondence between two clerics. He knew what the monastic life could be, and he knew what it often was, and the chasm between the two, so frequently the result of impoverished imaginations and unholy dread, could drive him to distraction. On June 25, 1963, he wrote to Berrigan:

> Obviously the monastic life is nothing if it does not open a man wide to the Holy Spirit. In actual fact, the head-in-the-ground type of monk is usually in practice the most damnable fascist you ever saw. This was true of Solesmes and of Maria Laach: the one was Action Française and the other Pro-Hitler, so I am told.
>
> In a word, it is all right for the monk to break his ass putting out packages of cheese and making a pile of money for the old monastery, but as to doing anything that is *really* fruitful for the Church, that is another matter altogether.[6]

Merton's quite palpable annoyance with institutional monasticism, as expressed in this letter to Berrigan, suggests that those who portray him as the *enfant terrible* of contemporary contemplatives are not wrong. But he was much more than a spiritual malcontent or renegade monk (it is not insignificant to note in this regard his attraction to both Rabelais and Villon). Merton was an apologist for both the anchoritic (hermit) and the cenobitic (communal) forms of monastic life, and an advocate for a revivified monasticism. To that end he worked assiduously to recover the ancient voices, to reappropriate for a new generation the thought and spirituality of the fourth-century Desert Fathers, as well as the great Cistercian Fathers, such as Guerric of Igny, Stephen Harding, Ailred of Rievaulx, and Bernard of Clairvaux.

He also knew that many of the ideas he brought with him to Gethsemani in 1941 were false. In a letter written to Dom Francis Decroix, abbot of the Cistercian monastery of Frattocchie, and dated August 21, 1967, Merton included "a message of contemplatives to the world" written at the behest of Pope Paul vi, long an ardent Merton admirer. It is a worthy summary of his thinking on the monastic ideal: "The contemplative life is . . . search for peace not in an abstract exclusion of all outside reality, not in a barren negative closing of the senses upon the world, but in the openness of love."[7] Blake would have said no less.

During his twenty-seven years as a monk, Merton explored the various types and expressions of monkhood. In 1948 his autobiography, *The Seven Storey Mountain*, was published, and its staggering popularity (six months on the *New York Times* bestseller list) made Merton an icon. His sudden yet enduring fame was partly of his own making and partly a consequence of his publishing success, yet as he was to discover, the life of the monk as icon was a mode of incarceration; his authentic self became the first victim of his celebrity status. The more he wrote about traditional monastic structures and spirituality, the more dissatisfied he became. He longed to leave Gethsemani for more rigorous and primitive forms of monastic heroism. He met resistance at every level.

There were occasions when the sombre prospect of a spiritual *auto-da-fé* must have seemed only too real, when the solitary walk to the spiritual stake was a moral imperative. Merton's mounting disquiet over the insufficiency of the cenobitic structures to ensure the kind of solitude and silence he felt called to, and his barely concealed outrage at the institutional intransigence of contemporary monasticism, clearly meant that his very identity was being reshaped, that in sharp contrast to his first monastic years in the 1940s and early 1950s, Merton's perduring struggle to know the true self would be increasingly defined less in terms of a conflict between the monastery and the world and more in terms of a conflict between the monastery and the monk.

In a letter dated July 18, 1967, to his friend and fellow monk the Benedictine scholar Jean Leclercq, Merton laments the setting in of spiritual rot both in American society at large and in the community at Gethsemani particularly:

> there is a stink of decay, not the decay of oldness, the enfeeblement of something past its prime: but rather a splendid cancerous fullness that shines with a kind of health, a richness and a flowering of something overgrown, overdeveloped, and lacking in basic intelligence, above all in living wisdom.[8]

The struggle for a "living wisdom" occupied the last decade of Merton's life, a struggle that would engage him in battles internal and external. He would pursue with unstanchable zeal the recovery of what he called "archaic wisdom"; he would, in the manner of Blake, "assist once again at the marriage of heaven and hell." Merton would become more and more the satirist, a writer with a genius for parody, the supreme "anti-poet" in English. He would become a modern Erasmus. In a 1964 diary entry he defended the great sixteenth-century Dutch church reformer, scourge of decadent monasticism, and humanist against the narrowness of his critics, but one senses clearly that Merton could just as easily be defending himself:

> He is a splendid writer and to my mind a deeply pious one. And his satires: are they after all too bitter or too extreme?
>
> One feels that his Catholic critics almost begrudge his fidelity to the Church; as if to satisfy them, Erasmus ought to have apostatized and given them an open-and-shut case against him!
>
> Always the same old narrowness: the Church is regarded as "pure" in the sense of "exclusive" — always excluding what is good but *not quite good enough!* Unfortunately, Erasmus *is* "good enough" still, even by their standards. And they bemoan it.[9]

Merton as an Erasminian critic denounced the inadequacies of an increasingly moribund institutional monasticism; he denounced the obsessive power politics of scheming prelates and abbots; he denounced the corporate mentality of Wall Street, the hegemony of U.S. mass culture, the contempt of genuine human freedom in American society; and he denounced the false superiority of Western civilization. Not surprisingly, there were many who in turn denounced him.

On the margins of society, a "guilty bystander," Merton needed the sustenance provided by monastic living in order to articulate an alternative to the mad rush of unreason that he saw as the premier mark of his time. No longer capable in his mature years as a monk of withdrawing from the concerns of humanity, he nonetheless found himself drawn increasingly to the solitary life of the hermit. Merton's life was fraught with contradictions, polarities, and wild paradoxes. He knew that wholeness or holiness, "final integration," would be achieved only through the careful balancing of what Blake called "the Contraries," of the "complementarity of opposites," the "marriage of heaven and hell." Psychological and spiritual health come *not* from the elimination of the tension, the creative polarities, but in their artful juxtaposition and harmony.

Merton was an "extraterritorial" writer, of the kind defined by the critic George Steiner as "unhoused," and "not thoroughly at home in the language of his production, but displaced or hesitant at the frontier."[10] Although Steiner is speaking specifically of being linguistically "unhoused" and has in mind such modern writers as Beckett, Nabokov, and Borges, metaphorically the designation of Merton as an "extraterritorial" and "unhoused" writer applies perfectly. His experimentation with "antipoetry," the extremes of parody, constitutes his linguistic displacement in American culture. In addition, Merton remains uncontained by boundaries — national, ethnic, or religious — exploring freely where he likes, mapping the contours of his own spiritual geography. Merton, in his writing and in his life, appeals to the ever-increasing multitude Milosz calls the "homeless religious minds" of this century and the next. His appeal is to be found in his frontier spirit, his "heretic blood."

In the early 1960s Merton observed in a letter to his friend Victor Hammer, an artist, that it is

> only the pseudo-saints that are oppressive. The real ones, from what I have read, are exceedingly lively. Of course, canonization manages to wash all the liveliness out of them and reduce them to safe limits, so that the *bien pensants* will not be disturbed.[11]

Merton is no pseudo-saint, nor is he likely to be canonized. He is the consummate post-modern holy one: flawed, anti-institutional, a voice for the voiceless. But he is also a classical traditionalist: centred, obedient, in search of stability.

In a brief diary entry dated June 1, 1960, Merton noted the following of his Russian friend and fellow writer Boris Pasternak: "Pasternak died Monday. His story is finished. It now remains to be understood."[12]

Thomas Merton deserves no less. *Heretic Blood* is my attempt to understand his story.

My exploration of Merton's life and work is based on Blake's Four-Fold Vision: Intellect (Urizen), Emotion (Luvah), Instinct (Tharmas), and Wisdom (Urthona), a "geography" of the spirit and of the imagination. As you will discover, Merton used Thomas Aquinas to understand Blake and I, in turn, have used Blake to understand Merton. A fearful symmetry.

Heretic Blood is designed to be an interpretation of a life, a primer for those eager to know more about Merton but intimidated by the sheer volume of his writings — journals, essays, letters, at least a thousand pages of poetry, and fifty-odd books. It is conceived as a guide to his life and thought: not a full-scale biography (though chapter one offers a quick sketch of Merton's life), but an interpretation of *the* towering spiritual figure of the century, sifted through the prism of Blake's typology. It is time, on the eve of a new century, for a fresh, even if unconventional, assessment of Merton, monk and poet.

Michael W. Higgins
Waterloo, Ontario, May 1998

1

THE PILGRIM

THE TRAVEL WRITER BRUCE CHATWIN argued that people are at their most sane and contented when journeying. He observed that as a general rule of biology, migratory species are less aggressive and more egalitarian than their sedentary, home-hugging counterparts.

> There is one obvious reason why this should be so. The migration itself, like the pilgrimage, is the hard journey: a "leveller" on which the "fit" survive and stragglers fall by the wayside.[1]

The twentieth-century monk Thomas Merton would perfectly appreciate Chatwin's analysis as it applied to his own condition: a perpetual wanderer and seeker of origins. Merton regarded humanity as instinctive wanderers. He saw the spiritual journey or pilgrimage as a metaphorical *peregrinatio* or "going forth into strange countries." He himself undertook the

hardest of journeys, and as a consequence became by the time
of his death the most spiritually fit of his age.

In his fifty-three years of earthly life Merton was not unac-
customed to journeys. He took many of them, from France to
England, from Long Island to Bermuda, from Cambridge to
Columbia University, from New York to Havana, culminating
in the journey that brought him from St. Bonaventure's University in Olean in the state of New York to the Abbey of Our
Lady of Gethsemani in the state of Kentucky. What inspired
these journeys was no doubt a combination of emotional restlessness, intellectual curiosity, and spiritual longing; even
when Merton had presumably found, in the Trappist vow of
stability, palliative for his disquiet, he yearned still for the
wisdom of the rimpoche and the insight of the lama, prompting
one final journey to the East.

To begin at the beginning: the First World War was in progress
when Merton began his first life on January 31, 1915, in Prades,
France. He was the elder of two boys, the son of an American,
Ruth Jenkins, and a New Zealander, Owen Merton. The Second World War was in progress when he began his second life
on December 10, 1941, in Trappist, Kentucky. He entered
the Order of Cistercians of the Strict Observance (ocso) at the
Abbey of Our Lady of Gethsemani. He began his third life,
the nature of which I will leave to the speculations of theologians, on December 10, 1968, in Bangkok, Thailand.

Merton was even born en route. His parents were both artists and they succeeded in conveying to him something of
the integrity and respect of the artist's vision of things. Of
his father in particular, Merton noted the parallels with
Paul Cézanne. Owen painted like the nineteenth-century
French artist and possessed a vision of the world that was
"sane, full of balance, full of veneration for structure, for
the relations of masses and for all the circumstances that

impress an individual identity on each created thing."²

Owen was (in the words of one of Merton's biographers, Michael Mott) "a painter of great promise up to the age of nineteen, at which point he seems to have slowed down." Certainly Owen had an unsteady, though romantic, start in life. He met Thomas Merton's mother at an art school in Paris, and after they married they moved to the small Pyrénées town of Prades, a site where Owen could indulge his love for the life of the French peasant and make a living from the tourist trade. War interceded. The tourists stopped coming and the peasants were conscripted. Ruth was drawn to the Quaker tradition of pacificism and persuaded Owen, possibly against his better judgement, not to join the French forces in the war effort. This stance was not appreciated by the New Zealand side of the family.

Merton's mother was a strong person and she left her stamp on young Tom at the very beginning. As Michael Mott observes:

> Thomas Merton's earliest memories were of his mother writing down everything that he did in a book. The record, the long record of Thomas Merton, begins with his *first* biographer, his mother, Ruth Jenkins. And the fact that everything he did was worthy of writing down, I think, had a profound influence on his life. Without playing the game of pop psychology, I think you can see Merton's autobiographical impulse growing out of his mother's attention to his singularity. Throughout his life he was certainly convinced that everything that he did was of sufficient importance to write down. All his life. He was fascinated by himself. Sometimes that brought an acute self-consciousness, a sharp egotism, but it also sharpened his memory. I have one bit in my biography, *The Seven Mountains of*

Thomas Merton, where I show how Merton was able to reconstruct from memory, about seven years after it happened, a bus trip that he had taken in England going from home to school, with every shop and important sight recorded. I don't know many of us who have that kind of memory whereby we can reconstruct whole streets — buildings, shop signs, and the rest — seven years after we've left the location.

One other thing that I think is very important about Ruth's influence on her son can be found emerging from her skill as a decorator. She was persuaded of the extreme importance of place or environment in shaping our lives. To that end she worked very hard, even though they had no money at all in Prades, to make the little room in which Tom was living as "right" as it could be. She would do this later when they were even in more straitened circumstances. The importance of place in his life he clearly inherited from Ruth.

His parents also managed to convey that need and taste for creative mobility that in other circles might be called instability. In 1916, barely a year after his birth, the family moved to the United States, living variously in Maryland and New York. Eventually the Mertons settled in Douglaston, Long Island, with Ruth's family. This was not a happy situation for Owen. He was a proud man, determined to keep his family fed and housed. Tension arose between Owen and Ruth's father, the formidably practical "Pop" Jenkins, who had made a small fortune in films, book publishing, and sales. Owen and Ruth moved to a "little shack of a place." On November 2, 1918, John Paul Merton was born. Tom's unassailable primacy of place in his mother's affections was at an end. In three years she would be dead. It would take him a lifetime to come to

terms with her death. Mott does not underestimate the powerful effect her death had on the impressionable Tom:

> Merton is still reeling from what must have appeared as the
> wilful withdrawing of his mother's affections following
> the birth of his brother and rival, John Paul, when she gets
> ill and leaves home. She was admitted to a public hospital
> with stomach cancer. And once again we are reminded of
> Owen's precarious financial state. It is a public and not a
> private hospital, although her parents stepped in to provide
> support for the funeral and burial.
>
> Although he visited Ruth frequently, Owen takes Tom to
> see his mother, I believe, only once. And then one day Owen
> comes back from the hospital with a letter to Tom from his
> mother saying goodbye and telling him that she will never
> see him again. He goes and sits under a tree and reads the
> letter. The effect is devastating. In a later scene that he
> recounts you see a similar response. After he goes to the
> Fresh Pond Crematory he sits in the car while everybody
> else goes into the wretched little chapel and he realizes
> somehow what is happening, that his mother is being turned
> into ashes. He has nobody to talk to; he smells the leather
> of the car; looks at the brick wall; and feels utter desolation.

A year after the death of his mother in October of 1921, Tom
left with his father for Bermuda, while John Paul remained
behind in the care of his maternal grandparents. Bermuda was
a nightmare. Owen was having an affair with the novelist
Evelyn Scott, who was the wife of his friend and fellow artist,
Cyril Kay Scott, and Tom found himself under the disciplinary
thumb of a woman whose claim on his father's love he saw as
both a threat and a betrayal. He identified in her many of
the characteristics he had loathed in his mother — she was

cerebral, detached, and cold — and because of his hostility, indeed hatred, the affair was doomed. At the age of ten, Tom returned with his father to the country of his birth, minus his mother and brother.

They lived in the ancient and picturesque Midi town of St. Antonin Noble Val, a site that Mott calls "a wonderful little medieval town" perfectly suited to the needs of the romantic Mertons:

> Owen loved France; he did not like England; and he loathed the United States. He loved France for its peasants and any country that did not have peasants was simply out of the running as far as Owen was concerned. St. Antonin was as near paradise as anyone was likely to get with its marvellous wood smoke smells and rich aroma of rabbit stews done in wine. Everyone in St. Antonin was either a saint or aspiring to be a saint, although everything was touched in some way by the spirit of Rabelais. Those splendid parties!

Merton found himself immersed in a world still marked by medieval culture. He was "constantly in and out of old churches, and stumbled upon the ruins of ancient chapels and monasteries."[3] In addition to the landscape, he had a three-volume set of picture books of the region, which he would peruse for hours, charmed by the mystique of ruins, rural isolation, and imposing majesty.

> I gazed upon the huddled buildings of the ancient Grande Chartreuse, crowded together in their solitary valley, with the high mountains loaded with firs, soaring up to their rocky summits on either side. . . . I had no curiosity about monastic vocations or religious rules, but I know my heart was filled with a kind of longing to breathe the air of that lonely valley and to listen to its silence.[4]

France instructed Merton in the peace, beauty, and serenity of a chosen solitude, for at an early age he was to suffer once again the pain of an enforced independence and self-reliance. Though surrounded by the generous spirit of a medieval peasant Catholicism, simple, faithful, and devout, the Mertons remained solidly non-Roman in their theological persuasion, or at least in their ecclesiastical sympathies.

In 1926 Merton was enrolled in the Lycée Ingres in Montauban. He found himself lifted from the warm tranquillity of life with his father in St. Antonin and dropped into the cold dormitories of the Ingres. He didn't speak the argot, he didn't know the rules of the game, and he was dismissed by his French peers as a snotty little English schoolboy. It was torture. The wounds would take some time to heal; perhaps they never did. He was daily beaten by his classmates; the teachers appeared indifferent to his plight; it was an ugly world of bullying and abuse of power. And then one day in the spring of 1928, Tom was plucked from the school by his father.

> To Tom this was the greatest jail delivery his father had ever organized. The very walls of the familiar houses on the way to the Villenouvelle station cried, "Liberty! Liberty!"[5]

Unable to make a living in France, and with an offer of support for Tom's schooling made by the Jenkins family, Owen decided to take up the opportunity to go to England and place Tom in Ripley Court, a private preparatory school in Surrey. He would be at Ripley for only a short time before moving on to Oakham School in Rutland, a public school of second-tier distinction. The headmaster, one F.C. Doherty, carefully prepared Merton, whose education was nothing if not diverse, for a Cambridge scholarship. The Oakham experience, as Mott notes, was very different from that at the Lycée Ingres:

Oakham was a very small school. You would not be lost at
Oakham. As soon as you arrived, even at the lowest form,
you were going to be an insider. Merton was *never* an insider
at Ingres. As well as the solicitous attention provided by the
masters of the school you had the pastoral setting, which
greatly appealed to Merton — in fact, its rural beauty con-
trasted sharply with the dark, Satanic mills of William
Blake's London. At this juncture in Merton's life London
held little appeal. But that would change with the Bennetts.

Dr. Tom Izod Bennett, Merton's godfather and ultimately
guardian, and his wife Iris Weiss accepted responsibility for the
cultural education of their young charge, in addition to providing oversight for his financial well-being. Bennett was an old
friend of Owen's from their boyhood days in New Zealand. But
whereas Owen enjoyed little public success with his artistic
life, Izod had made a considerable reputation as a Harley Street
surgeon. But all his skill could not save the life of his friend,
for Owen had developing within him a malignant tumour of
the brain. Although he had shown signs of being ill as early as
1928 at the time Tom was admitted to Ripley Court, the
progress of the disease was slow and undetectable. With Tom
happily ensconced at Oakham and with Izod and Iris ably
overseeing his son's welfare, Owen pursued every avenue to
find his artistic voice. But by 1930 he was confined to London's
Middlesex Hospital with little hope of recovery. As in the case
of Merton's mother, his father died at a distance, isolated and
sealed off. But there are differences between the two deaths,
as Mott makes clear:

> There is this desperate scene in Merton's autobiography
> when he describes receiving a call from his father saying
> that he will not be able to stay with him in Yorkshire and

has to get back to London. Later he rings up Tom, who at the time is alone in the house where he is staying, and his son listens to his father make no sense at all on the phone. He knows that his father's mind is gone. The smell of leather returns. He recalls the car, the crematorium, the death of his mother. He is absolutely devastated. He goes to see his father at Middlesex; there is no letter saying good-bye. His father is sitting up in bed drawing Byzantine saints and not his trademark landscapes. Tom is puzzled and pained but Owen insists that he has discovered a new style, one that will make him famous. It is pathetic. And then a few days later he is at his father's funeral.

Tom owed Owen much more than he at first realized. There is no indication that he ever felt his father had deserted him as his mother had done; he knew in his heart that his father was a warm, kind man who would be there if he could to spring him from such miserable prisons as the Lycée Ingres. Even though his admiration and affection for Owen were tempered by the episode in Bermuda with Evelyn Scott, he believed that his father was a man of struggling integrity, a "complicated hero," indeed a man of faith, of deep spirituality. It was Owen who introduced Tom to an artist whom he loved and wanted his son to love, the poet and revolutionary William Blake:

How incapable I was of understanding anything like the ideals of a William Blake! How could I possibly realize that his rebellion, for all its strange heterodoxies, was fundamentally the rebellion of the saints. It was the rebellion of the lover of the living God, the rebellion of one whose desire of God was so intense and irresistible that it condemned, with all its might, all the hypocrisy and petty sensuality and

scepticism and materialism which cold and trivial minds
set up as unpassable barriers between God and the souls
of men.[6]

Blake was seared into Merton's soul by his own artist-father,
whose death proved to be the occasion for a new restlessness
and a new liberty. Following Owen's death, Pop Jenkins once
more entered the stage, this time in a more directly inter-
ventionist way: he provided Merton with a private income,
encouraged him to travel in Europe and learn new languages
(this was one legacy that lasted: in addition to English and
French, Merton eventually became fluent in Italian, Spanish,
Portuguese, and Latin, and acquired a reading knowledge of
Greek and German), and insisted that he come to the United
States every second year. With Izod's agreement, the making
of the cosmopolitan Merton was assured. From the Bennetts
he would acquire a taste for jazz, modern writers, Russian
movies, and the art of Marc Chagall, in short, a feel for the
cultivated and for the *au courant*.

The freedom, or at least financial independence, that Pop and
the Bennetts made possible for Tom in the wake of his father's
death was a gift that he would squander in the years to come.
But his family and guardian's generosity allowed him experiences that would be fodder for both his spiritual and his
artistic life. During the Easter holiday break of 1932, at the age
of seventeen, he wandered through the Rhineland reading
Spinoza. Arguably a tactless thing to do and, not surprisingly,
he encountered the Nazis:

> With a pack on my back I was wandering down a quiet
> country road among flowering apple orchards, near Koblenz.
> Suddenly a car appeared and came down the road very fast.
> It was jammed with people. Almost before I had taken full

notice of it, I realized it was coming straight at me and instinctively jumped into the ditch. The car passed in a cloud of leaflets and from the ditch I glimpsed its occupants, six or seven youths screaming and shaking their fists. They were Nazis and it was election day. I was being invited to vote for Hitler, who was not yet in power. These were future officers in the ss. They vanished quickly. The road was once again perfectly silent and peaceful. But it was not the same road as before. It was now a road on which seven men had expressed their readiness to destroy me.[7]

This experience of the sinister would remain with him for decades.

After having acquired a Higher Certificate from Oakham and a scholarship to Clare College, Cambridge, in the same year, he returned to Europe in 1933.

Until now, Merton's religious training had been desultory — Episcopal through his maternal grandparents, Anglican through his education in England, and a smattering of Catholic influences in France. But on a visit to the Dominican church of Santa Sabina in Rome he underwent "a capitulation, a surrender, a conversion," not radical but subtle, not overwhelming but suggestive, poetical but unpersuasive, and not lasting. His religious instincts were ignited by Catholic art, but the fervour quickly waned. His impressions of Rome were warm and imaginative and he occupied himself, as he had done when a young child in France, with visits to churches, cloisters, and abbeys, seldom searching out the ruins of that other Rome — classical and imperial.

In the summer of the same year, still a teenager unsure of himself but hungry for experience, he left for the United States where he visited his mother's family, travelled widely, worked, lost the interest in religion he had briefly discovered in Europe, and returned to England on the *Manhattan*, "a garish and turbulent class steamer full of Nazi spies working as stewards and detesting the Jewish passengers." Once again the Nazis. No wonder he wrote about them — however obliquely — in his one published novel, *My Argument with the Gestapo*, or as it was originally titled, *Journal of My Escape from the Nazis*. He arrived in Cambridge sour and apprehensive. Cambridge itself was a "planned disaster." Nominally studying modern languages, he made the wrong sort of friends, spent inordinate amounts of money in the company of rich rowdies, acquired unmanageable book debts, and womanized like mad, or so he would have us believe. The story that while at Cambridge he fathered an illegitimate child who subsequently perished, with his mother, during the Blitzkrieg seems, in the view of his official biographer at least, to be of dubious veracity. Mott is persuaded that a good deal of his reputation for carnal exuberance, for womanizing, is simple boasting:

> Merton's close friend and fellow convert and poet, Bob Lax, told me that when he and Merton were students at Columbia University in the mid-1930s he had heard, long before he actually met Merton, that he was forced to leave Cambridge because of his having fathered at least one, and very possibly two, illegitimate children. Merton himself told many people that his son, not a daughter, mind you and in the singular, died during the Blitz. Well, to be honest, the only *solid* evidence that I have for any of this is a letter from Iris Bennett talking about it, although the letter proper is lost and all we have are extracts in one of Merton's journals. In and of itself, not very reliable. But there is some rather more compelling evidence with the will that he was required to make out prior to taking his Simple Vows as a Cistercian monk on March 19, 1944. In the will he makes

provision for money to be given to a person known to Tom Bennett. That's about all we've got.

Certainly Merton's career at Cambridge was less than auspicious. He had a falling out with the Bennetts, provoked the academic authorities at Clare College once too often with his wayward behaviour, and generally made a muck of it all. And so in November of 1934 he left England and the Europe of his birth and his travels, "a sad and unquiet continent, full of forebodings."

Although his stint at Cambridge was not a success, it was not a failure from an academic point of view. He did passably well in his studies, though he fell short of the expectations many had for him. The dream of a diplomatic or legal career nurtured by the Bennetts disappeared from the horizon. He himself believed that the most positive contribution the university made to his intellectual growth was his exposure to the "lucid and powerful genius of the greatest Catholic poet," the rare and inestimable Dante. The Italian poet represented for Merton an integrity of art and mind and a thirst for spiritual wholeness that he would in time more clearly associate with William Blake, *his* Blake. The very comprehensiveness of Blake's private mythology and cosmic vision became neatly coupled, for Merton, with the rigour and intellectual thoroughness he found in the writings of the contemporary French metaphysician and aesthetician Jacques Maritain. In fact, Maritain's *Art and Scholasticism* exercised a key role in Merton's effort to cope with the esoteric and heretical genius of Blake. Maritain was there for Merton at the beginning of his critical and imaginative appropriation of Blake in the 1930s and he was there for him in the last years of his life in the 1960s. In a letter to a friend, the publisher James Laughlin, in 1966, Merton wrote:

Jacques Maritain and I both agreed that we thought perhaps the most living way to approach theological and philosophical problems now (that theology and philosophy are in such chaos) would be in the form of creative writing and lit criticism.[8]

Blake was the model for such an approach — in the early years when Merton was struggling for his own voice and in the mature years when his identification with the "Blakean agenda" was complete.

Blake would also figure at his new university: Columbia in New York. He enrolled there in February 1935, just four months after leaving England. Pop encouraged him to get a job at a newspaper, but he discovered that many of them would prefer he come with a degree. Columbia gave him some transfer credits for his work at Cambridge, but far less than he had anticipated. His chosen course in English literature was not going to be the academic breeze he thought it would be. In fact, he fell in love with Columbia, a "big sooty factory full of light and fresh air." At Columbia he came under the influence of a figure who was to play a major role in the making of Merton the literary man: Mark Van Doren. As Merton saw him, Van Doren was a poet and critic with a Scholastic bent, a frame of mind schooled in philosophical rigour and clarity, "looking directly for the quiddities of things." Van Doren was as approachable as Columbia and equally lacking in pretension. Merton found everything about Columbia more congenial to his spirits than Cambridge and he inhaled liberally and wholeheartedly "the genuine intellectual vitality in the air."

Van Doren actively encouraged both Merton and the poet John Berryman to write, and became a literary mentor for both of these promising young men. Merton felt unleashed. His energy for writing was uncontainable. He became in quick succession editor of *Columbian*, the university yearbook, art editor of the literary magazine, *Jester*, a contributor to the *Spectator*, a literary quarterly, and a reviewer for the *New York Times*. A revealing snapshot of these Columbia years is provided by his friend, editor, and publisher, Bob Giroux:

> We were both undergraduates at Columbia, although I was a year behind him. He was in every literary circle, including the visual people. After all, amongst other things, he was a cartoonist. At first, I only heard of him from classmates and by reputation. And then we met in one of Van Doren's classes. But it was when he brought me a piece of writing for the *Columbian* that I recognized how truly distinctive he was. In appearance, he was of average height, very sturdy and solidly built, blond, and with a slight British accent. He was very well-educated, a Charlie Chaplin and Marx Brothers fan, peppering his conversation with all kinds of literary and cinematic allusions. Well, he left his submission with me and I remember being struck by its strong autobiographical flavour and its realism. We published it, though cut, which he didn't like, and our long literary association began.

During his Columbia undergraduate years Merton came to realize that his interest in the religious sensibility was not restricted to aesthetic reflections of St. Antonin; he was already a kind of pilgrim. A Hindu monk-philosopher, Dr. Bramachari, proved to be instrumental in helping Merton appreciate the riches of the mystical traditions of the West, while many of his peers sought solutions to their spiritual quandaries in the East. In fact, Edward Rice, the earliest Merton biographer and an old Columbia friend, observed simply that Merton "seemed to be the only person who talked sensibly to Bramachari about religion."

Just prior to his baccalaureate graduation in 1938, Merton read two books that impressed him deeply and whetted his appetite for communion with Rome, although he would not have put it in such a baroque fashion. One of these, *The Spirit of Medieval Philosophy* (1936), was by the historian, follower of St. Thomas Aquinas, and French Catholic luminary Etienne Gilson; it is a study possessed of both a sensitivity to the medieval imagination and an enticing intellectual clarity. The other book was far more controversial, impressionistic and daring: to wit, Aldous Huxley's *Ends and Means* (1937). Merton found Huxley's detailed familiarity with diverse mystical traditions fascinating and generally sound, but "the speculative side of the book . . . was full, no doubt, of strange doctrines." Gilson and Huxley can be understood as Merton's spiritual polarities, one rooted and the other fluid, one grounded in a scholarly tradition and scouting religiously for intellectual error, the other roaming uninhibitedly, celebrating the superficial freedom of eclecticism, but both of them conscious of the limitations of reason. Gilson and Huxley merge in Blake.

> As Blake worked himself into my system, I became more and more conscious of the necessity of a vital faith, and the total unreality and unsubstantiality of the dead, selfish rationalism which had been freezing my mind.[9]

Blake erupted in his heart, taking over both his soul and his mind. Blake became the subject of his master's thesis, "Nature and Art in William Blake: An Essay in Interpretation." This thesis has a controversial history, however. The poet and critic Eli Mandel judged it brilliant, but Michael Mott calls it a work of plodding scholarship, perversely lacking in any discussion of Blake the visual artist. It is very obviously an M.A. thesis, and its pedestrian and uncharacteristically cautious prose betrays its origins. It is the only sustained and systematic study of Blake that Merton ever wrote. In the thesis Merton attempted to better understand Blake's ideas about art by comparing him with the "aestheticians I think he most resembles." The originality of the thesis can be found in his use of the aesthetic ideas of St. Thomas Aquinas as a "touchstone by which to test Blake's thought." And to better understand St. Thomas, Merton turned to Jacques Maritain. Merton sought to "dispel the illusion that [Blake] lived exclusively in the tabernacles of ecstatic puritan cranks." Blake, in Merton's view, was a mystic in the tradition of the Augustinians and the Franciscans and, as such, a Neoplatonist. But it would be a Thomist like Maritain, a disciple of Aquinas, who would guide him through the esoteric pathways of the Swedenborgian genius of Romantic England, who would help him root Blake in Christian history and western intellectual thought. Quoting Henry Adams from his *Mont St. Michel and Chartres*, Merton observes of Blake: "Children and Saints can believe two contrary things at the same time." In years to come, the same could be fairly said of Merton.

He was not so much a scholar of Blake's work as a disciple, an interpreter, of his "visionary" approach to life. Merton appropriated what *he* understood to be the Blakean perspective on art, politics, and spirituality. This would be a lifelong undertaking, an internalizing enterprise rich with imaginative and spiritual insights. In short, the heretic Merton!

In a letter to Bob Lax, Merton confessed to his obsession with Blake:

I have studied William Blake, I have measured him with a ruler, I have sneaked at him with pencils and T squares, I have spied on him from a distance with a small spyglass, I have held him up to mirrors, and will shortly endeavor to prove the prophetic books were all written with lemon juice and must be held in front of a slow fire to be read.[10]

There isn't a thesis writer anywhere who would not appreciate Merton's full absorption in his subject, who would not understand something of his obsession. But Blake was more than a temporary obsession, a scholar's preoccupation, a passing fascination; Blake was at the core of Merton's self-definition both as an artist and as a religious visionary. Blake provided the working myth, the architecture of Merton's thought, his eschatology. Years of reflecting on Blake and his enterprise of healing and integration would result in some surprising achievements — literary, emotional, spiritual — in the mature Merton. But even in the rediscovered Blake of the Columbia years Merton saw in the English visionary the resolution, even if incomplete, of his many self-contradictions. And so, on November 16, 1938, at Corpus Christi Church in Manhattan, in the presence of Bob Lax, Ed Rice, Bob Gerdy, and Seymour Freedgood, all Columbia friends, Merton was baptized a Roman Catholic.

I have to acknowledge my own debt to him, and the truth which may appear curious to some, although it is not really so: that through Blake I would one day come, in a roundabout way, to the only true Church, and to the One Living God, through His Son, Jesus Christ.[11]

Throughout his life Merton was prone to extravagant responses, uncontainable enthusiasms, and occasionally intemperate judgements, but Blake was a "constant," the substratum that allowed his spirituality and artistry to cohere. In time, his religious sentiments and intellectual convictions would be less triumphalistically expressed, but his spiritual indebtedness to Blake and his fidelity to Blake's task of assisting at "the marriage of heaven and hell" were unswerving.

In 1939, after taking his master's degree, Merton immediately began doctoral work. It was his intention to write a dissertation on the Victorian Jesuit poet Gerard Manley Hopkins, for whom he had developed an admiration and with whose poetic outsider's temperament he was strongly in sympathy. At the same time, he took a minor teaching position at Columbia's University Extension, wrote numerous book reviews for the *New York Times Book Review* and the *New York Herald Tribune*, as well as for many literary magazines, and took on duties as an English instructor at St. Bonaventure's University, a Franciscan institution in Olean, New York. Merton played with the thought of a religious vocation, tossing the idea about with Bob Lax, who seemed similarly inclined at the time. He continued to live and socialize as a graduate student, and then decided while recovering from several tooth extractions (he had chronic problems with his teeth) to take a trip to Cuba. It was there that Merton had a second experience of the transcendent, something like but more deeply and intensely felt than the experience at Santa Sabina in Rome years earlier. At the Church of St. Francis in Havana he had a profound apprehension of the presence of God:

> the unshakable certainty, the clear and immediate knowledge that Heaven was right in front of me, struck me like a thunderbolt and went through me like a flash of lightning and seemed to lift me clean up off the earth.[12]

When he returned to New York, he decided to apply for admission as a Franciscan friar. He was turned down. In a conversation with a Father Edmund, and later and more devastatingly following a confession with an unidentified Capuchin friar, Merton was told that his Cambridge sins were perhaps too great to be so easily erased. There were obligations. The consequences of his sexual escapades at Cambridge were not to be set aside. His temperament, sexual immaturity, and recent convert's zeal were all suspect. This was a serious blow to Merton; after his unceremonious exile from England, here was another setback. It appeared that he was floundering. There were, however, other options in his life.

He had found Communism not without appeal in his early Columbia days, and now in his Catholic days found himself increasingly drawn to the apostolate of the puzzling, devoted, and not particularly irenic Baroness Catherine de Hueck — a Russian emigrée of noble connection and recent Catholic credentials. She was formidable. Merton was drawn to her strength, holy resolve, radical poverty, and deep social conscience. He worked for a short time in 1941 at Friendship House, her urban outreach centre on 135th Street in Harlem. This social apostolate was an orthodox Catholic's answer to communism's panacea for social ills, the preaching of violent revolution.

But the allure of the priesthood had not disappeared, it had merely receded. Dan Walsh, a Columbia philosophy professor who became one of Merton's most intimate friends and confidants, had once spoken movingly to Merton about the Trappists of Our Lady of Gethsemani Abbey in Kentucky, and after the collapse of his Franciscan ambitions, Merton decided to make a retreat at Gethsemani. The bonding was immediate. Merton wrestled with the demands on his loyalty and his conscience. Harlem or Gethsemani? The despair of the slum or the serenity of the enclosure? Friendship House or the Abbey?

He chose the cloister.

Today I think — should I be going to Harlem or to the Trappists? Why doesn't this idea of the Trappists leave me?

. . . I would have to renounce perhaps *more* to enter the
Trappists. That would be the one place where I would give
up *everything*. . . . And Harlem will be full of confusions —
and I don't particularly like the idea of working with a lot
of girls.

Or do I want to go to Gethsemani because it is a perfect
society, even in the natural order? . . . Going to Harlem
doesn't seem like anything special — it is good, and is a
reasonable way to follow Christ: but going to the Trappists
is exciting and fills me with awe, and desire: and I return
to the idea "Give up *everything* — *everything!*" and that
means something.[13]

Gethsemani won out: no girls, utter self-sacrifice, and a
romantic's spiritual self-immolation; and all this in the very
shadows of the Draft Board of the United States Armed Forces,
for it was a time of world war even though the U.S. was still
on the periphery of full involvement. In March of 1941 Merton's classification, I-B, meant that he would have at most
limited service because of his problems with his teeth. But
then the Draft Board changed the health rule about teeth, and
in December of the same year issued a notice to Merton that
he was to appear for a re-examination, with the real possibility
that he might be reclassified an I-A. By the following month
he could be in the army. Merton began to sweat. On December
2, 1941, he wrote:

Before the notice came there was the desire for the cloister.
Since the notice of reexamination for the draft — a funny
thing: a terrific combination of fear that I might *not* get to
the cloister, and of confidence that the vocation is true and
from God — and the trial is from God.

And if you had a true vocation for the cloister, and yet were
taken off for the army? Simply have to suffer it. I don't know

how. God would have to show me how. There is no force in me, but in Him is all strength.

But before I got this surprise notice from the Draft Board, I had a great desire, for the cloister. After the notice I also got *confidence* in the vocation![14]

On December 7, 1941, Japan attacked Pearl Harbor. The United States was now at war. Merton arrived at Gethsemani on December 10. He was admitted as a postulant on St. Lucy's Day, December 13. He was safe. Merton was finally at home, away from the world.

The Trappists, long termed the "Foreign Legion of the Church," were an austere offshoot of the Cistercian Order. He entered a world unlike any other. As the Merton scholar William Shannon notes:

It is important in assessing Merton's history as a monk to recall his first impressions of Gethsemani. He tells us how a Brother Matthew met him at the door, allowed him to enter, and then closed the door letting him into the place of new freedom. It's an interesting way of describing freedom — closing a door.

I think that what happened to Merton can be best appreciated when you consider that he had been living a quite undisciplined life prior to becoming a Catholic, in fact one of the reasons why he converted to Catholicism can be discovered in his reading of Aldous Huxley's *Ends and Means* wherein he learned that a truly human life is a disciplined life. And so he became the ideal monk, for a short time at least, obeying all the rules, fervently following the principle that if you keep the Rule, the usages or monastic regulations that govern every aspect of communal life, you are doing God's will. You don't have to think for yourself. The Rule of the Order will do the thinking

for you. Well, he was too intelligent to live very long with
that.

Life at Gethsemani in the 1940s was raw. Meat, fish, and eggs
were excluded from the diet. The monks froze in the winter
and were often overcome by heat in the summer. They fasted
regularly and with rigour; physical labour alternated with
hours of singing the Divine Office. If anything, life for the
postulants and the novices was even stricter. Michael Mott
succinctly outlines this rarefied world:

> Gethsemani was extraordinarily austere and extraordinarily
> inefficient. Dom Frederic Dunne, the abbot at the time
> Merton entered, was a very humane and wise abbot. He
> encouraged writers and was very helpful to Merton. But he
> was a management disaster. The place was falling down. It
> had been built a hundred years before for approximately
> forty to fifty monks. At the time Merton joined, the Abbey
> had about eighty and within a very short period of time it
> would have over two hundred and climbing. The buildings
> were ancient and about ready to collapse. They cut down an
> inordinate number of trees in order to feed an inefficient
> boiler for a heating system that was incapable of producing
> heat. The monks froze in the dormitories; they froze in
> the Abbey church; they froze everywhere they went. And
> yet vast numbers of trees were being sacrificed to keep
> them in this state. This condition of benign malfunctioning
> would only change following the election of Dom Frederic's
> successor.

But if Merton was unlucky in his choice of monastery, he was
fortunate indeed in having Dunne as his first abbot. Almost
immediately Merton found himself immersed in writing rather
than cheese-making. His abbot understood the psychological

necessity and spiritual urgency that together defined Merton, the silent one, as the Abbey's newest wordsmith. Bound by a vow of obedience, Merton had no choice but to accept Dom Frederic's orders and write.

Merton was determined, however, to abandon poetry, about which he had been serious during his Columbia days. Nonetheless, through the combined efforts of Lax and Van Doren he succeeded instead in having his *Thirty Poems* published by New Directions in 1944, an achievement in which he took great, if slightly guilty, pleasure. It is not insignificant that his first published work was a collection of poems; the most moving and the most technically perfect work in the volume is his elegy for his brother John Paul, to whom he had drawn closer since entering the monastery, and who was killed returning from a bombing raid on Mannheim. "For My Brother: Reported Missing in Action, 1943" is a cathartic vindication of profound faith and of fraternal love, a poem of which Van Doren writes:

> For Merton there is another world beyond this one where his brother died, and where he himself writes poetry. But the poetry is a way to that world. Indeed, given his endowment, his may well be *the* way, so that mystic and poet, seer and singer, in his case are one.[15]

"For My Brother" is a wrenching tribute to the brother whose mad sacrifice has now left him utterly alone. John Paul, the young fighter full of heroic virtue, has been claimed by death, by Christ:

> When all the men of war are shot
> And flags have fallen into dust
> Your cross and mine shall tell men still

Christ died on each, for both of us,
For in the wreckage of your April Christ lies slain,
And Christ weeps in the ruins of my spring[16]

Mother, father, and brother: Merton is now orphaned. The
world is fully dead to him. All he has now are the consolations
of religion and of art. Over the next decade he will produce
scores of books and pamphlets, impressively catholic in their
range. He will publish three volumes of poetry, *A Man in the
Divided Sea*, *Figures for an Apocalypse*, and *The Tears of
the Blind Lions*; two biographies, *Exile Ends in Glory* (a life of
Trappistine Mother Berchmans) and *What Are These Wounds?*
(a life of the Cistercian mystic Lutgarde of Aywieres) — hag-
iographies of such pious tone and sugary prose that they later
embarrassed Merton, who would rank them at the very bottom
of his list of writings; a spiritual handbook that many would
consider a devotional classic, *Seeds of Contemplation*; a history of Cistercian monasticism, *The Waters of Siloe*; a rather
laboured study in ascetic theology, *The Ascent to Truth*; an
exquisitely wrought diary, *The Sign of Jonas*; and most important of all, in 1948, his celebrity-creating bestseller, *The Seven
Storey Mountain*.

Mountain is a remarkable work for a young writer. Its success
speaks much for its skilful evocation of the temper of the times.
Merton captured the post-war angst of the age, the enervating
feeling of spiritual dislocation that accompanied the slaughter
and exile of millions. Although Merton chose to turn his back
on a world mired in blood and rage, the death of his brother
brought the barbarity and capriciousness of the war into the
heart of the cloister. Merton was a child of his time.

Although there is a certain arrogance in publishing your
autobiography at the age of thirty-three, Merton was acting
under the instructions of both Dom Frederic, his abbot, and

Dom Robert, his novice master, when he undertook the task of writing his own life. Neither he nor his religious superiors, nor indeed his publishers, had any idea that *Mountain* would prove as stunningly successful as it did. Mott marvels at its cinematic technique, its capacity to draw you in with a distant shot here and a close-up there. It betrays something of Merton's interest in films, but it is also an extraordinarily accurate reading of the temper of the times. Through his own personal experience, Merton expresses the deepest feelings of his contemporaries. He instinctively, viscerally grasped the spiritual longing of a generation, and gave it voice. It was *his* story, the story of a lost sheep that was now found. But legions of readers found *their* story in its pages. Publishing history was made.

Columbia contemporary Bob Giroux, later Merton's editor at Harcourt Brace, observed in an interview with journalist Paul Wilkes:

> when the book was published on October 4, 1948, it did not seem to me, nor to anyone else in the firm, that it would become a national phenomenon. It merely looked as if the book would "do all right". . . . But meanwhile something was happening: readers were discovering the book for themselves and we had to reprint several times. . . . New readers, all over the country, averaging *two thousand* every business day, wanted the book out of season, for its own sake, and they wanted it in extraordinary quantities. The process continued during 1949. In May of that year, when I visited Thomas Merton at Gethsemani, I presented him with Copy No. 100,000. In the original cloth edition, the trade sale exceeded 600,000 copies.[17]

Even before the book appeared, various literary and social notables had judged it a work of significance. Giroux sent galley proofs to three famous people who "not only all replied, but . . . used extraordinary terms." Evelyn Waugh wrote that *Mountain* "should take its place among the classic records of spiritual experience"; the novelist Graham Greene, who like Merton was a convert to Catholicism, observed that it is "an autobiography with a pattern and meaning valid for all of us"; and Clare Booth Luce predicted that future readers "will turn to this book to find out what went on in the heart of a man in this cruel century."[18] Some enthusiastic critics at the time of publication likened it to Augustine's *Confessions* and Newman's *Apologia pro Vita Sua*, although it lacks the profundity of the former and the elegance of the latter. In later years commentators have been divided over its value, with Harry Cargas of Webster College arguing for its recognition as a work of "near genius because of the intensity crammed into [its] pages" and Harvey Cox of Harvard lamenting this "disgustingly triumphalist and even arrogant" work.

Merton himself entertained contradictory assessments of his autobiography's importance. He often despised it and deplored the myth that it created for him. He was the "Seven Storey Mountain Man," forever trapped by its certitudes and apologetical zeal. But he also knew that it was a work of his youth, that it could not be undone, that it had to be accepted for what it was. In the 1963 preface to the Japanese edition, Merton makes his peace with a work that both made and unmade him:

Perhaps if I were to attempt this book today, it would be written differently. . . . Certainly I have never for a moment thought of changing the definitive decisions taken in the course of my life: to be a Christian, to be a monk, to be a priest. If anything, the decision to renounce and to depart from modern secular society, a decision repeated and reaffirmed many times, has finally become irrevocable. Yet the attitudes and the assumptions behind this decision have perhaps changed in many ways.

For one thing, when I wrote this book, the fact uppermost in my mind was that I seceded from the world of my time in all clarity and with total freedom. The break and the secession were, to me, matters of the greatest importance. Hence the somewhat negative tone of so many parts of this book.

Since that time, I have learned, I believe, to look back into that world with greater compassion, seeing those in it not as alien to myself, not as peculiar and deluded strangers, but as identified with myself.[19]

From the time of the publication of *The Seven Storey Mountain* in 1948 until his death twenty years later, Merton bore the stamp, the signature, of the celebrity-monk. It was impossible to erase. He was the child of his success.

On May 26, 1949, Merton was ordained a priest. He was both monk and cleric, a dual role over which he felt some ambivalence. Still, his ordination day was a moment of sweet triumph for the one-time reprobate who had been denied admission to the Franciscan friars, and a moment of finality, of acceptance, in a life marked by few constants and a fragile continuity.

In May 1951 Merton was appointed master of scholastics. This position was alternately called master of juniors or master of students; it was the fourth most important position in the Abbey hierarchy after abbot, prior, and master of novices, and entailed responsibility for the formation of junior monks in temporary vows. Merton would continue as master of scholastics until September 1955, providing lecture conferences, private conferences, and intellectual and spiritual oversight for those under his care. Dom John Eudes Bamberger, abbot of the Abbey of the Genesee in upstate New York and a psychiatrist, recalls the Merton style:

Merton was Master for the whole time I was a junior and he was my teacher and spiritual director. At the time I found I could move on the same wavelength as he, that I could empathize with him. I felt that I could interpret his many inconsistencies as a kind of higher consistency. But I did that more instinctively than analytically. Later on, much later in fact, after his death, the natural dynamism of life made me analyze him more.

I always felt that he operated quite simply and straightforwardly with the brothers. He was an extraordinarily gifted person, highly intelligent and quick. There are a lot of intelligent people who don't give you the impression of thinking with their skin. But he did. There was intelligence pulsating throughout his whole body. He reacted with great energy and promptitude to all kinds of stimuli. He was brimming full of new ideas.

But he could shift gears easily depending on the company. A lot of monks, and others as well, readers, correspondents, etc., felt he was inconstant. In fact, they derived a very false impression of him because they failed to see that precisely because he was *so* sensitive to people's personalities, needs, and expectations, he would automatically assume any relationship that would gratify their needs and aspirations as far as he could. This could be self-defeating.

Still, psychologically speaking, he was a natural self-corrector. In a way, only a few of the juniors could appreciate his complexity.

Following his stint as master of scholastics, Merton was appointed to the more influential role of master of novices, with responsibility for forming the monastic candidates who had yet to make simple vows. This position he held for a decade. Timothy Kelly, the Canadian abbot of Gethsemani since 1973, remembers a playful, enthusiastic, original, magisterial, and yet humble novice master:

> When I had my first interview with the Novice Master I knew him only as the Novice Master. I did not know I was speaking to Thomas Merton or Father Louis or Louie as he was known in the monastery. It was the custom of the time to be given a name other than your own — your name in religion as it were — and Merton was given the name Louis after the sainted King Louis IX of France. So, here I was with a monk I knew only as the Master of Novices.
>
> At the end of our interview he asked me what I knew about the life of a Trappist monk. I told him that I had read all of the books of Thomas Merton as well as those of Father Raymond, another Gethsemani author with a large readership. He asked me what I thought of them and I said that I thought that they were both romantics but from different perspectives. I told him that I liked Merton's style much more than Raymond's. He simply responded by saying that one should always be careful with what one reads and how one interprets what one reads. With that our interview was over.
>
> It was only next morning that I found out that the monk I had been speaking to, my Novice Master, was Thomas Merton.

Throughout the fifties Merton wrote on largely Catholic themes, exploring the ancient truths and traditions of his adopted faith in a manner that was rich but generally conservative, often provocative but still safe. Not a professional theologian by training or inclination, Merton was really a religious thinker, having more in common with Blaise Pascal and Simone Weil than with the methodologies of systematic theologians. He found a ripe subject for study in the personalities and writings of the Early Church Fathers, the Desert Fathers, the Cistercian mystics of the twelfth century, the Rhine mystics of the fourteenth century, and the Spanish mystics of the sixteenth century. He translated select Latin and Greek texts that moved him with their grace, simplicity of style, reverence, and mystery of vision; among these were *Clement of Alexandria: A Selection from the Protreptikos* and *The Solitary Life: A Letter of Guigo the Carthusian.*

Although he was a cloistered monk, Merton was also a celebrated writer, and he was more and more in touch with the world he had formally renounced. Columbia friends corresponded with him regularly, and indeed on occasion made the trek to Gethsemani to visit him. Countless readers of his many books initiated correspondence with him, and fellow writers and religious figures sought his counsel. He, in turn, wrote to other authors and those public figures who piqued his interest or inspired him. The solitary maintained his social contacts, to the degree that monastic enclosure allowed. And for all his complaining, the monastic authorities were more tolerant of Merton's formidable correspondence, periodic visitations, and later telephone calls than they were with any other of the brethren.

By 1959 Merton, the reliable monk, the sane Catholic voice, spokesman for the mainstream American Catholic sensibility, had become highly restive. He came increasingly to feel that answers to the great questions of meaning were no longer at the ready, that a time of judgement was at hand and genuine Catholic thinkers no longer in a position to offer rock-hard truths. In a diary entry for January of 1959, Merton unfavourably contrasts the amiable Catholic writer G.K. Chesterton with the Swiss theologian Msgr. Romano Guardini. GKC is found sorely lacking.

A very fine interview with Guardini was read in the refectory
— a wonderful relief from the complacent windiness of
Chesterton (*St. Thomas Aquinas*). Guardini spoke of power
poisoning man today. We have such fabulous techniques
that their greatness has outstripped our ability to manage
them. This is the great problem. Difference between Guardini and Chesterton — Guardini sees an enormous, tragic,
crisis and offers no solution. Chesterton evokes problems
that stand to become, for him, a matter of words. And he
always has a glib solution. With Chesterton everything is
"of course" "quite obviously" etc. etc. And everything
turns out to be "just plain common sense after all." And
people have the stomach to listen and to *like* it! How can
we be so mad? Of course, Chesterton is badly dated: his
voice comes out of the fog between the last two wars. But
to think there are still people — Catholics — who can talk
like that and imagine they know the answers.[20]

Merton is rather hard on Chesterton. He dismisses him as a
sanguine dogmatist, an optimist on a day of doom. Clearly
Chesterton had become the Catholic author of choice for
many, who found in his writings palatable certainties in an age
of intellectual and spiritual chaos. Chesterton struck a com-
bative stance, armed with wit, good cheer, a whimsical love of
paradox, and a deep solemnity, carefully measured for popular
consumption. Merton fell for the caricature. By the late fifties
he abominated the complacency represented by Chesterton
and his kind. Merton was primed for the doubt, radical self-
scrutiny, and anti-institutional bias of the coming decade.
Chesterton was a symbol of the old Catholicism. Merton was
looking for something new.

We can see as early as 1957, two years before the entry on
Chesterton, a new disquiet uprooting the old certainties in

his volume of verse *The Strange Islands*. The centrepiece of
this volume, "The Tower of Babel," is a verse play that spares
nothing and no one. It is a vigorous denunciation of the misuse
of language and the failure of meaningful and intelligible
communication. While trying to recover the primitive purity
and integrity of the word — both as vehicle of understanding and organ of salvation — Merton saw in the political
rhetoric and commercial jargon of these civilized days something worse than the rape of language; he saw its ugly spawn,
the spiritual chaos that results from the distortion of truth. It
was this slow, unthinking, deliberate destruction of language
that occasioned a new direction and tone in Merton's writings.
As he would later note in his correspondence with the European thinker Hans Urs von Balthasar: "I am very much in
agreement with you on the importance of poetry as being, ever
so often, the locus of Theophany."[21] Still, poetry more often
obscures than illuminates the divine presence. The word must
be stilled. The "babble" of the mid-fifties would become the
"torture" of the mid-sixties:

> The Cross is the exclamation that nobody understands, and
> it is also the prototype of torture as "speech." But Christ
> said nothing, except ritual words and quotations that were
> pure and full of silence. They had no political implications,
> they defined nothing, they uttered no program. They abol-
> ished all programs: *consummatum est.*[22]

From his early forties to the time of his death at fifty-three,
Merton occupied himself more and more with social and political issues, in the light of both his contemplative vocation and
his understanding of Blake's vision of integrated harmony. At
the same time as he took on the world, he returned to the sources
of his monastic self-understanding. In 1960 he published a

work particularly close to his heart, *The Wisdom of the Desert*, a translation of sayings of the fourth-century Desert Fathers of Syria and Egypt. This work captured with Zen-like precision the Christian paradox in which the twentieth-century American monk found himself:

> It would perhaps be too much to say that the world needs another movement such as that which drew these men into the deserts of Egypt and Palestine. Ours is certainly a time for solitaries and for hermits. But merely to reproduce the simplicity, austerity and prayer of these primitive souls is not a complete or satisfactory answer. We must transcend them, and transcend all those who, since their time, have gone beyond the limits which they set. We must liberate ourselves, in our own way, from involvement in a world that is plunging to disaster. But our world is different from theirs. Our involvement is more complete. Our danger is far more desperate. Our time, perhaps, is shorter than we think.[23]

It was during this time — the last decade of his life — that Merton came increasingly to realize the importance of clearly distinguishing between a monk's solitude, which is designed for the service of humanity, and the *contemptus mundi* that would isolate him from the human family. The monk's gift to humankind can be found in the quiet, transforming witness to transcendence that is the monk's creed, the stuff of a true humanism.

The life-source of the monk's vocation is silence; his destiny is realized in silence; his vision is fed by silence. Yet Merton was driven to speak; he knew that to speak is not to clamour, to proclaim is not to harangue. He knew that the false prophets — the antithesis of the Desert Fathers — were those who made of society's need their assurance of success. Merton saw language mangled by the power-hungry and twisted by professional propagandists. He wrote with renewed purpose, convinced of the redemptive effects of the word for the soul. If he could, he would cleanse language of her many maladies, make of her again a tower of understanding and unity, no longer Babel, the tower of confusion and division.

His essays and poetry betray an apocalyptic urgency. His tone no longer reflects the detachment of a monk, distant from harried humanity, and the occasional arrogances of the past, of the self-imposed exile looking haughtily upon a fractured world, are now absent. In such disparate works as *Hagia Sophia, Original Child Bomb*, and *Seeds of Destruction*, Merton writes with fire, sympathy, and understanding. In *Original Child Bomb*, for instance, that Swiftian prose poem on atomic annihilation, controlled fury underscores deep alarm, combined with a sense of the radical witness of the monk, as sentinel on the last frontier, that characterized Merton's writings of the early sixties. In a revealing correspondence with the philosopher Leslie Dewart — about Cuba, U.S. warmongering, and ecclesiastical intransigence — Merton both fears and welcomes the self-demolition of decadent structures both spiritual and temporal:

Are we really so identified with a rotten and crumbling edifice that we are bound to collapse with it?

This is where I stop. I think that if the thing collapses, and it must, a great deal of what we have called "Christianity" will go with it, and if we are around to rub the dust out of our eyes we will finally see that it wasn't Christianity at all. Who will deliver us from the body of this death? . . . I have to go along with policies that are often so inert, so blind, so stupid that they utterly stifle the true life of the

Church and make it *impossible* for the most clear-sighted
and courageous of her members to do anything that will
further the real manifestation of the truth and charity of
Christ in the world. . . . behind all this spurious Pentecostal
wind one can hear, if he listens a little carefully, the hideous
merriment of demons.[24]

Within a short time Merton became one of the most out-
spoken and respected critics of the scourge of racism, the
nuclear arms race, and the wild proliferation of unfettered
capitalist and imperialist ambitions. He set his face against
authoritarianism in any form — in the state as well as in the
church. Although it was never easy for Merton the monk to
take on Caesar in all his guises and variants — the monastic
authorities, the U.S. episcopate, and the relevant Roman dicas-
teries were all eager to censor the political Merton, and indeed
to silence him directly when he wrote on peace matters —
when he took on the church, as he did frequently in his private
diaries and in his correspondence, his criticism was merciless.
To Dan Berrigan he wrote, complaining about the infantilizing
strategies of superiors, the trivializing preoccupations of most
monks, and the trepidations of nervous bishops:

Look, I hate to be vulgar, but a lot of the monastic party line
we are getting, even where in some respects it is very good,
ends up being pure unadulterated —— crap. In the name of
lifeless and graven letters on parchment, we are told that
our life consists in the peaceful and pious meditation on
Scripture and a quiet withdrawal from the world. But if one
reads the prophets with his ears and eyes open he cannot
help recognizing his obligations to shout very loud about
God's will, God's truth, and justice of man to man. I don't
say that this has to be done in a journalistic way or how, but

it has to be done somehow. I don't say it is the dish of every individual monk, but certainly it is incumbent on some monks. I don't say it necessarily means going out of the monastery but I don't say that one can rightly confine the monk completely to his monastery in the name of a literalist and antiquarian concept of the contemplative life. . . . In the beginning I was all pro-contemplation, because I was against the kind of trivial and meaningless activism, the futile running around in circles that Superiors, including contemplative Superiors, promote at the drop of a hat. They will have the whole monastery humming with kindergarten projects and assure everyone that this is "contemplation." But try anything serious, and immediately you get the "activism" line thrown at you. Or, rather I have been told . . . that I am destroying the image of the contemplative vocation, when I write about peace. Even after *Pacem in Terris* when I reopened the question, I was told: that is for the bishops, my boy. The bishops meanwhile are saying, "That is for the theologians". . . .[25]

But Merton remained the faithful monk despite his frequent ventings of spleen. At the same time as he was recording his acerbic commentaries on the worldly follies of the mighty inside and outside the cloister, and at the same time as he was publishing his fiery and caustic essays on the social evils of the day, he produced in 1964 the small enchiridion or spiritual handbook, *Life and Holiness*, which provided concrete direction for the spiritually unsettled. It would appear that in the throes of his severe castigations of the politically corrupt, in the midst of his assaults on the structures of organized hate and the ruthless pillaging of the weak, Merton wrote this work to express his own craving for balance, for an integrated and comprehensive humanistic spirituality.

Merton knew that the route he took to spiritual wholeness was fraught with controversy. Both in the monastic enclosure and out in the world he had many followers, who looked to him for direction. His votaries and his critics were legion. To celebrate the individual over the corporate or conventual collectivity was antimonastic. At the same time, to allow his views, his convictions, and his vision to be submerged in the community was to be unfaithful to himself. Pitted against a despotic, even if benign, abbot, Merton spoke often for the fearful, the intimidated, and the inarticulate. The indomitable James Fox, who succeeded Frederic Dunne in 1948, was to be his superior for twenty years. The conflict that existed between the poet from Prades and the Harvard Business School graduate was fierce and long-lasting, a drama of near epic proportions. Merton lived in the shadow of his abbot's inflexible will; Fox lived in dread of his charge's experimental imagination. "I am a plane," Merton wrote, "to be brought down. And I fly constantly surrounded by a cloud of ethical *Flak!*"[26]

Although Merton never took a direct hit, he was often knocked off balance. The conflict between him and Fox was a *necessary* conflict, though infused with his penchant for the dramatic and the self-referential, and, as Mott points out, ultimately grounded upon their mutual respect:

Dom James and Father Louis, for all their anguish, worked together most of the time and by the time of Merton's death they were clearly friends. And I *mean* friends. Friends who had put up with one another, who had slanged at one another, who, in Merton's words, were like "a couple of cats spitting and hissing." Merton needed Fox; he needed him to say "no" so that he could react; he needed his opposition.

Merton took his role as the lone sentinel on the boundaries of apocalypse with the utmost seriousness, but he also knew that his obsessed, interminable writing was a mode of defence. There was a pathological dimension to it that was emotionally and spiritually debilitating.

> I am simply surfeited with words and typescript and print, surfeited to the point of utter nausea. Surfeited with letters, too. This is so bad that it amounts to a sickness, like the obsessive gluttony of the rich woman in Theodoret who was eating thirty chickens a day until some hermit cured her. The only hermit that can cure me is myself and so I have to become that solitary in order to qualify as my own physician.[27]

The antidote to his maniacal busyness — seclusion as a hermit — had been a dream of Merton's since the early fifties when he became increasingly disgruntled with the monastic life at Gethsemani, a life that was communal, cenobitic rather than anchoritic or eremetical. His quest for the solitary life now achieved a measure of success. Fox gave him his first, partial access to a hermitage, with several restrictions attached. Over time, these restrictions were waived and in August of 1965 he was given permission to live full-time as a hermit on Gethsemani grounds. It is what he had longed for, or so he thought. As Mott indicates:

> once the monks honoured his desire to be a hermit and to live outside the community, his monastic family, he then felt neglected and accused them of turning their collective backs on him. There is another delicious irony in the fact that while the novices were listening to tapes of Father Louis extolling the virtues of community life he is off in the woods living as a hermit.

If he thought the hermit life would stanch his torrent of words, he was wrong. Merton maintained his publishing commitments, his correspondence responsibilities, his diary entries — those for private and those for public viewing — as he had done prior to commencing life as a full-time hermit. Not much had changed, it seemed. In many ways, the isolation afforded by the hermitage provided Merton with the uninterrupted time to perfect his considerable skills as a diarist. In a highly revealing passage written on September 20, 1965, Merton provides a fine distinction between a journal entry and a pensée. He explains the metamorphosis and acknowledges the role exercised by structured spontaneity and achronological patterning necessary to create the perfectly formed meditation.

> I have been working on "Conjectures [of a Guilty Bystander]" in the afternoon — at moments it gets to be like Cantares Hopscotch — criss-cross itinerary of the various pieces taken out of time sequence and fitted into what? An indefinite half-conscious pattern of associations which is never consistent, often purely fortuitous, often not there (and not sought in any case). A lot of rewriting. For instance rewrote an experience of March 18, 1958 (entry of March 19) in light of a very good meditation of Saturday afternoon, developed and changed. A lot of telescoping, etc. In a word, transforming a Journal into "meditations" or "Pensées."[28]

Blake would understand this technique perfectly; he had practised it. And Blake would also understand Merton's increasingly desperate need for the life of the complete solitary. His engagement with the world demanded the consolation of withdrawal from it.

Relieved of his decade-long duties as novice master in 1965, Merton now held a position in the hierarchy of the monastery that was marginal in every way; he was a solemnly professed monk-hermit. This was the way he wanted it. Although one of his finest works, and one of which he was especially fond, *The Way of Chuang Tzu*, appeared in 1965, Merton was only on the cusp of a new and furious wave of energy which would drive him for the remaining three years of his life. His mid-decade reflections have an "eye of the storm" tranquillity about them. He seemed, if only temporarily, to be settled. He mused on the past, what could have been, his creaking body, his melancholy litany of ailments. In one journal passage penned on the Feast of St. Thomas the Doubter, Merton's intimations of mortality are bittersweet, mordant, and even lugubrious. He had received an old snapshot from a relative showing him with Bonnemaman, his maternal grandmother, standing at the back porch of their house in Douglaston, Long Island, thirty years before. Bonnemaman was within a couple of years of her death.

And there am I: it shakes me! I am the young rugby player, the lad from Cambridge, vigorous, light, vain, alive, obviously making a joke of some sort. The thing that shakes me: I can see that that was a different body from the one I have now — one entirely young and healthy, one that did not know sickness, weakness, anguish, tension, fatigue — a body totally assured of itself and without care, perfectly relaxed, ready for enjoyment. What a change since that day! If I were wiser, I would not mind but I am not so sure that I am wiser: I have been through more, I have endured a lot of things, perhaps fruitlessly. I do not entirely think that — but it is possible. What shakes me is that — I wish I were that rugby player, vain, vigorous, etc. and could start over again!! And yet how absurd. What would I ever do? The other thing is that those were, no matter how you look at it, better times! There were things we had not heard of —

Auschwitz, the Bomb, etc. (Yet it was all beginning, nevertheless.)

And now what kind of a body! An arthritic hip; a case of chronic dermatitis on my hands for a year and a half (so that I have to wear gloves); sinusitis, chronic ever since I came to Kentucky; lungs always showing up some funny shadow or other on ex-rays [sic] (though not lately); perpetual diarrhea and a bleeding anus; most of my teeth gone; most of my hair gone; a chewed-up vertebra in my neck which causes my hands to go numb and my shoulder to ache. . . . What an existence![29]

Although self-pitying, awash in nostalgia, and a fine indicator of Merton's love for dramatic overstatement, the journal entry does nonetheless betray Merton's twofold anxiety: the draining of his physical vigour and the downward spiralling of the century's morality. These were the end days.

Merton had long been occupied with the sense that he would die young. He mentioned it often. But when he wrote his entry on the Feast of St. Thomas in 1965, three years to the month before his death, he could not have known that the greatest challenges to his emotional, intellectual, and spiritual vigour were still before him. And he would rise to them.

In late March of 1966 Merton was in St. Joseph's Hospital in Louisville for back surgery. The neurosurgeon performed an anterior cervical fusion to correct Merton's cervical spondylosis. He regained consciousness and entered a world very different from that which he had previously known. For, "after all, to fall in love again after twenty-five years of isolation was, to me at least, an event."[30] Let me be clear: it was not the neurosurgeon he fell in love with, but a student nurse who cared for him. His feelings were reciprocated. They longed for each other's company; relished their playful banter; connived to meet. Merton's lover — called S. in Mott's official biography, named M. by Christine Bochen in her edition of the restricted journals of 1966–1967 published under the title *Learning to Love*, and identified as Margie Smith in John Howard Griffin's posthumously published portrait, *Follow the Ecstasy: Thomas Merton, The Hermitage Years, 1965–1968* — aroused in him a devotion he initially conceived of as a "profound spiritual friendship." But it was more complicated than that.

> What disturbed a man of his honesty was the already pas-
> sionate nature of this devotion. He tried to argue that he
> was not seeking happiness with her as opposed to his choice
> of seeking happiness in God alone. For the moment, this
> opposition seemed curiously confused. But it was not
> merely the question of his vow of chastity. It went far
> deeper, to the very roots of his being. "To seek happiness
> in human love would be as absurd as a fish getting out on
> the beach to walk. . . . My chastity is not merely the renun-
> ciation of sin or of sexual fulfillment but the renunciation
> of a whole mode of being, a whole conception of life and of
> myself."[31]

The devotion became an obsession. Merton was hooked. Mott explains:

> So many people thought the nurse had initiated the whole
> thing, but clearly he did. If that was as far as it had gone,
> then it would have pleased Dom James. He said, you know,
> that when one of his monks went to hospital he expected
> him to fall in love with one of his nurses, but the minute
> he returned to the monastery that was to be the end of it.
> Obviously, as in all things, Merton's case was to be different.
> A very attractive young woman was drawn to Merton and

he was flattered. She, in turn, was flattered by his attentions, his interest in her opinions about his work, etc. A nice situation. Dom James would have approved.

But it didn't end; there was no farewell; their love followed him *into* the monastery.

In fact, their love intensified. Over the coming months both Merton and M. would struggle to make sense of their singular passion. What compromises would be made? What would be the cost of their love?

Merton's love for S. [M.] was not something he wanted to terminate, or could terminate. He tried to preserve it in a new solitude, though there were times when he seemed ready to risk even this to join her during the next year. He saw her, briefly, twice when he was in hospital in October 1966. There was a period of silence toward the end of 1967. In the summer of 1968 he telephoned her once more. By then there was nothing she could do to help him, and he hung up on a note of desperation. "We are two half people wandering / In two lost worlds." (Merton's "Evening: Long Distance Call")[32]

Merton's sexual reawakening revealed the uncharted depths of his own emotional dislocation, his need for genuine and reciprocated love. Ron Seitz, a fellow Kentucky poet and friend of many years, has no doubts that Merton the romantic and Merton the monk were on a collision course:

I aspired to be a monk of Gethsemani on several occasions, and realized that I could not manage the celibacy vow. The authorities could see my preoccupation with women and sex and my acceptance into the monastery simply did not come to pass. I confided my difficulties to Merton because I felt he would understand what I was going through. He spoke to me very freely about his pre-monastic years and I learned first-hand about his appetites for sex and drink.

Indeed, even as a monk of many years, he still had an eye for female beauty. I remember one time when we were driving down the road and he caught sight of a farm girl with the blue jeans bleached out in the buttocks area and he commented on the beauty of it all. He confessed to me on more than one occasion that his relationships with women prior to entering the monastery were self-indulgent or narcissistic. He used women as sexual objects.

His love for M. was different. It was an innocent thing. I think that he was quite naive about all the implications of the relationship and at one point flirted with the idea of leaving his monastic life and getting married. That would have been disastrous. And he knew it.

Merton was changed utterly by this love, the ramifications of which would percolate meaningfully through the remaining years of his life. Christine Bochen comments on Merton the love poet and assesses the long-term impact of the relationship on him:

M. was a young woman and not a teenager. She was not a giddy student nurse but a woman of some experience. I have often wondered what it would have been like to receive the many love poems that he wrote for her. In the poetry, far more than in the prose, we have a kind of honesty that Merton was confident with, a true and deep and profound expression of love. Merton was far more trustful of the poems than he was of the journal writing. He was doubtful of the capacity of his prose to adequately state what was in his heart. He entertained no such doubts about his poetry.

At one point, Merton wrote that he was at war with his own heart and I wonder if that doesn't provide us with a vivid way of capturing his own interior struggle. M. was at the heart of that struggle and if we situate this period in his life within the larger frame we can see that all of his life was an exercise in learning to love.

I think that the episode with M. was an experience waiting to happen because Merton at this time in his life was already becoming increasingly aware that there were areas of his life, particularly as they concerned his relationships with women, which had not worked out well and needed to be revisited. Merton was conscious of his inability to accept love at the time he was at Cambridge and later at Columbia, and now at the age of fifty-one, in mid-life, with a new clarity born of solitude and mature prayer, he saw what had hitherto been obscured: *that he had not allowed himself to be loved*. The episode with M. revealed for the first time what intimacy actually means. He allowed himself to love and be loved, to know and be known.

The year 1966, then, was a watershed year for the maturing monk — emotionally and spiritually — and 1967 would bring no respite from the new and bold challenges facing him.

In these last years of his life he was at work on his two great Blakean "myth-dreams," *Cables to the Ace or Familiar Liturgies of Misunderstanding*, what he calls his "long poetic retch," and *The Geography of Lograire*, "my summa of offbeat anthropology." With *Geography*, in particular, James Laughlin understood Merton to be engaged in nothing less than a life-long "work in progress, his *Cantos*, his 'Patterson.'" These Blakean works reflect Merton's conviction that the tyranny of mind and power in Western culture suppresses the genuine spirituality and life-affirming imagination, the meaning-generating capacity of words and silence, so integral to other cultures: aboriginal; oriental; extinct.

In both these long poems Merton's imagination is let loose. Grammar is scattered; ideas poured into a macaronic stew; parody freed to run riot; the idiosyncratic becomes the commonplace. And there is a fury of purpose embedded in these poems that reveals the poet's spiritual anguish and macabre delight in mad experimentation. *Cables* and *Geography* are both antipoetic epics, not easily accessible to the reader, subversive, jarring, outrageous, maddeningly ironic. It was the Chilean poet Nicanor Parra who provided Merton with the idea of antipoetry, a poetry replete with irony and protest, a method of coping with the contemporary disarray of language and meaning, a latter-day Blakean strategy. As Merton wrote in his posthumously published *Asian Journal*:

> the antipoet "suggests" a tertiary meaning which is *not* "creative" but a deliberate ironic feedback of cliché, a further referential meaning, alluding, by its tone, banality, etc., to a *customary and abused context*, that of an impoverished and routine sensibility, and of the "mass-mind," the stereotyped response by "mass-culture."[33]

Much as he was the antipoet, Merton was also the antimonk. In a correspondence with the theologian Rosemary Radford Ruether, at the time of the composition of *Cables*, Merton commiserated with her over the many demands made upon their time by worthy groups, movements, etc., and observed that contrary to public perception he is

> probably much more in communication with people all over the place, all over the world, than most active lifers are. . . .

My way is to be notoriously offbeat and inconsistent, but to
be able to establish a kind of consistency within the offbeat-
ness, which people gradually come to recognize and
respect. . . . I don't comfortably wear the label of monk . . .
because I am now convinced that the first way to be a decent
monk is to be a non-monk and an anti-monk. . . .[34]

There is something frivolous, something of braggadocio
about Merton's claim to be a non-monk living his monkish
existence in his rural retreat, but in touch with everyone
everywhere. This is playful and a bit irritating. Merton *was* a
monk and he *was* sequestered, by his own desire, away from
the kinds of professional and domestic tensions that were only
too common in the busy life of Ruether, mother, scholar, wife,
and activist. But Merton does have a point if you consider that
his antimonk stand is predicated on his resistance to a narrow
stereotyping of the good Catholic monk in the popular imagination, a stereotyping that was, in good measure, the result of
his success as a writer. One way Merton found to implode the
constricting and reductionist definition of monkhood that
identified it exclusively with the Christian tradition was to
view it from the perspective of the East, in whose spiritual
tradition contradictions and negation cease and the Contraries
live in harmony. This is the East that is, in Hermann Hesse's
phrase, "the mother of all things," the East of Zen where one
chooses between madness and innocence, the East where "you
are lost, for you are, at last, nowhere," the East where reason's
summit is paradox.

That the East represented the fulfilment of a dream, a yearning for knowledge and growth, can readily be attested to by
Merton's own zealous absorption of the wisdom of Eastern
spirituality and his total immersion in the contemplative's
common quest for God. This is not to suggest that Merton was

oblivious to the dangers of doctrinal compromise, indifferent-ism, syncretism, and the like, but rather that he realized that the quest of the mystic, the journey to the heart of all reality, the searching for the *total other*, is shared by all authentic traditions.

In a life brimming with paradox, the Trappist monk vowed to stability became a wanderer. He understood that one must travel to go nowhere:

> Follow the ways of no man, not even your own.
> The way that is most yours is no way. For
> where are you? Unborn! Your way therefore
> is unborn. Yet you travel. You do not become
> unborn by stopping a journey you have begun:
> and you cannot be nowhere by issuing a
> decree: "I am now nowhere!" (Cable 38, *Cables to the Ace*)

Merton was about to arrive at the heart of nowhere country.

The year 1968 was to be the journey's end. And it began auspiciously enough with the election on January 13 of the new Abbot of Gethsemani, the successor of James Fox, Merton's onetime novice, Flavian Burns. Dom Flavian's relationship with Merton was very different from that of Dom James. Whereas Fox had kept Merton on a short leash, the new abbot was disposed to release the restive wanderer for the occasional trip. Save for his not infrequent visits to physicians and specialists in Louisville, his hospital stays, and two brief visits out of state — one to St. John's University, Collegeville, Minnesota, in 1956 to attend a conference on psychiatry and the religious life given by the controversial convert Dr. Gregory Zilboorg, and the other to New York City in 1964 to meet the eminent Zen authority Daisetz T. Suzuki — Merton had not left the monastery for close to twenty-seven years. He was about to make up for lost time.

In May he visited both Our Lady of the Redwoods Monastery in Whitehorn, California, and the Monastery of Christ in the Desert in Abiquiu, New Mexico; in late August he was invited to meet Dr. Soedjatmoko, the Indonesian ambassador to the United States, in Washington; in September he returned to Christ in the Desert, gave a conference at a convent of Poor Clares in Chicago, spent two weeks in Alaska giving talks to several religious communities, and travelled along the California coast from Santa Barbara back to Our Lady of the Redwoods. He flew out of San Francisco on October 15 on his much anticipated Asian tour: he had been invited to attend and give a principal address at a meeting of monastic superiors in Bangkok held under the auspices of a Benedictine body, Aide à l'Implantation Monastique (AIM).

The Bangkok conference was scheduled for December but Merton had been given permission to build an itinerary that would include several stops prior to and immediately after the AIM event. He accepted an invitation to speak at the Spiritual Summit Conference scheduled in Calcutta and sponsored by the Temple of Understanding; he travelled to New Delhi; had a meeting with the Dalai Lama at his home in Dharamsala; spoke about William Blake and his Four-Fold Vision with Dr. V. Raghavan, the distinguished Sanskrit scholar, in Madras; spent several days in Sri Lanka and visited the ancient ruined city of Polonnaruwa where he experienced a shattering theophany: "I don't know what else remains but I have now seen and have pierced through the surface and have got beyond the shadow and the disguise";[35] journeyed on to Singapore and then arrived in Bangkok on December 7. The stage was set for the last act, indeed the last performance.

Looking tired, Merton delivered his paper, "Marxism and Monastic Perspectives," at 10:45 a.m. on December 10 for not only the assembled delegates but two television teams as well.

The presence of the Dutch and Italian television crews disturbed him, because he had promised Dom Flavian that there would be no television. But it was out of his hands.

At the end of his presentation, he observed, "So, I will disappear from view and we can all have a Coke or something." Merton had lunch, walked back to his cottage with fellow delegate François de Grunne, had a shower, and then, very possibly with the soles of his feet still wet, grasped a large standing fan that was defective and took a full 220 volts of direct current. He cried out and fell to the floor, where he was discovered with a long burn mark along the right side of his body, a discoloured face, eyes and mouth open, the fan lying on top of his body. When Odo Haas, Abbot of Waekwan, lifted the fan he too received a severe electrical shock and was held to the shaft of the fan until Celestine Say, Prior of the Abbey of Our Lady of Montserrat in Manila, unplugged it. The Abbot Primate, Rembert Weakland, gave Merton the last anointing and the Prioress of Taegu Convent in Seoul, the Austrian internist Edeltrud Weist, pronounced him dead.

As Mott notes, however, there were several peculiar things done to the body:

It seems to me very obvious that when you just step out of a shower you are naked and that when you have been electrocuted you urinate involuntarily. When the Thai police arrived, and it took them a stunningly long time to arrive, they discovered that the body had a pair of drawers on. In fact, it is a second pair. The first pair they put on him must have been put on while the fan was still running because they have burn marks. So he is given a second pair. He's all cleaned and ready for inspection. The naked monk is made modest. Other strange things happen: the position of the body has changed; there is a virtual demolition job done on the premises by the Thai servants, even to the point of removing several inches of dirt from the flowerbeds around the building. Anybody who went to the death site an hour after Merton had died would see a totally transformed scene.

It is all a bit of a mystery story. Still, I have no doubts that his death was an accident.

No autopsy was conducted; the body was flown back to the U.S. on an army jet from Vietnam — an ironic note that Merton would have appreciated. The funeral liturgy and interment occurred at Gethsemani on December 17, fully one week after his death. His grave is marked with the simple white cross accorded all deceased Trappists irrespective of their rank or prominence.

Rumours abounded that Merton would not have returned to Gethsemani in any other way, that his departure to the East was a departure from Gethsemani. Certainly Merton was conscious of these rumours. He had informed his friends by circular letter and by postcard that he intended to remain a monk of Gethsemani. Wilber H. ("Ping") Ferry, Merton's friend and correspondent who accompanied him on his trip along the California coast, noted in a letter written twelve years later that

he was coming back, for sure. He raised the question himself . . . and his answer was invariably, "I'll always be a monk of Gethsemani." At the same time, he had hoped to have two or three years in (probably) Japan at a Zen Center. And he hoped to find a place alone, and away from Gethsemani, to take the solitary road for several years. Whether he intended some time to return physically to G. I don't think he had decided yet himself. But he certainly wanted to have forever the identification of a monk of Gethsemani.[36]

As a poet Merton lusted for experience and he saw its apotheosis in the word; and as a monk he sought as *the* apotheosis of experience final integration with the Word. A writer of words and yet a seeker of silence, under a vow of stability and yet burning with the fever to travel, "ascetic, conservative, traditional, monastic [and] radical, independent, and somewhat akin to beats and hippies and to poets,"[37] a "guilty bystander" yet an "alter Christus," Merton intimated the future consummation of dream and reality, division and unity, in his use of the mandala as a personal symbol of integration and rest:

> Better to study the germinating waters
>   of my wood
> And know this fever: or die in a distant
>   country
> Having become a pure cone
> Or turn to my eastern abstinence
> With that old inscrutable love cry
> And describe a perfect circle. (Cable 74, *Cables to the Ace*)

Not only Dan Berrigan was stunned by Merton's death. No one who knew him was prepared for it. Brother Paul Quenon, a poet and former novice of Merton's, recalls the day he heard of Merton's death as if it were yesterday:

> Everyone remembers where they were when they first heard of the death of President John F. Kennedy. And so with Merton. I was in the refectory or dining hall with the rest of the community. Abbot Burns came up to the microphone at the end of the meal and announced that Father Louis had

had an accident in Bangkok, that he had died, and that we were waiting for further news.

The first thing that I did was to say the penitential psalms for him. It is a monastic custom to do so, but Merton had once said that when *he* dies we will have to batter heaven with our psalms. So I did as he asked. I went into the abbey church, knelt down, and prayed the seven penitential psalms in a way I had never done previously or have done since.

And then I went into the scriptorium or study room and time seemed to be standing still for me. But just as I entered through the scriptorium door the safety valve on the boiler released a great gush of steam. It was a symbol for me, a likeness to the death of Jesus on the cross when he breathed forth the Spirit into the world.

And Merton? A Zen death, an unconsciously organized suicide? A political act, an organized assassination?

Donald Grayston, the Anglican theologian and Merton scholar, has long been struck by the significance of Merton's death:

T.M.'s death was certainly unusual. Many people have asked me if it was suicide, or if not, whether he was murdered by the CIA or some other politically motivated group disturbed by Merton's peace writings.

What's the thing about Merton's death that continues to fascinate so many?

I have read widely and deeply on the subject, including some contemporary theorists about death. The point made by some that in the West we have only four kinds of death was particularly interesting: natural death; murder; suicide; accident. But in the East, the religious East that is, there is a fifth kind of death: the death of the master. There are certain elements by which the death of the master can be identified: the master gathers his disciples around him; does something absurd with bread and wine; says it's his body and blood; and then dies the next day. I am not comparing Merton to Jesus, but when you consider the circumstances of his death you find that the conditions necessary for the death of the master are there for the discerning. Almost all of the Catholics who were at his Bangkok session were his disciples. They had been reading him for years. They had been disciples at a distance and now they were disciples in the presence of the master. And then he does something absurd. He says, "So, now I will disappear and we can go get a Coke or something," and then he dies.

In addition to meeting these terms of the death of the master, we have all the incidents of synchronicity that surrounded his final days — the dreams that people had, the things that they saw, the letters that they wrote each other, the photographs taken, many by Merton himself, that together make up a kind of collage of words and images that scream out for all who would hear: *this was an unusual and highly significant death*!

Once again the wagging tongue, the wild proliferation of rumour, the groundless speculation. Merton was to the end the monk who left his mark on a generation, on a culture, on a century.

2

THARMAS:
The Rebel

TO UNDERSTAND the significance of Thomas Merton for our time, to appreciate his spiritual geography, as it were, it is necessary to know something of the affinity between his vision and art and that of William Blake, *his* Blake. The Romantic poet and engraver was unlike any of his contemporaries, and he exulted in the eccentricity of his views and his craft. He was keen on dethroning reigning monarchs of all kinds: of taste and thought and rule. He created an elaborate mythology of gods and heroes, including Urizen; Enitharmon; Los; the Spectres and Emanations; Beulah; Oothoon; the Limits of Contraction & Opacity, and many more, not to confound his contemporaries but to radically expand our constricted vision.

Blake abominated the sad rule of the Academy — a reliance on "Mathematical Proportion" to the detriment of "the Imagination" — in all its forms: painting, poetry, philosophy. Accordingly, he attempted to reawaken our dormant senses, to challenge the rigid rule of Logic, to free the passions that

institutional Christianity and the Enlightenment conspired to
suppress. Blake was not in sympathy with his age. He saw its
life-denying contradictions only too clearly and they called
him mad for it. He was largely undervalued by his contemporaries, not infrequently scorned by his artistic peers, indulged
by the larger public as quaint and incomprehensible, feared
as a dotty subversive by a few, and generally ignored. He and
his wife Catherine lived most of their lives on the brink of
insolvency. Not a success story.

But Blake's reputation has fared much better in the twentieth
century. Scores of artists and scholars have sought to decode
this most singular and maddening of poets and dreamers and
in so doing have claimed him for their own. Merton's reading
of Blake was strikingly original, but more important still,
it was unlike many scholarly interpretations of Blake's art.
Merton appropriated, made his own, Blake's visionary poetics
and radical spirituality. In short, Merton became *the* twentieth-
century heir to Blake's vision and poetics. As Merton observed
as early as 1939, in his master's thesis — "Nature and Art in
William Blake: An Essay in Interpretation" — Blake "was
entirely individual, perhaps because he was the most deeply
religious artist of his time in England."

> It is impossible to understand Blake with the analytical
> tools his own century used — by judging him by precon-
> ceived and arbitrary standards, and, worst of all, by seeking
> out his moral ideas and attempting to judge his art by them.
> He must be approached with a broader, deeper, more flexible
> understanding. Hold Blake up beside the Scholastic philos-
> ophers, and many of his apparent contradictions resolve
> themselves out, many dark places become light. . . . But
> if we approach him as materialists and skeptics — as
> his enemies, Blake will mock us as he mocked many of

his unenlightened friends, teasing us with more and more extravagant visions until we are forced to walk away shaking our heads and murmuring like Dr. Trussler: "Blake, dim'd with superstition."[1]

And so Merton approached his Blake via the a priori and systematic methodology of the great Schoolmen, principally Thomas Aquinas, aided by the work of the twentieth-century neo-Thomist and aesthetician Jacques Maritain, who would in time become one of his dearest friends. Merton claimed Blake less for his century and more for himself.

What is it in Blake that so appealed to Merton? There is certainly some congruence of history, biography, and temperament between the two: they were both poets; each of them had a special bond with a brother who died young: Blake's brother Robert, who probably died of consumption, and John Paul Merton, killed during the Second World War. Merton and Blake both possessed the spiritual qualities of the biblical prophet and rebel: the capacity for righteous anger mingled with insight. But far more important than this is the congruence of strategy, of vision, to which Merton refers in his last critical piece on Blake, a review of the Death-of-God theologian Thomas J.J. Altizer's *The New Apocalypse: The Radical Christian Vision of William Blake*, in which he wrote:

Blake saw official Christendom as a *narrowing* of vision, a foreclosure of experience and of future expansion, a locking up and securing of the doors of perception. He substituted for it a Christianity of openness, of total vision, a faith which dialectically embraces both extremes, not seeking to establish order in life by shutting off a little corner of chaos and subjecting it to laws and to police, but moving freely between dialectical poles in a wild chaos, integrating sacred vision, in and through the experience of fallenness, as the only locus of creativity and redemption. Blake, in other words, calls for "a whole new form of theological understanding."[2]

In his art and in his spirituality Blake offered Merton, his artistic and mystical descendant, a "new form of theological understanding," a strategy to redress a shattered humanity, an integrated vision. What Peter Ackroyd observes of Blake can with equal justice be applied to Merton: "He was, above everything else, an artist and not an orthodox 'thinker': he was attracted to images or phrases as a means of interpretation, and never espoused a complete or coherently organized body of knowledge."[3] But both did espouse a new way of seeing, a way of perceiving and understanding that stood in marked contrast to the prevailing orthodoxies of taste and theology, art and spirituality. They both opposed the constricting rule of what Blake termed the "Ratio, the generalisation, the use of abstract reason, 'Mathematic Proportion' that is the negation of 'Living Proportion.' "[4] And they both found it necessary in the development of their alternative mythologies — alternative to the dominant modes of thinking — to be wildly exploratory and decidedly idiosyncratic in their respective poetic styles because they found themselves expressing original and provocative ideas that "could not be contained within the inherited forms of verse; no conventional prosody could have held it, and no cadence could represent it."[5]

Blake and Merton are poets rich in paradox, fed by deep, strange, and mystical sources, defiant and yet profoundly conservative at heart. They both accept the reality of the Fall — of a sundered humanity, riven by false oppositions — which must be overcome by a new and higher unity: Universal Man; Four-Fold Vision; Jesus Christ. For Blake, the Fall is best seen in the fragmented state of each individual human. In Blake's mythology every human consists of four components, each struggling for ascendency over the others; they are identified as the Four Zoas, Urizen (Reason), Urthona (Wisdom), Luvah (Emotion), and Tharmas (Instinct). They are the "Four Mighty Ones" in every human. The trick for Blake is not to eliminate the opposites, to subsume the warring Zoas under one of their number, to perpetuate the tyranny of Single Vision, but rather to create "the fourfold creative and prophetic vision in which opposites do not merely come together and fuse in synthesis, but are restored to a higher unity, an alchemical wedding of loving and fiery elements made all the more ardent by separation."[6]

Merton's poetic and spiritual vision consisted of his own central "myth-dream" as he called it: the disunity of the word /world and its reparation by the poet; the role of silence in this lifelong act of reparation; the tyranny of intellection and its dethronement by "archaic wisdom"; the ultimate realization of that Four-Fold Vision which is imaginative and spiritual integration/wholeness.

It is interesting to note that though Blake is often alluded to in the journals, diaries, and letters and appears occasionally in both theological and literary essays, he receives sustained critical treatment only at the beginning and the end of Merton's writing life. And although nearly thirty years intervened between his master's thesis on Blake and his review of the Altizer book, his appreciation and understanding of Blake remained remarkably consistent. In his Altizer review his enthusiasm for the heterodox Blake lacks something of the more cautious and conservative approach characteristic of his convert days, but in two specific ways his reading of Blake remains the same.

One is his stalwart defence of Blake's belief in supernatural or revealed religion as opposed to the "Natural Religion" of the Deists of the eighteenth century, a religion devoid of vision and imagination, a religion of rational construction alone. In his thesis, Merton contends that J. Middleton Murry's critical writings on Blake's concept of nature suggest that the poet was an atheist. Merton pointedly asks whether Murry is questioning the validity of Blake's visions. Does the critic wish them to be "despiritualized"? "If Blake's visions were not visions of a supernatural world, why did he pray for them to be restored when they would not come to him? Or how could he say such a thing as 'The Lord our Father will do for us, and with us according to his divine will, and for our good'?"[7]

In his Altizer review of 1968 Merton takes issue with the author's Hegelian reading of Blake and warns that such a reading in effect forces Blake into the arms of the Antichrist. Merton has Blake himself respond to Altizer's charge by quoting from his "Annotations to Bacon's Essays":

When Bacon claims to reason in favour of religion, Blake calls him "An Atheist pretending to talk against Atheism," and when Bacon praises social rituals Blake comments: "Bacon supposes that the Dragon Beast & Harlot are worthy of a place in the New Jerusalem. Excellent Traveller, Go on and be damned!" Blake's conclusion is that "a Lord Chancellor's opinions are as different from those of Christ as those of a Caiaphas or Pilate or Herod." I think this should be kept in mind by anyone who wants to praise Blake as a "Christian atheist" or an apostle of purely secular Christianity, in the sense in which this is understood by some popular theologians.[8]

The second way in which Merton's interpretation of Blake remains constant is his essentially Scholastic reading of Blake's aesthetics and theology. In the preface to his thesis

he makes it clear that he has used the aesthetic ideas of
St. Thomas Aquinas as a "touchstone" in his assessment
of Blake's thought and poetics. And when in his Altizer review
he speaks of the Godhead he chooses the terminology of the
Scholastics, a language of essence, substance, being, and accident, over that of the Death-of-God theologians, a language of
process and becoming. Once again we see his indebtedness to
St. Thomas, an indebtedness due in no small part to his admiration for the writings of his friend Jacques Maritain.

> Afflicted as I am with an incurable case of metaphysics, I
> cannot see where the idea of Godhead *as process* is more
> dynamic than that of Godhead *as pure act*. To one who has
> been exposed to scholastic ontology and has not recovered,
> it remains evident that the *activity of becoming* is con-
> siderably less alive and dynamic than the *act of Being*. Far
> from regarding "pure Being" as static quiescence, tradi-
> tional metaphysics is in accord with Blake in regarding it as
> a source and ground of all life:
>> The pride of the peacock is the glory of God.
>> The wrath of the lion is the wisdom of God.
>> The lust of the goat is the bounty of God.
>> The nakedness of woman is the work of God.[9]

Blake, therefore, is to be found at both the beginning and at
the end of Merton's life. In *The Seven Storey Mountain* he
publicly appropriated Blake's rebellious posture, his strategy
of response to the materialist and myopic evils of his day:

> It was Blake's problem to try and adjust himself to a society
> that understood neither himself nor his kind of faith and
> love. More than once, smug and inferior minds conceived
> it to be their duty to take this man Blake in hand and

direct and form him, to try and "canalize" what they recognized as "talent" in some kind of a conventional channel.
And always this meant the cold and heartless disparage-
ment of all that was vital and real to him in art and in
faith. There were years of all kinds of petty persecution,
from many different quarters, until finally Blake departed
from his would-be patrons, and gave up all hope of an
alliance with a world that thought he was crazy, and went
his own way.[10]

Blake was the model of rebellion; his way was the standard.
Like Blake, Merton understood that

true holiness and redemption . . . lie in the energy that
springs from the reunion of Contraries. But the Negation
[Urizen, the "Abstract objecting power that Negatives
everything"] stands between the Contraries and prevents
their "marriage." Holding heaven and hell apart, Urizen
infects them with his own sickness and nothingness. True
holiness, faith, vision, Christianity, must therefore subvert
his power to Negate and "redeem the contraries" in mercy,
pity, peace. The work of this reversal is the epiphany of God
in Man. The God that "is dead" is therefore the Negation
set up in solitary and absolute authority as an idol and
Spectre. But this God is endowed with life in proportion as
men invest him with (earthly) power and adore him in his
separateness and isolation — even putting one another to
death in his honour. The beginning of faith must obviously
be a "no" to this idol, this Negation of life and of love. But
the negation of the Negation and the restoration of Contraries is not just the work of intelligence. In Blake it was, and
had to be, a mystical and prophetic experience involving
the whole man.[11]

It would be some time before Merton felt sufficiently confident to move (as he put it in his Altizer review) "freely between dialectical poles in a wild chaos, integrating sacred vision," but his dangerous poetics and subversive spirituality would eventually find expression in his *Cables to the Ace* and *The Geography of Lograire*. Blake's poet, who seeks to "assist once again at the Marriage of Heaven and Hell," here finds his counterpart in Merton. In these last two poems the function of the poet, in my view, is clearly a prophetic and mystical one, "integrating sacred vision" [Blake's Four-Fold Vision] in and through the very condition of humanity's fallenness. This necessitates an unrestrictive sympathy for the authentic religious impulse irrespective of culture, sect, doctrine or history. It entails a wholesome respect for diverse religious traditions and a deep imaginative daring that finds in "wild chaos" the "only laws of creativity and redemption."

Cables, in particular, underscores Merton's Blakean and cosmic eschatology. Only those truly liberated from a "narrowing of vision, a foreclosure of experience" can appreciate the imperative for a "new form of theological understanding." Like Blake, Merton worked for the dethronement of Urizen — the abstract power that negates everything — and for the overthrow of the tyranny of logic, law, and generalization. He worked for the creative revitalizing of the tension of the necessary separation, the legacy of the Fall, and of redeeming the Contraries or "the marriage of heaven and hell." But this reversal of the power of Urizen, of a fallen history, though it be seen in the epiphany of the incarnated Word, must not be seen as occurring outside human history and therefore succumbing again to the abstract reasoning of Urizen. The radical reversal of fallen history requires not only the acceptance of the Fall as an ontological fact — and both Blake and Merton clearly do accept it — but also an acceptance of the world as the geography of redemption.

As Merton acknowledged in *The Secular Journal* and *The Seven Storey Mountain*, it was William Blake who brought him into the Roman Catholic Church and made him "conscious of the necessity of a vital faith," but the Blakean temerity and bold experimentation of his mature thought and exploration remained largely hidden during the early and formative years of his monastic life. It was as if, in embracing Blake, Merton established his monasticism as an act of spiritual and intellectual rebellion. His appreciation of the *full* significance of Blake's rebellion for his art, his life, and his spirituality would come later.

But Blake didn't figure only in Merton's thought and mysticism, he also figured prominently in his life. Blake helps us to understand Merton, and he helped Merton to understand himself. In short, Merton is a Blakean character, the contours of his personal geography mapped by Blake himself.

The remainder of this chapter will look at Merton under the heading of the Zoa, *Tharmas*, or instinct, and each subsequent chapter will examine Merton under the separate heading of each of the remaining Zoas. In this way we shall see Merton for what he was: not only a twentieth-century Blake, but a poet-mystic shaped by his understanding of Blake's deliriously heretical genius.

Although in Blake's mythology it is Orc who embodies the fiery spirit of rebellion, Tharmas represents something of that rebellious instinct in its coarser and more primitive state. Tharmas, Merton wrote in his thesis, represents the "world of perishing, blind, created things." Tharmas is instinct, nature, loins, the desperate struggle for self-assertion, for identity, that we see most clearly in youth and in the unsettled questions of our formative years.

Merton's rebellion began at Montauban. When Owen Merton enrolled his son in the Lycée Ingres in 1926 he introduced him to a world marked by "sly bullying . . . bad language, and the tyranny of Monsieur le Proviseur and his henchman, Monsieur le Censeur."[12] Merton was the solitary stranger, a daily butt of jokes, sneers, and fists. He learned the sting of insult and obscenity. He never forgot the misery he endured at the Lycée, nor did he forgive. In his autobiography he would excoriate the barbarity of that prison known as the Lycée Ingres, a microcosm of the corruption of the French ideal itself:

> The experience of living with the kind of people I found in the Lycée was something new to me [he was eleven at the time], but in degree, rather than in kind. There was the same animality and toughness and insensitivity and lack of conscience that existed to some extent in my own character. . . . But these French children seemed to be so much tougher and more cynical and more precocious than anyone else I had ever seen. . . . I suppose the most shocking thing about France is the corruption of French spirituality into flippancy and cynicism; of French intelligence into sophistry; of French dignity and refinement into petty vanity and theatrical self-display; of French charity into a disgusting fleshly concupiscence, and of French faith into sentimentality or puerile atheism. There was all of this in the Lycée Ingres, at Montauban.[13]

Merton's gift for irritating overstatement is amply displayed in this easy judgement. In his post-conversion zeal he is quick to record the injuries he suffered as the foreign youngster, prey to the villainy of corrupted French youth and quick to lambaste the authorities who supervised the dormitory-prison that was his home, his hell, for nearly three years until rescued by an English private preparatory school. It wasn't quite as horrific at the Lycée as Merton describes it, and he did arrive at a *modus vivendi* with the school bullies, though he had to be constantly on his guard, ever poised for the next pummel, obscenity, or derisive remark. As noted earlier, when his father "sprang" him, as it were, from his French incarceration and settled him anew in the pleasant pastures of England, "to Tom this was the greatest jail delivery his father had ever organized."[14]

He now found himself in Ripley Court in Surrey, where he stayed for a year before going to the pastorally situated Oakham Public School in Rutland in 1929. Merton had by now fine-tuned the science of acclimation, and he very quickly learned the rules and mores of an English public school. He did not abominate its culture as did his contemporary C.S. Lewis (who wrote witheringly of its sadistic élan in his autobiography, *Surprised by Joy*); to him its peculiarities, rites, and quasi-military regimentation were recognizable and he was able to make the appropriate adjustments. Oakham was no Lycée Ingres.

While at Oakham, Merton demonstrated to the satisfaction of his masters that he was university material. He competed for the Johnson Exhibition at Clare College, Cambridge, a scholarship named after the founder of Oakham and Uppingham, another public school, and open only to students from these two schools. Merton won, and thus it was decided that he would go to Cambridge. It was to prove a bitter experience.

One of Merton's poems, "Sports without Blood: A Letter to Dylan Thomas" (1948), captures the conflicting moods that defined his Cambridge years. The poem is partly written in the style of the Welsh poet himself:

> Hush-hush water cripple the world that's
>   upside down,
> And lives are flights on the face of

> motherofpearl heaven
> Until old crossbones get their skulls in
> greysize capture

"Sports" serves as both a recollection of impressions made during Merton's sour Cambridge University days and a general lament for a world gone awry — his personal world and the world of nations. In part one of the poem, "When evening drowned and sang in the peeled water / Hate took place in Cambridge" and many gathered to watch the much-honoured sport without blood: the regatta. The regatta is a metaphor for life, the success of which depends on the quality of the competition. The fury of the competing oarsmen shatters the gentle symmetry of nature as reflected in the serene waterways, "White blades replace the upside down cathedrals / With a wallop of bells," and the intoxicating fever of those driven to win, "With dog-drunk gasbodies winning under the tank," marks "old King George's June" as a "night without religion."

The world of Cambridge is pictured in part two of the poem as a "spell between two bombs," a world peopled for Merton with satirist Evelyn Waugh's BYTS or Bright Young Things and critic Martin Green's "children of the sun," a sparkling and privileged priesthood of aesthetes and decadents:

> . . . here we bloom, amid the marigolds
> Sad, with the central doll of an old photo. . . .
> Oh, the bald lawns, and the enclosure
> The green we had to smell!

It was a world indifferent to the decay that was eating England, and Merton for that matter, where men and women "slept in the cloud without Christ." Only the Welsh minstrel, the poet Thomas, untouched by the languor of the elite,

. . . proceeded to the burial.
Night by night in Camden Town
Up and down the furry buildings
In and out the boxing alleys, dark as tea
You walked with murder in your music box
And played the pieces of blind England all
   around the town.

In the poem's third part the speaker addresses aristocratic England:

. . . whose hopeless manor
Fox and grouse have come to own,
Bred hand in glove with pestilence
The ivy eats your castle down.

The deterioration of England's once proud manors and ancient values can be briefly arrested on the day of the regatta, just before the "formal racers come," by staring into the unruffled water that mirrors the upside-down, topsy-turvy, world of our own past making. *This* world is an illusion, however, mirroring the spiritual illusions we have feasted on:

Come, let us drink our poisoned home
And swim in the face of a glass world.

In the concluding part of the poem the speaker resolves to go in another direction, to "turn again to waters brown," to leave "this people to its own calm." He rejects the "dark, sinister world of Cambridge" and the spiritually sterile culture of the landed nobility and seeks now the "soundless song" of his "fens."

What Wales was for Dylan Thomas, Gethsemani became for Merton, and he was determined to achieve in his own work and life the poetic and spiritual integrity that he saw in Thomas. "Sports without Blood" is Merton's deliberate effort to achieve something of that integrity, which was best defined by Dylan Thomas himself in answer to a question posed by an inquirer:

> What I like to do [he told his questioner] is to treat words as a craftsman does his wood or stone or what-have-you, to hew, carve, mold, coil, polish and plane them into patterns, sequences, sculptures, figures of sound expressing some lyrical impulse, some spiritual doubt or conviction, some dimly realized truth I must try to reach and realize.[15]

"Sports without Blood" contrasts the suffocating world of a sinister Cambridge with the genuine freedom of the minstrel, but this clever conceit only disguises the fundamental problem that Merton had at Cambridge: alienation from himself.

When Merton arrived at his next port of call, Columbia University, in February of 1935, the sooty, noisy, hectic world of Manhattan acted like a purge, a necessary release from the social pressures and high expectations of Cambridge. He could be more himself — if only he knew who he was.

Tharmas/Merton was the intrepid rebel. He couldn't settle down; he loved to probe and provoke; and ultimately he moved perilously close to the brink of self-dissolution, of irrecoverable despair. The year 1938 was the year of his conversion to Roman Catholicism, a watershed year as Merton undertook a radical remaking of the self, a casting off of the old vesture and a donning of the new. He created a shockingly unpredictable persona: the Catholic zealot. The wastrel was now an aspirant to sainthood; the city he once celebrated for its vitality, its alluring rhythms of adventure and accomplishment, he now derided as a den of thieves, slick operators, and crass materialists.

Merton came to loathe the New World as much as he did the Old. By the early 1940s Merton's contempt for secular society was complete and admitted of no remedy but rejection.

He placed no trust in the capacity of the world to rise; it seemed capable only of sinking. In the opening stanza of "Dirge for the World Joyce Died In," from a collection of early poems dated 1940–42, the poet speaks of the carnage of the age — "ravel up the roots," "rack apart the knotted limbs," "Ravish the kingdoms," "scan their ruins" — inviting the reader to enter the realm of the living dead, abandoning all hope as we enter the Inferno.

In the second stanza Merton asks us with irony to "Rescue the usurers from the living sea" for "Their dead love runs like life" as they prepare with calculated concern "To blast the harvest of our prettiest year." In the third stanza the doctors, blind and deluded, "Count the course their shining zodiacs go," oblivious of death's sinister undoing, deaf "to the worms' red work." While the physicians "in their disinfected city" prognosticate with a charlatan's authority, there is one who will "Suffer no drug to slack his idiot eyestring," whose diagnosis cannot be attested to by astrological certitude, but only by sight, and he is James Joyce, the "Proud spy in the cursing kingdom of the dead." The "cursing kingdom," for Joyce, is the middle class, and those who share its value system:

> the middle class is as sacred as the Mystical Body of Christ and indistinguishable from it, so *everything* he says seems to be blasphemous.[16]

Joyce is not the only "proud spy," however. Like him, Merton/ Tharmas despises the gods of commerce and politics, the idols of secular ambition and urban living, the Baal of mediocrity and spiritual torpor.

Merton's apartment building on Perry Street in Greenwich Village, New York City, during his student days at Columbia University in the 1930s.

A 1930s photograph of Thomas Merton (left), Bob Lax, and unidentified student in the *Jester* office, the Columbia University student publication.

A partying Merton (left) holding a glass and cigarette at a Columbia bash.

Robert Giroux of the New York publishing firm, Farrar, Straus & Giroux, in 1997. Giroux was a Columbia friend of Merton's and later the editor of *The Seven Storey Mountain*.

Merton (centre) and colleagues — Franciscan and lay —
at St. Bonaventure University, Olean, New York.

Merton, a young
tonsured Trappist,
standing in front of
the gate of Our
Lady of Gethsemani
Abbey in Kentucky,
in the 1940s.

Merton and Sister Thérèse Lentfoehr, poet, amanuensis,
soulmate, and keeper of the flame, probably in the late 1950s.
PHOTO COURTESY OF THOMAS MERTON CENTER

Merton on picnic with friends beside unnamed lake.
PHOTO COURTESY OF THOMAS MERTON CENTER

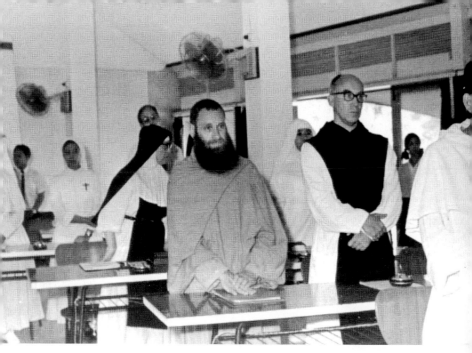

Merton in company with other monastics at the conference in Bangkok, Thailand, December 1968, from which he would not return to Gethsemani alive.

PHOTO COURTESY OF THOMAS MERTON CENTER

Flavian Burns, ocso, was abbot of Gethsemani at the time of Merton's death.

BERNIE LUCHT

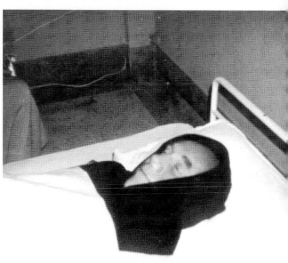

Merton lying "in state."

PHOTO COURTESY OF THOMAS MERTON CENTER

Patrick Hart, ocso, was Merton secretary, friend, and latterly, his editor.
BERNIE LUCHT

Poet Paul Quenon, ocso, was a novice under Merton and is a kindred spirit.
BERNIE LUCHT

James Fox, Merton's abbot for two decades, was a significant force in
modernizing Gethsemani. He was
Merton's necessary polar opposite in
both temperament and spirituality.

COURTESY GETHSEMANI ARCHIVES

Abbot Timothy Kelly, current abbot
of Gethsemani and a Canadian from
the Windsor, Ontario, area.

BERNIE LUCHT

Matthew Kelty, OCSO, October 1997. Kelty was
Merton's one-time confessor and a discerning admirer.

BERNIE LUCHT

The abbey at Gethsemani,
February 1998.
BERNIE LUCHT

The graveyard at Gethsemani
where Merton is buried.
BERNIE LUCHT

The bell tower.
BERNIE LUCHT

The Abbey of Gethsemani today.
BERNIE LUCHT

The poet's contempt for modern materialist values and the props that sustain such a cardboard kingdom is the contempt of the Hebrew prophet Amos for the neighbours of Israel and indeed Israel itself. Merton denounced Miami and that other Sodom, New York, with a fury not unlike Amos's denunciation of Judah and Bethel.

In "Dirge for the City of Miami," Merton outlines afresh the consequences of the Fall. Miami was once a garden, where "The simple grapefruit in the grove / Shine like the face of childish love." There was a time when the sunflowers leaned "toward the south / With the confidence of early youth." But the "red hibiscus" and the "copper apple" have changed this and the garden now houses a society that is "all but rude / To this [once] delicious Solitude."

The garden is now an enclosure where the drunkard, "gentle murderer," forger, "weary thief," bank robber, perjurer, and "limping whore" "Lie down upon the windy shore." The contrast of "jungles full of golden bells" with the "wealth of stucco flowers" highlights the generosity of nature as opposed to the unnaturalness of the human kingdom. Among people enticed, lured by the offerings of Babylon, the false Eden, only "the downcast palms recall / The tears that Magdalen let fall." The very opening of the poem poses the question "Where will you find an iron wreath / Appropriate to such a death?" — the death of a dream, the death of innocence. What was said of Christ may also be said of the derelict, the passenger, the "gentle creature buried there" — that this person's memory will, as the seventeenth-century English poet Richard Crashaw would have it, be dated not like others "by moments, months, and yeares / Measure their ages; thou, by TEARES."

Merton reserves his bitterest invective, however, for the city that was his home: New York. In the poem "Hymn of Not Much Praise for New York City," Merton makes the "children of the city" invoke the mercy of their "Queen of our hopped-up peace." Far less a queen and far more a rich whore — "Rich as a cake, common as a doughnut, / Expensive as a fur and crazy as cocaine" — New York whirls with decadent frenzy superseding "the waltzes of more shining / Capitals that have been bombed." New York's indifference in the early 1940s to Paris rotting in prison and London dying of cancer is exacerbated by her love for "metal money," a love that guarantees her pleasure in the face of her desperate children, who plead in vain for a cure beyond aspirins.

They — the children — petition to be locked "in the safe jails of thy movies"; confined to the "semi-private wards and white asylums of thy unbearable cocktail parties"; sentenced for life "to the penitentiaries of thy bars and nightclubs," the "pale infirmaries," clinics and operating-rooms that are the locations for their learning, pleasure and life nourishment, with "the blue, objective lights" that leave them "stupefied forever" — because only when senseless can they endure this madness. New Yorkers are hollow people, insensate and lost, desiring no answers, no explanations, "even when we ask." They prefer the stupor of their incarceration, which prevents them from inquiring, from attending in awe to the wonder about them.

This poem reads like a parody of a prayer or a litany in praise of the Queen of the Kingdom of the Saved, the Blessed Virgin Mary. For Thomas Merton, Catholic convert and poet, we are Mary's spiritual children, dependent on her for compassion and intercession. But New York is not a benign protector like the Virgin Mary. New York does not liberate, she enslaves, like Circe, the hoarding enchanter with her "big face like a shining bank" transfixing her prey.

Merton's New York is like the New York of the Spanish poet, Federico Garcia Lorca, a "New York of slime / . . . of wires and death." Born in the shadow of the Great War and now resident in a city wallowing in its unspecified misery, its spiritual malaise, the fervent new Catholic poet knows what the English war poet Wilfrid Owen wrote: "All a poet can do today is warn." Merton would do plenty of that. And he would do it, warn that is, most especially in his autobiographical "Journal of My Escape from the Nazis," the one novel of his that eventually saw publication, although not in his lifetime. Submitted to his agent in 1941 the "Journal" appeared as *My Argument with the Gestapo* in 1969.

My Argument with the Gestapo is a work of rebellion, of youth's unreasoning rage, written with the fury of Tharmas. The novel's hero is a barely disguised Merton. An angry young man, reminiscent of Franz Kafka's Joseph K. in *The Trial*, he deplores the numerous efforts made to circumscribe his liberty, to define him by what he does and what he possesses. His is the classic outcry of the individual in the Mass Age. The hero excoriates his befuddled interlocutors, a couple of investigating officers cast in the Kafkaesque mould:

> You think you can identify a man by giving his date of birth and his address, his height, his eyes' color, even his fingerprints. Such information will help you put the right tag on his body if you should run across his body somewhere full of bullets, but it doesn't say anything about the man himself. Men become objects and not persons. Now you complain because there is a war, but war is the proper state for a world in which men are a series of numbered bodies. War is the state that now perfectly fits your philosophy of life: you deserve the war for believing the things you believe. In so far that I tend to believe these same things and act according to such lies, I am part of the complex of responsibilities for the war too. But if you want to identify

me, ask me not where I live, or what I like to eat, or how I comb my hair, but ask me what I think I am living for, in detail, and ask me what is keeping me from living fully for the thing that I want to live for. Between these two answers you can determine the identity of any person. The better answer he has, the more of a person he is.[17]

The "better answer" will be found in the most perfect act of repudiation, of rebellion. The more thorough one's loathing of the world, the better the opportunity to find one's true identity. The young protagonist of *My Argument* is the ideal existentialist hero, railing against the iniquities of an oppressive society and resolved to sustain his freedom by radically resisting the blandishments and proscriptions of the temporal order. The hero's cry is a cry of the heart, a cry in the wilderness, Tharmas's act of primordial rebellion, a defiant assertion of the "I" against the crushing forces of Nature and Society:

Have you ever asked yourself what you would put in your Time Capsule (for eventually every family will sink a capsule of its own in the barren earth of their backyard, no longer any use for the growing of living plants), have you ever asked what little souvenir of yourself you will like to have dug up in 6939: think of it, you, five thousand years from now, that same unassuming, unimaginative, pathetic, miserly, envious little hypochondriac that you are, dug up as a present to the future, your own simple gift to mankind, the unembellished snapshot of your completely unimportant self! How would you like to be looking?[18]

Merton gave very serious thought to how he would look. He entered the Trappist Order on December 10, 1941.

There was no effort on Merton's part to "redeem the contraries" when he wrote *My Argument*. Blake's apocalyptic rebellion has been only partially internalized. Merton condemns, and only condemns, his society. He deplores its risible preoccupation with the paltry tokens of its "high culture."

> By these, the future will know you as you are; for after all, what is a modern human being but a collection of objects which he possesses and is proud of? You are a pair of glasses, a little bridge of iron teeth, a watch, a tiepin, a belt, a secret bandage of rubber, a box of toothpowder, a half-empty pack of cigarettes, a lighter, twenty-seven cents, a class ring, a pair of shoelaces, a tiny box of aspirins, and clippers for your nails, and a card giving the address of a psychiatrist, and, on the back, the name of an oil to prevent the falling out of hair.[19]

This is a society defined by its possessions with a moral authority of no greater value than a litany of trinkets. For Merton/Tharmas the antidote to a community obsessed with ownership is to be found in the cloister: "The renunciation of the right of ownership on the part of the monk, should . . . have a symbolic, or shall we say a prophetic significance. It is a silent and implicit condemnation of the misuse of ownership."[20] The monk is a *type* of the just person, standing in judgement on the rampant inequities and follies of the age. Such reasoning as this must have had enormous appeal to Merton in his revulsion against the corruption and opulence of the United States and the irrational unleashing of the dogs of war on the continent of his birth.

My Argument is an expiatory novel, situating the hero in the heart of the European maelstrom, vicariously making amends for his abrupt departure from the "sad and unquiet continent, full of forebodings." The hero is an outsider, a marginal figure, a rebel, eager to reconstitute his identity according to a new plan, a divine blueprint. And what better way to make reparation, to remould identity and recast the future, than by redefining the ideals that govern one's life, especially when the old ideals have been riven by great violence?

Although the hero is not a monk, the novel is an apologia for monasticism. It is about the casting off of an old identity and the adoption of a new one. For the psychologically and spiritually displaced Merton, no more radical a critique of the prevailing myths and ideologies of the world he detested could be found than in the *contemptus mundi* of the Order of Cistercians of the Strict Observance. The poor "burnt men" of the Abbey of Gethsemani were his models of pure rebellion: they overturned the priorities and values of the world and lived as a sign of negation. As he later wrote in "Monastic Peace" in 1958: "In the night of our technological barbarism, monks must be as trees which exist silently in the dark and by their vital presence purify the air."[21]

The monk, for Merton, is the perfect rebel. Monasticism itself is a form of institutionalized rebellion, precariously situated on the fringes of society, a stark and disturbing reminder of those truths obscured by human self-absorption and rapacity. The monk exists in paradox. Vowed to stability, he is nonetheless a wayfarer, ever yearning for the centre. The monk is the point of intersection, the necessary link, the bridge to the transcendent. As Raimundo Panikkar, a scholar of world religions observes in *Blessed Simplicity*:

The monk is the expression of an archetype which is a *constitutive dimension of human life*. This archetype is a unique quality of each person, which at once needs and shuns institutionalization. . . . The great monks have always been worried when the monk becomes a well-accepted figure in the world and receives the blessings of society.[22]

The monk is present to our culture in a critical and prophetic manner, a silent guardian of our humanity. Ideally the monk is a mature realization of that quality of monkhood that we all possess — openness to the transcendent. But the ideal seldom obtains: there are immature monks and there is decadent monasticism. Throughout the history of Catholicism there have been golden periods when the monastic ethos flourished, and there have been periods when monasticism was moribund and no longer a vital force in the spiritual leavening of society. A countercultural presence, monasticism can turn in upon itself and become a self-perpetuating institution given not to radical witness but to spiritual complacency.

But in 1941 Merton's thoughts were far from seeing the underside of monasticism. The monastic vocation was the supreme act of rebellion in a society that deprecated spiritual truths. Merton wanted *his* act of rebellion to be as dramatic a repudiation of his old self as he could manage. The Trappists were the answer. They allowed no compromise, they were severe in their discipline, and their silence was complete; their "No" to the world was definitive. For the moment, Merton saw only flaws in the world he now solemnly abjured. The monastic way was perfect in every regard. The poet-monk of Gethsemani was herald to the Apocalypse.

His eight-part poem "Figures for an Apocalypse," published in 1947, opens with an invocation calling the Bridegroom to appear: "Come down, come down, Beloved / And make the brazen waters burn beneath Thy feet." The poet burns with a desire for judgement and can already taste the sulphur of conflagration. The dread of the Apocalypse is the poet's secret delight as the Bridegroom comes,

Splitting the seven countries
With the prism of Thy smile,
Confound all augury
Sever the center of our continents
And through that unpredictable gate lead in
The world's last night,
Clad in the wrath of Armageddon
And in Thy fires arrayed.

In the second part of the poem the speaker implores the "thin, unprofitable queens," the rich women, to "come to your windows" and see the arrival of the Bridegroom. These rich women are like the rich men of "Hymn of Not Much Praise for New York City" of whom it was remarked that it is difficult to know which "are still alive, and which the dead." They are the converse of the wise virgins of Matthew's gospel, unprepared for the arrival of the Bridegroom, squanderers of the "promise." They are "grey, artificial Shebas, spurious queens" who have prostituted their hope with a life of excess: " 'We had not planned to have so great a Lent / Bind us and bite us with its heavy chain.' "

The third part of the poem is titled "Advice to My Friends Robert Lax and Edward Rice to get away while they still can" and reads as a bitter warning to these two writer-friends. Bob Lax was a poet who converted to Catholicism following Merton's conversion, and Ed Rice, a journalist and a cradle Catholic, was Merton's godfather when he was received into the Roman communion.

Win pity for the poor pilgrims,
Or forge a paper to Paradise
From the gates of the smouldering jail.

Merton warns them that writers and intellectuals must look about them, for the mark of the Beast is everywhere:

The skylights of our intellect
Have gone as grey as frost,
While the dawn makes ready, with coated tongue,
To mutter the last alarm.

Oblivious of the omnipresent danger, "fearing to look where the windows ache / With the sight of the Babylon beast," secure in the spiritual myopia that protects them, Rice and Lax are warned that, alas, "it is too late to fly away / From the city full of sulphur." Like T.S. Eliot's speaker in the "Unreal City" of *The Waste Land*, Merton "had not thought death had undone so many." Though he has made it clear that "it is too late to fly," Merton appears to contradict himself by saying that indeed, "it is the hour to fly without passports / From Juda to the mountains." Although it is too late to fly literally or externally, perhaps it is never too late to fly metaphorically or inwardly. Merton chose to flee literally to the woods of Gethsemani where "We'll arm for our own invisible battle / In the wells of the pathless wood." In Gethsemani he found it possible to shoot "the traitor memory" and therefore to flee metaphorically the constraints and illusions of the past.

In the fourth part, "Apoc. xiv, 14," Merton meditates on this passage from the Book of Revelation: "Now in my vision I saw a white cloud and, sitting on it, one like a son of man with a gold crown on his head and a sharp sickle in his hand." The speaker exhorts us to "look in the night, look, look in the night," for there is one clothed in a garment of silver holding in his hand a sickle of which it can be said:

The steel is cleaner than ice,
The blade is sharper than thought:
The curve is like an intellect, neat.

The wielder of the sickle thrusts this scythe in threatening judgement "in the most quiet harvest in the midnight world," and the soul of the speaker stands poised for the fearful sound of "some far furious trumpet" heralding the dread moment of judgement on an indifferent world. Pierced to the core of his soul by this fearful annunciation, the speaker is captive to a wild note that "bites my soul with lightnings live as steel."

In the fifth part of the poem, "Landscape, Prophet and Wild Dog," Merton paints a nightmare scenario right out of a play by Samuel Beckett. It reads as a commentary on the absurdity of modern political messianism, and with its stark backdrop "at the edge of the salt lands," with trees that "stand like figures in a theatre," the drama of ideas is played out on a stage of desolation. A prophet scurries across this wasteland, pursued by a wild dog that succeeds in getting its teeth into his ankle and bringing him down. In this humbled position the prophet is reminded that his assured prognostication that we shall tonight witness the millennium, the "withering-away of the state," when the skies shall embrace the world "melting all injustice in the rigors of their breezy love," has not come true either now or in the afternoon of our expectations. As the wild dog nails "his knives into the prophet's shoulder," the prophet is mockingly reminded of his golden age, with its material success, general leisure and utopian indifference, and finally of a cosmic fraternity in which "the whole will die of brotherly love." But when the day dawns and the mist of illusion dissipates, it is not a pastoral setting that meets the eye but the "Satanic mills" of William Blake:

What flame flared in the jaws of the avenging
    mills!
We heard the clash of hell within the gates
    of the embattled Factory
And thousands died in the teeth of those
    sarcastic fires!

And there is no answer forthcoming, for the prophet is now carrion — "and the air is full of wings."

The secular dreams of political theorists and reconstructionists, of utopian revolutionaries and anarchic idealists, have long nourished the hope for a millennium marked by universal liberation. Prophets such as these, however, have nothing to offer, each new movement being but a slight historical variation on a common theme. The cravenness of the human heart will remain but fleetingly mollified by the paper dreams of false prophets and ultimately will exact a terrible revenge, "burying the prophet's meatless shin." Merton's wild dog dismembering the modern liars is intentionally evocative of the Catholic poet Francis Thompson's "hound of heaven" in its aspect as devourer of false prophets:

Whether man's heart or life it be which yields
    Thee harvest, must Thy harvest-fields
    Be dunged with rotten death?[23]

In part six, "In the Ruins of New York," however, Merton returns once again to the city that represents for him the culmination of all power, greed, success, and godless ambition. He speaks of this post-apocalyptic paradise with a mixture of foreboding and with the righteousness of a Hebrew prophet. Like Jeremiah addressing the citizens of Jerusalem, the unfaithful heirs to the promise who had "filled this place with the blood of innocents" (Jer. 19:4), Merton reminds those who look to New York as the city of promise that they shall be sorely tried by the desolation to come.

The moon, a haunting overseer of destruction, leans, benignly quizzical,

> . . . to catch the sham brass
> Of your sophisticated voice
> Whose songs are heard no more.

Once the hectic arena of commerce and exchange, New York has now been rendered mute, its proud towers of "silver and steel" levelled, and its "black boils of Harlem and the Bronx" lanced by an avenging heaven. Merton recalls the callous, mercenary, and utilitarian spirit of a city "with nickels running in her veins," how with indifference to the suffering of her poor millions she has merely sealed her doom and "has died in the terrors of a sudden contemplation." New York is no Nineveh. She has rejected her Jonas and has no ear for salvation.

Merton sees in the "bosom of Manhattan" the perfidy of Sodom. New York is a city wholly given over to the pursuit and worship of money, daily crucifying the poor who are her victims:

> Can we console you, stars,
> For the so long survival of such wickedness?

When final judgement has been passed on this "city / That dressed herself in paper money," then perhaps we shall see emerge from the fallen towers and the smouldering ash "a place in the woods," "an acre of bannering corn," and "virgin glades of Broadway for the lynx and deer." But for now the harbingers of the caves, the "hairy ones," have come out to frolic amidst the ruins of a once proud city:

> And we believe we hear the singing of the
>   manticores
> Echo along the rocks of Wall and Pine.

The manticore, half-lion and half-man and not possessing the full dignity of either, seems only too fitting an inhabitant of the "wastes of Jersey." In contrast, Merton reflects in tranquillity overlooking a glen in his claustral home, the woods of Gethsemani, far from the singing manticores and Jersey's wastes:

> It was quiet as the Garden of Eden. I sat on a high bank, under young pines, and looked out over this glen. Right under me was a dry creek, with clean pools lying like glass between the shale pavement of the stream, and the shale was as white and crumpled as sea-biscuit. Down in the glen were the songs of marvelous birds. . . . The echo made the place sound more remote, and self-contained, more perfectly enclosed, and more like Eden.[24]

Gethsemani, Merton's Eden, is an arresting counterpoint to the mad rot of New York.

In the next section of *Figures for an Apocalypse*, part seven, entitled "Landscape: Beast," the poet provides a map picturing the comprehensiveness of the Antichrist's advances. In the east "where smoke melts in a saucer of extinguished cities," the remnant can be found "Waiting to see those horns and diadems / And hear the seven voices of the final blasphemy." In the west, "the last men wait to see the seven-headed thing," preparing to receive the "indelible brand" of the accursed Beast, "the dolour of that animal's number," 666, and as such

be evermore "burned with her disgusting name." In the interior
of the land, in the interior of the private soul, "a blue-green
medium dragon" roams the land, rolling "in the ashes of the rav-
aged country." But it attracts little attention and little fear, for

> Who shall gather to see an ordinary dragon,
>   in this day of anger,
> Or wonder at those scales as usual as sin?

  In the south the horsemen of the apocalypse and the angels
of vengeance are unobserved, and "no one hears or fears the
music of those blazing swords." Who in the north will recount
"the terror of those ruined streets?" Who will recount the
murder of the prophets and the saints by the servants of
the great city of Babylon?
  In the eighth and concluding section, "The Heavenly City,"
Jerusalem becomes "the new world's crown." And Babylon
will be dethroned, its hegemony permanently shattered, and
death itself will die:

> Because the cruel algebra of war
> Is now no more.
> And the steel circle of time, inexorable,
> Bites like a padlock shut, forever,
> In the smoke of the last bomb:
> And in that trap the murderers and sorcerers
>   and crooked leaders
> Go rolling home to hell.
> And history is done.

  With the consummation of history and the triumph of the Lamb
over the Beast, the "heavenly city" will stand as the "new
creation's sun,"

While all the saints rise from their earth
  with feet like light
And fly to tread the quick-gold of those streets.

The Book of Revelation prophesies that the messianic Jerusalem will stand upon her twelve foundations, each bearing the name of one of the apostles of the Lamb, and the conquest of Babylon and her minions will be complete.

But until the moment arrives when all will be either reduced or transformed, the Christian must live on the threshold of the Last Judgement, and Merton the monk, by his dramatic and desperate gesture of preparation in isolation, serves as the vanguard of the faithful host. The monk-poet is especially sensitive to his role as prophet and witness to the dissolution of time. What Northrop Frye wrote of Blake could be appositely said of Merton:

> Visionaries, artists, prophets and martyrs all live as though an apocalypse were around the corner, and without this sense of a potentially imminent crisis imagination loses most of its driving power. The expectation of a Last Judgment in the New Testament does not mean that the Christians of that time were victims of a mass delusion, or that they were hypnotizing themselves in order to nerve themselves for martyrdom, but that they saw the physical universe as precariously balanced on the mental cowardice of man. And when Blake and Milton elaborate theories of history suggesting that time is reaching its final crisis during their own lives, they are only doing what Jesus did before them.[25]

In rejecting the world the monk-as-herald rejects the values of the world and seeks in solitude those immutable truths the world knows not of. For Merton, the monk has his face turned toward the desert. His ears are attuned not to the echoes of the apostolate that storms the city of Babylon but to the silence of the far mountains on which the armies of God and the enemy confront one another in a mysterious battle, of which the battle in the world is only a pale reflection.[26]

Steeled for the final conflict, Merton spurned human intercourse as the world defines it in order to discover himself in the hidden god, the *Deus absconditus*. It was a radical decision, an outsider's act of defiance, and his monasticism a statement of rebellion. But even before he sought admission to the monastery he knew that the world cried out in anguish for saints, that nothing short of an heroic response to this call should be made, and that such noble self-giving can be found here and now in the midst of suffering humanity. As he notes in a journal entry of May 26, 1940:

The only thing that can save us is an army of saints — and not necessarily Joan of Arcs or military saints. Where will they come from? Nobody can really say, except those who think about it seem to believe (like Maritain) the saints will come from the poorest of the laity, from the depths of the slums, from the concentration camps and the prisons, from the places where people are starving, bombed, machine-gunned and beaten to death. Because in all these places Christ suffers most. Maritain adds, I think, that they will also be found in a few religious orders — the contemplative ones.
    And the rest of us, what should we do? Fall down and pray and pray over and over to God to send us saints![27]

For Merton the choice was to be between the slums of Harlem, with the Baroness, and the rustic cloisters of a Trappist abbey in Kentucky. Although he could sympathize with the bombed and machine-gunned, and indeed fictionalize their horror in *My Argument with the Gestapo*, his personal response to the rallying call for saints had to be expressed in the most dramatic of terms and his post-conversion romanticism had to find an outlet in a gesture as extreme in its unconventionality as it was severe in its simplicity. The Trappists were the answer.

Merton/Tharmas — embodiment of the rebellious impulse and native restlessness — found in the monastic way of life a structure, a culture, that could articulate his rage and harness his energy. But in tracing Merton's life as a monk we discover that his views on monasticism shifted, transmuted, collapsed, regenerated, in short, were a barometer of his own quixotic, self-destructive, and wildy creative monastic life. Monasticism was not a static condition for Merton but a vital one full of contradictions and crises, a ceaseless struggle to balance the contraries, his own marriage of heaven and hell. To that end, monasticism as rebellion means more than a categorical and definitive repudiation of the world; it means adopting a stance of scrupulous self-critique, of positioning yourself on the periphery of the peripheral, of living on the margins as monk both vis-à-vis the world and vis-à-vis the monastery; it means that the monk *qua* monk is a maverick of the mind, of the will, and of the spirit.

A healthy monasticism requires vigilance, emotional equilibrium, a sense of humour, and a natural abhorrence for misplaced zealotry. Even at the height of Merton's monkish success, the year of publication of *The Seven Storey Mountain*, he entertains no illusion about the underside of monastic regulations and spirituality. The story of Frater Damian is Merton's 1948 cautionary tale.

Frater or Brother Damian arrived at the monastery in 1943, a one-time sailor, and was given a goodly measure of hard labour because of his strength. He studied, prayed, and persevered in his vocation. Although he contracted tuberculosis and was confined to the infirmary for two months, he seemed on the mend. And then he had an emotional breakdown. The monks were mystified. One monk opined that he must have been reading too much St. John of the Cross, another that the devil was behind it all, and still another that he was a nervous fellow. Detectives were called; Damian was handcuffed; and Merton was deeply saddened. Damian was no threat. After all here was a young monk, a hard worker and seemingly pious, preparing to make his solemn profession, and now he was to be sent away where Merton hoped he would be "treated nicely and not just kept in a cage." The event was rather unsettling for Merton, partly because he could easily imagine himself "waking up some fine day with a pair of handcuffs" on him like Kafka's Joseph K., and partly because at the time of Damian's breakdown, Merton was engaged in reading about the seventeenth-century abbot of the Cistercian Abbey of La Trappe, an aristocratic former libertine and court wag, Armand Jean le Bouthillier de Rancé. Having renounced his dissolute ways, de Rance was predictably a rigorist like St. Augustine, and with a purist's vengeance, he initiated a reform of Cistercian monasticism that was designed to return the order to its roots. He introduced a severe regimen of ascetic practices that were designed to offset what he saw as the laxity of the order as well as to exorcise his own lingering guilt as an ex-courtier turned abbot. Although the de Rancé reforms helped to consolidate the newly minted Order of Cistercians of the Strict Observance or Order of Reformed Cistercians, they became popularly known as the Trappists. Merton joined the tough branch of the firm but does not appear to have had much taste for the French reformer's style. Frater Damian's plight generated both puzzlement and sympathy on Merton's part; there was something strangely unChristian in the de Rancé method:

> That old Trappist business of trying to starve and beat your way to sanctity and [of] assuming that your own efforts and energy are practically everything — beating your head against a brick wall at the end of a dead end in order to fulfill some negative ideal . . .
>
> Our Cistercian Fathers and St. Benedict knew better. So did the Little Flower [St. Thérèse de Lisieux]. So did our Lord.[28]

Merton's misgivings regarding the muscular monasticism of the La Trappe tradition may seem perplexing; he was, after all, only a year from ordination when he entered the above passage in his diary. But Merton was a post-modern monk in a pre-modern tradition. His choice of the monastic way of life as his vocation was not an act of penitence and submission but of rebellion; it was his way of defining his natural rebelliousness. He was the monk as subversive — subverting the values both of the world and of the monastic status quo, in the latter case encouraging the establishment of the hermitage vocation in a community that valued only the communal life, advocating a return to the earliest sources in order to eliminate the numerous excrescences to pure monastic life accumulated throughout the centuries, and extending the fruits of contemplative existence outside the cloister.

Not too many years after his ordination in 1949 Merton was eager to leave the Trappists for a more robust community of contemplatives. He discovered that the Camaldolese were just what the Spirit ordered. The Camaldolese are hermits and the names associated with their "founding" include some illustrious medieval monks and reformers like St. Romuald, John

Gualbert, and Peter Damian. An offshoot of the Benedictines, they first appeared on the scene in 1012 in the Apennines near Arezzo. Merton was drawn to their "desert" spirituality. Following a conversation with his Chicago psychiatrist friend, Philip Law, Merton was determined to look into the Camaldolese option. Law encouraged him; in fact, in 1952 he encouraged Merton to establish his own contemplative order, but Merton demurred.

In 1955 Merton was still restive. He began to confide more and more in the Benedictine historian Jean Leclercq about his spiritual disquiet and his insatiable yearning for a deeper monastic culture than Gethsemani's. He was dissatisfied with the communal life of the Trappists and wanted a more solitary life, a life he thought he could find with the Camaldolese hermits. His abbot opposed the request for a transfer — a *transitus* — to the Camaldolese, but Merton was far from resigned. James Fox temporarily placated the disappointed Merton by telling him that he would bring to the higher superiors of the order his proposal that Merton become a hermit in the Gethsemani woods. Merton characteristically enthused:

> If this permission were ever granted it would solve all my problems, I think. The forest here is very lonely and quiet and covers about a thousand acres, and there is much woodland adjoining it. It is as wild as any country that would be found in the Ardennes or the Vosges, perhaps wilder. I could be a hermit without leaving the land of the monastery. One could begin the project gradually and imperceptibly, for the government is putting up a fire-observation tower on one of our hills and the future hermitage could be in connection with this. One could begin simply by being the watchman on the tower and gradually take up permanent residence

there. Unfortunately the higher superiors, as far as I can see, are absolutely closed to any such suggestion and even refuse to permit a monk to work alone on the observation tower. Dom James is placing the matter before the Abbot General.[29]

Merton was right. The abbot general, Dom Gabriel Sortais, said no to Merton's request. In addition, Merton was appointed master of novices, thereby securing him firmly to the very bosom of the monastery. This delicious irony was not lost on Merton and he observed to Leclercq that "strange things can happen in the mystery of one's vocation." Merton was clearly, and not for the last time, outFoxed by his abbot.

By 1958 the wanderlust again got the better of him. He was frustrated as much by his own self-ignorance as he was by the intransigence of his abbot. He asked plaintively in his journal:

What is it that moves me? The thirst for stimulation? The need for a new country and wider horizons? I don't pretend to know what is really eating me. Partly temptation, and partly something immeasurably more solid than that.[30]

By the late 1950s Merton was desperate for new challenges. Spiritual complacency threatened to engulf him; the theological atmosphere of the pre–Second Vatican Council church was stuffy if not suffocating; though he was as prolific as ever, there was a tired and derivative quality to his writing, and he knew it. Suddenly his journals are full of Cuernavaca.

Mexico was the scene for some of the most daring experimentation in monastic living in the Roman Catholic Church. The Benedictine monastery at Cuernavaca was under the energetic, indeed iconoclastic, leadership of its abbot, Dom Gregorio Lemercier. The abbot encouraged Merton to consider joining the community as a hermit and the idea greatly appealed to him. Merton petitioned the appropriate Vatican department or dicastery, the Congregation for Religious, for an indult of exclaustration (permission to live outside the cloister). Once again Merton was hopeful for a positive adjudication. Would Dom James interfere? Would his request for the indult be denied? Would he ever be a hermit? Things looked bleak; in fact, a favourable decision was never in the cards.

If Merton anticipated support from the abbot-general he was sorely misguided. Gabriel Sortais, although appreciative of many of Merton's gifts as a writer and spiritual father, disapproved strongly of the American monk's public reputation. A monk should be quiescent, modest, self-effacing, anonymous, and most definitely not a celebrity. In Sortais's view a monk's theological opinions are best kept to himself; self-censorship should make official censorship unnecessary. Merton and Sortais crossed swords in 1960 over the publication of an article Merton wrote on *The Divine Milieu*, by the controversial and still unrehabilitated French Jesuit-scientist and mystic, Marie-Joseph Pierre Teilhard de Chardin. Teilhard, as he was known, was a master synthesizer of theological and scientific insight, an evolutionist who spoke not only of the evolution of biological species but of the mind and the spirit as well, a palaeontologist with a flair for mystical prose, and a priest who endured censorship, silencing, exile, and misunderstanding. He saw very little of his work published in his lifetime; it was only after his death in 1955 in New York that he became the darling of the Second Vatican Council and the sixties counterculture. *The Divine Milieu*, an abstruse and idiosyncratic work of private spirituality, both alarmed and puzzled the ecclesiastical authorities. Merton chose to write about the book, and in doing so threw down the gauntlet. After consulting a professor in Rome, Sortais forbade Merton to publish. He accepted but seethed.

A book in itself "harmless" they admit. But one must not say anything in favor of T. de C. One must "make the silence" regarding T. de C.

The decision means little to me one way or the other, and I can accept it without difficulty. Less easily the stuffy authoritarianism of Dom Gabriel, who cannot help being an autocrat, even while multiplying protestations of love. I rebel against being treated as a "property," as an "instrument" and as a "thing" by the Superiors of this Order. He definitely insists that I think as he thinks, for to think with him is to "think with the church." . . . I have *no obligation* to form my thought or my conscience along the rigid lines of Dom Gabriel. . . . It may be quite correct that T. is a theological screwball. But I refuse to form part of an indignant chorus against him, and I refuse even to form part of a silently disapproving or hostile assembly of righteous critics. I refuse to draw back from him shaking my garments. I have nothing but sympathy for his attempt to take a new view of things . . . but as far as I am concerned the book is generally healthier and more deeply, genuinely *spiritual* than anything that has ever emanated from the authoritarian mind of Dom Gabriel.[31]

The efforts at thought control by Dom Gabriel, Dom James, and other ecclesiastical authorities outraged Merton/Tharmas, prompting the rebel to consign for the moment his private views and rather unmonastic candour to his diaries. He abhorred the efforts of religious leaders to suppress engaging new thought whether "screwball" or not. The exercise of institutional censorship diminished all the players. Merton could see in the decisions of his superiors the same kind of repressive techniques employed by the nameless authoritarians who peopled *My Argument with the Gestapo*. Merton had discovered early on that he needed to remain as vigilant inside the monastery as he had outside against the authoritarian instincts that threaten genuine spiritual freedom. Having fought his war against Sortais and lost — it was an easy capitulation, because of the vow of obedience — he was delighted by the move on the part of the Gethsemani authorities to at least in part recognize his need for some solitary time. A small hermitage was built in the fall of 1960 for the express purpose of *rencontres* and dialogue with Protestant clergy and academics, "but it also serves for solitude and I have at least a limited permission to use it part time." The concession was a small but meaningful one. But if it was intended to placate Merton or subdue his need to speak to the people of his time, it was an unsuccessful ruse. Merton would not be silenced. He admitted to his friend Wilbur Ferry that clearly "a contemplative monk should have a quiet though articulate place in the discussions of his time, when the time is one like ours."[32]

The consolations of withdrawal from the world, a premier motivation of the early monastic years, were waning fast. Merton's monastic rebellion would need to be further mutated; he would need to redefine his foundational "no" to the world. This redefinition was arrestingly telescoped around the issue of peace. As the 1960s unfolded and the Cold War heated up Merton found it increasingly difficult to subscribe to what he called "the monastery as dynamo concept." This pious notion conceived of the monastery as a spiritual power centre, generating grace and blessings, with each monk performing his required spiritual tasks unquestioningly and all working together in holy harmony under one head. By the early 1960s Merton had repudiated this notion unequivocally, and had come to believe that the monk as spiritual cog in the great machine was a vicious caricature of monasticism. The idea that Merton had earlier embraced with equanimity, if not zeal, that the monk is called to sacrifice his individuality, he now rejected. He felt that the elimination of the individual voice in the mass society of the twentieth century was an evil that must be denounced — that the individual voice must be heard, and heard loudly. All the more reason why Merton found the suppression of his own contributions in the public arena on the matter of peace a particularly onerous burden to bear. Merton refused to toe the official Catholic line; he was increasingly pacifist in his thinking, arguing vigorously against the "just war theory," which originated with St. Augustine and was then refined by St. Thomas Aquinas, and had been standard Catholic teaching for centuries. To Merton, episcopal timidity could not be justified with nuclear incineration on the horizon.

His superiors were disturbed by Merton's increasingly forceful and decidedly political reflections on peace in the nuclear era, and Sortais and Fox, under pressure from the American episcopate but also out of their own sense of disquiet, ordered Merton to publish no more articles about peace issues. He obeyed, but only just. For some time he had been writing pointed, highly critical letters to various correspondents which he had gestetnered or mimeographed, collated, compiled, and widely but circumspectly circulated with the help of obliging younger monks like Paul Quenon:

> This was the time when many of his writings were banned. He was writing letters to many significant people and I often found myself slowing down the process of mimeographing simply because I kept reading what he wrote. It was really an intense thing for me to read this profoundly prophetic and important voice in a context where everyone else seemed to be dangerously oblivious to the kinds of issues he was addressing.

They came to be known as the "Cold War Letters" and they

were 111 in number, written between October 1961 and October 1962. The definitive order forbidding him to write any further on politics and peace issues was enacted in April 1962. His experiment in *samizdat* or underground literature was over. At least officially. In a letter to the peace activist James Forest, Merton gave eloquent and personally outraged vent to his annoyance with abbatial myopia:

> I am being silenced on the subject of war and peace. . . . It reflects an astounding incomprehension of the seriousness of the present crisis in its religious aspect. It reflects an insensitivity to Christian and ecclesiastical values, and to the real sense of the monastic vocation. The reason given is that this is not the right kind of work for a monk, and that it "falsifies the monastic message." Imagine that: the thought that a monk might be deeply concerned with the issue of nuclear war to voice a protest against the arms race, is supposed to bring the monastic life into *disrepute*. Man, I would think that it might just possibly salvage a last shred of repute for an institution that many consider to be dead on its feet . . .[33]

Merton castigated the monastic authorities for reducing the monk to a supine prayer producer with no function other than to obey the "purposes and objectives of an ecclesiastical bureaucracy," and "to affirm his total support of officialdom." To Merton, for whom monasticism was always a form of rebellion, the figure of the monk as portrayed by his superiors did violence not only to his sense of self but to his very understanding of monastic spirituality in both its primitive and its twentieth-century forms. He watched with horror the gradual and effective transformation of a community of contemplative monks into an industry — Trappist Corp.

The basic issue is ... the conservation of the large, prosperous, active, business-like abbey-corporation in which the individual monk is a contented functionary, more and more tendency toward a monastic bureaucracy, and centralized organization — a population content with the externals which are "satisfactory," and not desiring a "more contemplative life" or any "new formula" — in fact an assertion of the Trappist Corporation, against the new primitive Benedictine monasteries which have a young and exploratory outlook, and are willing to experiment.[34]

Stunned by the administrative effort to secure a future for the monastery based on a corporate model, Merton sought ways to deconstruct a crushing style of monastic lordship, ways that were ostensibly respectful of abbatial authority while at the same time subverting it. His "Cold War Letters" were one response, his poetry another. He embraced models and icons of rebellion and holy disobedience, like the scatological French firebrand and author of satirical romances, the Renaissance monk François Rabelais. He found in his monkish compatriot a refreshing sanity, a healthy sensuality, and "a fine active irrepressible imagination and mind," in short, all those qualities he saw in limited supply amongst his religious contemporaries. Loath to endorse the kind of monastic ideal espoused by his abbot and like-minded monks, and adamant that retreat from the world did not mean retreat from its concerns, Merton anguished over the future of Gethsemani. At the same time, as a jotting in his journal of December 17, 1963, makes clear, Merton had vanquished his need to locate himself outside Gethsemani:

I find I still have great confidence in my community and my abbot though one thing is definite — I no longer have any

questions in my mind about changing stability. I have no
desire to even see the gatehouse of any other monastery of this
Order, or of the Camaldolese, or of the Carthusians. . . .[35]

And yet within a few months of having penned this affirm-
ative entry, Merton found himself once again ruminating on
failed monasticism. Interestingly, this time around, the object
of his sharp critique was not success-mad abbots, censorious
French authorities, dull and pious brothers, or even Catholic
apologists of the old school disappointed in a wayward monk,
but rather himself. On February 22, 1964, he celebrated the
twenty-second anniversary of his reception of the habit of a
Trappist, but what should have been a moment of celebration
became rather a moment of self-reproach. He reviewed, with
the painful honesty that was typical of him, his two decades
as a monk and found himself seriously deficient in motive and
accomplishment. After all, he had entered the monastery to
become a saint, he had told his Columbia contemporaries. The
portrait he now painted of himself in the winter of 1964 fell
far short of that exalted ideal:

> I must admit that the twenty-two years have not been well
> spent. . . . twenty-two years of relative confusion, often
> coming close to doubt and infidelity, agonized aspirations
> for "something better," criticism of what I have, inexplica-
> ble inner suffering that is largely my own fault, insufficient
> efforts to overcome myself, inability to find my way. . . .[36]

The passage marks a low point in the whirligig of Merton's
ever-fluctuating emotional and intellectual life. He goes on to
speak of his resolve to reclaim something of the asceticism of
his early years and to lose himself in the liturgy, which is "deep
and real, and one thing that I have learned to trust." His dream

of the solitary life, however, has not been abandoned. Although not dissatisfied with his temporary solitude, he longs for the day when the life of the hermit will be recognized as a "legitimate prolongation of what begins in the cenobium"[37] and hopes that complete rather than occasional hermit will be seen as a rare but authentic expression of monastic life.

Although Merton continued his musings on the relevance of monastic spirituality throughout the 1960s, sometimes strident and iconoclastic and sometimes serene and nostalgic, he never allowed himself to drift too far from the moral crises of the day — peace, justice, racism. Following a special gathering at Gethsemani of leaders of the peace movement in November of 1964, Merton wrote to Jim Forest, who had also attended the event, likening the nuclear engineers, physicists, and nuclear military personnel to a "monasticism in reverse":

> These are the monks of the twentieth century: the fellows cloistered in the bomb silo, with their communal life, their silence, their austerity, their separation from the world. The monk is supposed to dig into the earth to find the sources of life in hiddenness, and these dig into the earth with the power of death. They become seeds like the seeds of hell that are in people's minds.[38]

These false monks, denizens of the silo, stand in macabre contrast to the true monks, denizens of the desert. The monk must explore the desert area of the human heart, the "arid, rocky, dark land of the soul":

> the contemplative is the man not who has fiery visions of the cherubim carrying God on their imagined chariot, but simply he who has risked his mind in the desert beyond language and beyond ideas where God is encountered in the

nakedness of pure trust, that is to say in the surrender of our poverty and incompleteness in order no longer to clench our minds in a clamp upon themselves, as if thinking made us exist.[39]

The image of monk as desert-dweller as opposed to the monk as nuclear warrior draws a sharp distinction between an isolationism that purifies and humanizes and an isolationism that confirms individual and state autonomy to the exclusion of all else. By 1968 Merton had pursued the concept of the monk as rebel to its climax. In a letter to the Quaker scholar June J. Yungblut, he remarked that "even in the most static and established kinds of Christendom, monks have tended to be mavericks"[40] and outsiders, even, as he observed in Bangkok, revolutionaries like the Marxists. But unlike revolutionaries, monks are engaged in the transformation not of structures but of human consciousness itself. In this task of transforming consciousness, Merton saw the monk participating in the same critique as the disciples of theoretical guru Herbert Marcuse. The political radical and author of *The One Dimensional Man* was, in Merton's view, an heir to William Blake. Both of them "recognized the two-dimensional character of Western logic and also the endemic temptation to reduce this tension to a one-dimensional and authoritarian system."[41] This reduction results in the creation of Urizen, the "Abstract objecting power that Negatives everything," the univocal, single-focused, oppressive rule of reason. And Urizen equals Authoritarianism.

Although the face of Urizen can be seen in oppressive power structures outside the monastery — mass society, the totalitarian state, Single-Vision ideologies — Merton also found the shadow of Urizen in his own abbot. His relationship with Dom James Fox was a turbulent one that lasted most of his monastic

life. In 1948 Fox succeeded the much-loved Frederic Dunne —
the abbot who had initially encouraged Merton to write — and
quickly established an abbatial style noted for its nuanced
rigidity, organizational finesse, spiritual conventionality, and
paternalism. Fox, a graduate of the Harvard Business School,
presided over the unprecedented growth of Gethsemani following the war, a growth in numbers, buildings, and outside
contracts — tobacco, dairy, fruitcake, etc. — all of which made
the abbey a seat of prosperity, at least materially.

In Merton's view all this success was failure. The marketing
strategies of "Gethsemani Inc." profoundly undermined the
genuine monastic quest that motivated the majority of men
who sought life in its cloisters. Fox and Merton were at intellectual and spiritual loggerheads from the beginning. But the
power imbalance weighed in the abbot's favour, and Merton
resented it. The abbot always had the trump card.

Brother Patrick Hart, Fox's secretary from 1957 to 1966, and
Merton's secretary from shortly before the fateful trip to Asia
in 1968, observed the dynamics of the relationship at close
quarters:

Merton's appeals to go to either the Camaldolese or to the
Carthusians were blocked mainly by Dom James who felt
that he would never persevere, that he would become a
rolling stone, consumed by wanderlust, looking for the ideal
place where he could find contemplative leisure. If you have
lived the monastic life for some time, you know that such
a place does not exist. What often happened is as follows:
Merton would come to Dom James with his request to leave
the Cistercians and join a more contemplative order. Dom
James would listen, tell him that the call to greater contemplation was not necessarily a call to leave but to withdraw
further into the interior life; he would skilfully capitulate

on some points by allowing him to become a forester on Gethsemani grounds thereby getting more solitude. Merton would leave satisfied, for the moment. Until the next time. Merton was often frustrated by Dom James' efforts to prevent him from leaving. He knew, for instance, that when he would apply to go elsewhere the local authorities would contact the abbot and he would get nothing in the form of an endorsement. In fact, Dom James would reply to those inquiring as to Merton's worthiness as a potential hermit that he does not have a vocation to a pure solitary life, that he needs a certain amount of activity, that he is very good as Master of Students and as Master of Novices, that he has an active mind, a very great intelligence, and he writes well. Application dead. On the whole Merton behaved as a good monk in a public way; he would rebuke monks who attacked Fox; he did not adopt a sour and frustrated posture in chapter or choir. It was only later when I read the restricted journals and letters that I realized *how* frustrated he often was and *how* important his private writings were as an outlet for this frustration.

And these private outpourings could be quite acerbic and angry. Repeatedly denied permission to transfer to a different order and prevented thereby from becoming what he felt he was called to be — a hermit — he lashed out at the "astute and ruthless politicians" in Rome and at Gethsemani who stymied him because of their prejudice in favour of the "unchangeable holiness of power." Fox, in particular, earned some scorching prose:

I am therefore kept from seeking any kind of a personal ideal by a man who is convinced of his own rightness just as he is completely convinced of the rightness of Wall Street and big business, *Time* and *Life*, the Spellman and Sheen type of Catholicism etc. etc. Anything else is to him *inconceivable*, and for one to seek a primitive, non-American, eremitical kind of life is simple folly.[42]

Fox, it seems, existed to frustrate Merton the monk from maturing into a full-time solitary. In Merton's estimation his abbot was one of that number made *"unassailable by their goodness,"* their reputation protected by the purity of their intentions, and capable of a terrible cruelty blasphemously justified by their "sweet unconscious inhumanity." Dom James was the necessary polarity, the defining opposite, who both contained and directed Merton's rebellion. Merton needed Dom James and this need accounts for the painful ambivalence he felt towards his abbot. He oscillated wildly between deep resentment and affectionate understanding. Patrick Hart sees in their relationship something more than a study in contrasts:

They did very well together considering where they came from. Merton came out of a bohemian, artistic kind of existence with very little formal religious training, whereas Dom James came from Boston with a deep Irish Catholic background. Even so, Fox and his brother were sent to Harvard by his parents and his three sisters to Radcliffe because they wanted them to break out of the Catholic ghetto. His vocation — his brother became a Jesuit and his three sisters became nuns of Notre Dame de Namur — was nurtured by his parents, unlike Merton who, although baptized, was allowed to construct his own faith. Their early and formative years were stunningly unlike. They were unlike too in their gifts. Dom James graduated with a degree in history but stayed on at the Harvard Business School emerging fully equipped to handle himself professionally.

When he became Abbot of Gethsemani, and I think this was providential, he immediately began to offset the damage done by the near bankruptcy of the order. Acting on the advice of Ethel Kennedy's father, Dom James decided to move away from simple agrarian management into organized industry: first the cheese, then the fruitcake, and then the bourbon fudge. This was Dom James' strategy for making us self-supporting. But Merton was unhappy with the abbot's business enterprises. After all, he was a poet and a prophet and not a business graduate. They were both prima donnas, one forging ahead heedless of the traffic and the other a coordinator, cautious, applying the brakes. One was a genius and the other highly intelligent but essentially pragmatic. And their relationship, although filled with tensions, was also full of ironies and touching signs of trust. For instance, in spite of the fact that Dom James prevented Merton from realizing his desire to be a hermit for so many years, he eventually agreed to read a paper Merton had written on the topic at a General Chapter, saw the official approval of hermit life in the Trappist tradition, granted Merton the privilege to live as a hermit, and then when he retired as abbot retreated to a hermitage as well. In addition, Dom James asked Father Louis, "Louie," to be his confessor. This was a real vote of confidence in Louie; it demands great trust to be confessor to a monk. It speaks to how Dom James trusted Merton.

But the level of trust that motivated the abbot to ask Merton to be his confessor does not gainsay the fact that during most of his abbatial rule Dom James was deeply suspicious of his famous charge and demonstrated great cunning in controlling him. Merton knew his brother/adversary very well and at one point in 1965 defined him in terms evocative of Blake's Urizen:

Because of a certain sado-masochism in his character, he associates love with negation and suppression, with "captivity." His mind circles around the idea of power and authority, the capacity to possess and be possessed. As Abbot he cannot believe in himself unless he feels that in some sense he *owns* the hearts of the monks. . . . he has *force*, this one has to admit. A perplexity, smooth and unbending will, more a passion than a volition. A passion for a certain kind of disguised self-affirmation-in-restriction.[43]

Merton the rebel, the maverick monk, struggled to "balance the contraries," to mix compassion with judgement, idealism with tolerance, the institutional with the charismatic. Dom James fought to keep Merton a "prisoner of Gethsemani," but his successor as abbot, Flavian Burns, freed him to travel. Merton is the prophet Elias in his poem "Elias — Variations on a Theme":

> Under the blunt pine
> Elias becomes his own geography
> (Supposing geography to be necessary at all),
> Elias becomes his own wild bird, with God in the center,
> His own wide field which nobody owns,
> His own pattern, surrounding the Spirit
> By which he is himself surrounded:
>
> For the free man's road has neither beginning nor end.

Merton/Elias, prophet, maverick, and "wild bird," found "God in the center" and geography dissolved.

3

URIZEN:
The Marginal Critic

ON MAY 20, 1963, a frustrated Thomas Merton noted in his private journal the full measure of his annoyance with Abbot Fox:

> Everyone can come and see me in my cage, and Dom James can modestly rejoice in the fact that he is in absolute control of a bird that everyone wants to hear sing. This is the way birds stop singing — at least those songs that everyone wants to hear because they are comforting and they declare that all things are good just as they are.
>
> One's song is forced at times to become scandalous and even incomprehensible.[1]

By the early 1960s Merton, the canary in his cage, was changing his song; the melodies were increasingly dissonant, the tone sharp, the songs provocatively experimental. It was total war against the rule of Urizen.

But who or what is Urizen? In Blake's world he is Reason in its most narrow and constraining form, the savage constriction of imagination, the murderous dominance of logic to the exclusion of creative empathy. Urizen is the legacy of the Enlightenment. According to the Blake scholar David Bindman, Urizen's

> tyrannical personality and resemblance to traditional depictions of Jehovah imply that 18th-century Deism is nothing more than the legalism of the Old Testament in new garments — the Letter of the Law rather than the Spirit, which is Christ. Urizen's response to the threat of revolution is that of an aged tyrant, propping up a discredited social order of which he is both creator and creation. He is not, however, a force external to humanity: he is also the reasoning faculty, which in man's Fallen state becomes separated from his imagination.[2]

Merton understands Urizen to represent

> empiricism and doubt, and also dogmatism, because he is blind to imagination, passion, spirit. Consequently, he cannot really understand life or experience at all.
> He in darkness clos'd viewed all his race
> And his soul sicken'd and he curs'd
> Both sons and daughters, for he saw
> That no flesh nor spirit could keep
> His iron law one moment. (*The Book of Urizen*)

And Urizen himself says:

> Read my books, explore my constellations,
> Enquire of my sons and they shall teach thee how
>   to war. (*The Four Zoas*)

The tyranny of Urizen consists in trying to govern by abstract codes based on mathematical reasoning and materialism, and it brings about a vicious circle of oppressions and wars.[3]

The presence of Urizen can be found everywhere, not least in the Roman Catholic Church. In a sharply Blakean critique of the church's complicity in tyrannical rule, Merton wrote to the philosopher Leslie Dewart, following the publication of Dewart's *Christianity and Revolution: The Lesson of Cuba*, a study of the relationship between the church and the Castro overthrow of the corrupt Batista government:

[I]n order to safeguard and defend the faith, indeed my immortal soul, I have to accept certain undeclared assumptions implicit in a political policy, and I have to accept them as if they were of faith. . . . I have to go along with policies that are often so inert, so blind, so stupid that they utterly stifle the true life of the Church and make it *impossible* for the most clear-sighted and courageous of her members to do anything that will further the real manifestation of the truth and charity of Christ in the world.[4]

What must collapse is Urizenic Christianity, a Christianity of law, logic, and control, a Christianity so utterly enmeshed in the established order that its prophetic power is muted irretrievably. The Cuban church was incapable of seeing the need for meaningful reform, and its pathological abhorrence of revolution prevented it from making the kinds of self-purging and self-correcting initiatives that could have spared it the fate of the *ancien regime*. The Cuban experience is illustrative of the church's desperate manacling by the temporal powers, its constitutional inability to effect the kind of liberative action characteristic of Jesus. It is deaf to the Spirit.

We cannot listen, because, after centuries of Holy Roman Empires and the rest, we cannot look upon history otherwise than as a force sustaining the Church's power to reach and *control* souls. The sin, hidden but real, is in this concept of the *absolute need for external control* over souls in order to save them.

And with that sin is another: our compassion for man has too much in it of secret contempt.[5]

Urizen's grip on the church may not be unshakable but it is firm, cemented by centuries. The failure to respond to the winds of change is a failure of the imagination and of the heart. By clinging to the structures of control, the Cuban church relinquished its moral right to direct the revolution and participate in defining its goals. Once again, the moment was lost, Urizen's grip too tight.

How to counter the hegemony or lordship of Urizen was a lifelong undertaking for Merton. As poet, spiritual writer, and social critic, he found Urizen's influence ubiquitous and deadly. But he also knew that his "rowdy Blake" would be there for him, that his "Blake is *never* merely indifferent. Always if not inspired, at least very alive. Never dead. I love Blake."[6]

But before the canary's song became strident, "scandalous and even incomprehensible," it was melodic, paradisal, lyrical. Before Merton launched his full assault on Urizen with his poetry of the sixties — *Emblems of a Season of Fury; Cables to the Ace; The Geography of Lograire* — he was first the poet of the choir and the poet of the desert, as the Canadian critic George Woodcock called him.

But, as always, Blake was with Merton at each new beginning: in France, in England, at Columbia; and Blake went with him into the monastery in 1941.

Horrified by the "plague of cerebration" that infected the world, Merton found in the Abbey of Gethsemani as much antidote as retreat, his Advent where he and the monks "have become more humble than the rocks, / More wakeful than the patient hills" ("Advent," *A Man in the Divided Sea* [1946]). Here in an obscure valley in Kentucky hidden from "the cities / Of the fire-crowded universe," the cleansing fires of purgatory prepare the anxious soul for full spiritual recovery:

> Rob me, and make me poor enough to bear my
>   priceless ransom;
> Lock me and dower me in the gifts and jails of
>   tribulation:
> Stab me and save me with the five lights of Your
>   Crucifixion! ("The Peril," *A Man in the Divided Sea*)

The five senses, enslaved by Blake's Urizen, will find their healing in the five wounds of Christ. This is the first stage in Merton's lifelong poetic and spiritual effort to effect a "reparation." Later he would refer to this reparation as his central "myth-dream." Blake is at the heart of it all. Just as Blake's Prophetic Books seek an answer to the dilemma of the "marriage of heaven and hell," of the spirit's disharmony, of the tyranny of logic and the loss of innocence, so too does Merton, in his own "prophetic books" (*Cables* and *Geography*), seek to unravel an answer in a mosaic, pure and bizarre, as he elevates fact to myth, illusion to truth, outside his "small blue capsule" of mystic insulation. "T.S. Eliot is vexed and cannot look." And Merton must do this for "it is written: 'To see the world in a grain of sand.' "

I have mentioned earlier Merton's indebtedness to Blake both as an agent of his conversion to Catholicism and as the subject of his M.A. thesis. For Merton, Blake was a religious artist and as such he wants to be not beautiful and appealing to him but intelligible. In other words, he does not love nature for and in herself, but looks at natural objects, *sub specie aeternitatis* as they are in God.[7]

Merton's reading of Blake via Thomas Aquinas coincided on this point, at least, with Northrop Frye's observation that

Reality is intelligibility, and a poet who has put things into words has lifted "things" from the barren chaos of nature into the created order of thought. The Preacher says wearily that of making many books there is no end: the Apostle John, in the full exuberance of the spirit released in him by Jesus, proclaims that the world is not nearly big enough to hold all that might be written about the Word.[8]

It is the relationship of the word with the Word (Jesus/Logos/ Spiritual Imagination) and the relationship of both with the Fall that underlie Merton's sympathy with Blake's vision and poetics. In his thesis on Blake, Merton writes that

it is common among mystics to identify the creation of man with the fall; that is, the creation of man in time and space. In Eden, man was eternal. But he fell from eternity into time, into matter, illusion, chaos and death. The creation of the universe as we know it resulted from the fall of one of the "eternals," Urizen, from eternity into matter, and he dragged all the others with him. . . . It is self-will that causes the fall from intelligibility into the blandness of matter: then the spirit is locked up in the flesh. The five senses are thus only "chinks in a cavern" and, whereas before the intellect contemplated Truth face to face, now "Five windows light the cavern'd man" and "if the doors of perception were cleansed, everything would appear to man as it is: infinite."[9]

The cleansing of the doors of perception is the work of the poet and the mystic, and for Blake as well as for Merton art and love alone can repair the division and disharmony of the Fall. To understand Blake's poetics and mysticism Merton turned again and again to St. Thomas. He used the categories and terms of Thomistic aesthetics "because [they] are so clear, so acute, so well-balanced, that they fill the whole subject with a light by which we may more clearly see into the depths of Blake's own more recondite thought."[10] This reliance on Thomistic ideas and terms was especially helpful in the case of *claritas*, a concept that proved a singularly valuable instrument whereby to measure the intention and execution of Blake's aesthetic:

> Since *claritas* implies essential beauty it implies also intelligibility, and this is what Blake always insists on when he defends imagination against scientific reason, "the philosophy of the five senses". . . . The work of reason (Matter) and logic which give us in the end only an approximate understanding of first causes does not interest Blake: he, rather, inextricably linking up the poetic instinct with his own mysticism, and all his religious feelings finds, through poetry, the possibility of direct intuitive contacts with pure intelligibility. . . . This seizure of intelligible realities without using concepts as a formal means is something analogous in both the poet and the mystic. . . .[11]

The association of *claritas* with Merton's own interest in language and the Word finds a special focus in the similarity of the mystic and poetic intuitions:

In poetic intuition objective reality and subjectivity, the world and the whole of the soul, coexist inseparably. At that moment sense and sensation are brought back to the heart, blood to the spirit, passion to intuition.[12]

The splendour of the Word and the truth of the word are not only the mystic's delight for in their unity they are the poet's dream. But this dream demands a Promethean effort: the reparation of the Fall. For Blake, the Fall entails the shattering of the Four-Fold Vision, the separation of inspiration from art, and the usurpation of Pure Wisdom. For Merton, the Fall is a "confusion of cries." As he laconically observed in *Cables to the Ace*: "Since language has become a medium in which we are totally immersed, there is no longer any need to say anything." But speak the poet will. The tone and the manner of the speaking will change with the urgency of the vision; in time he will become the antipoet, his voice madly satirical. But in the early years — the 1940s and 1950s — the voice is lyrical. It is the early Blake speaking.

For instance, in his "Aubade — Lake Erie" from his collection *A Man in the Divided Sea* Merton united in one lyric the tension and contrast that Blake developed in two separate but related poems. In the aubade, a traditional morning song, the "innocent children" are "Awake, in the frames of windows. . . . / Loving the blue, sprayed leaves of childish life." They are one with nature, dancing in the sun, walking through fields of barley "Turning the harrowed earth to growing bread," treading underfoot "the bleeding grape," "splicing the sweet, wounded wine." Their harvest is the pure communion with nature that only the innocence of children can achieve — an innocence, however, that can be recreated in the banquet of belief, the eucharist of faith. The children, "fugitives, and sleepers in the fields," free from the post-Fall consequences of labour, restraint, and harnessed energy, with "their shining voices, clean as summer," play and frolic while "a hundred dusty Luthers rise from the dead unheeding," searching for "the gap-toothed grin of factories" and "the wood winds of the western freight."

The poem, however, is not about the poet's romantic preference for a benevolent feudalism over a rampaging industrialism, for incorporated in it is the Blakean contrast of "Holy Thursday" from Blake's *Songs of Innocence,* where the children walk toward St. Paul's Cathedral in London on the feast of the institution of communion — "O what a multitude they seem'd, these flowers of London town" — with "Holy Thursday" from his *Songs of Experience,* where the children, enslaved by "cold and usurous hand," are reduced to a poverty in which

> . . . their sun does never shine,
> And their fields are bleak and bare,
> And their ways are fill'd with thorns:
> It is eternal winter there.

The joyless and guilt-ridden wardens who have imprisoned the children, the

> Priests in black gowns [who] were walking their rounds,
> And binding with briars my joys and desires
> > (Blake's "The Garden of Love")

are the "dusty Luthers" of mass production and grim Christianity, the fathers of a grinding capitalism and unholy faith. They are the ones who, for Merton and for Blake, have taught the children "to sing the notes of woe,"

> And because I am happy & dance & sing,
> They think they have done me no injury,

And are gone to praise God & his Priest & King,
Who make up a heaven of our misery.
    (Blake's "The Chimney Sweeper," *Songs of Experience*)

Blake and Merton found children, as indeed did Christ, particularly sensitive to spiritual truths, the transparent profundity of which often eludes sophisticated intellectuals who prefer abstraction to imagination. In a letter to Dr. John Trusler of August 23, 1799, Blake writes that

> I am happy to find a Great Majority of Fellow Mortals who can Elucidate My Visions, & Particularly they have been Elucidated by Children, who have taken a greater delight in contemplating my Pictures than I had even hoped. Neither Youth nor Childhood is Folly or Incapacity. Some Children are Fools & so are some Old Men. But There is a vast majority on the side of Imagination or Spiritual Sensation.[13]

As in the "Aubade — Lake Erie," where the children "in the frames of windows" perceive without obstruction, so too in Merton's poem "The Winter's Night," when in the dark "the frost cracks on the window," the children arise and confer "And all call out in whispers to their guardian angels." They wait for a New Age, one ushered in in the quiet of the Incarnation. The moment of Christ's entry into human history is the beginning of a new innocence. In the Lent of our discontent, in our "winter's night," only the children, bearers of our primordial or edenic innocence in commerce with their angels, wait for a star to sing "in the pane, as brittle as their innocence." The brittle innocence of the children and their capacity for spiritual sensation can also be found on the "barque of Gethsemani."

The monastery is both "the decayed hole among the mountains" and the ark-like "tame home" that offers rest in a world beset with the waves of tumult. Gethsemani is the harbour in the storm and the "dead grove." It is the visionary's Eden where the unity of a shattered humanity, or Albion as Blake would have it, can once again be imagined, a place or a condition wherein *claritas* assures the intellect a direct and intuitive enjoyment of beauty, the beauty of Blake's "human form divine." Eden is the Blakean "Four-Fold Vision":

> To see the splendor of form in matter is to look through matter into eternity, it is to abandon "single vision and Newton's sleep" and to realize that:
>> Every generated body in its inward form
>> Is a garden of delight and a building of magnificence.[14]

The loss of Eden, the shattering of the "Four-Fold Vision," is pictured in Merton's poem "Christopher Columbus" from his 1949 volume *The Tears of the Blind Lions*. This poem is a chronicle of a mythical America's rejection of Eden. For Merton, Columbus was "a great Captain with Mary [imagination] in his sails" who left the known world, the European world of constricted vision, in search of "the undiscovered continent." He dispensed with the ordinary means of traversing the ocean and "waded into the waters of the sea."

Having left the European imagination "like the pillars of Hercules / Standing westward on the way to the Azores," Columbus emerges from the sea on the shores of America:

> Suddenly the great Christ-bearing Columbus
>   rises in the sea
> Spilling the green Atlantic from his shoulders
> And sees America through a veil of waters.

Columbus is the Blakean Orc, a figure who embodies the power of human desire for a better world and as a consequence of the exercise of this power often precipitates revolutions that anticipate the Apocalypse. As Frye notes:

> In the Golden Age before the Fall, humanity or Albion dwelt at peace in its Paradise or Atlantis. The Fall produced a chaotic world and the central symbol of chaos is water. . . . The Atlantic Ocean, then, symbolizes the fallen world in Blake; he calls it the "Sea of Time and Space." The rise of a new civilization . . . in America indicates the reintegrating of Atlantis, the disappearance of the Atlantic Ocean, and the return of the Golden Age.[15]

"Rising from the harbor," Columbus is cheered by the natives who see him as "their noon-day sun, their giant Gospel." Thousands come to him with gifts of the land for he signals the dawning of the Golden Age, reaching "down to the citizens / The golden fruits of which his arms are full." However, as evening sets in, as innocence is eclipsed, "the little ones have wept him out of sight." The story of America is really the story of a false Golden Age, the story of a land and its peoples betrayed, with Columbus restrained in shackles like Blake's "red Orc":

> What will you do tomorrow, America
> Found and lost so soon?
> Your Christ has died and gone to Spain
> Bearing a precious cross upon his shoulder
> And there your story lies in chains.

Orc, the firebrand, has one grand apocalyptic sweep in overcoming the restraints of Urizen and his minions in Blake's epic *America*:

Stiff shudderings shook the heav'nly thrones!
  France, Spain, & Italy
In terror view'd the bands of Albion, and
  the ancient Guardians,
Fainting upon the elements, smitten with
  their own plagues.
They slow advance to shut the five gates
  of their law-built heaven,
Filled with blasting fancies and with mildews
  of despair,
With fierce disease and lust, unable to
  stem the fires of Orc.
But the five gates were consum'd, & their
  bolts and hinges melted;
And the fierce flames burnt round the heavens,
  & round the abodes of men.

Columbus, Merton's spiritual revolutionary, cannot consume the "five gates" with the "fires of Orc." Enchained, with his "sham discovery" and its natives "mapped and verified / Plotted, printed, catalogued, numbered and categorized," Columbus knows the awful truth of Urizen's power and the full loss of freedom:

In every cry of every Man,
In every Infant's cry of fear,
In every voice, in every ban,
The mind-forg'd manacles I hear. (Blake's "London")

Having been offered the liberty of Orc, the spiritual freedom of Columbus, and having then lost it, the America of "Christopher Columbus" becomes the nightmare world of a "Hymn of Not Much Praise for New York City." It is a world whose value can be gauged only in proportion to the value of its currency, the rate of its exchange. Columbus has been displaced by "devils . . . sailing to your harbors":

> They bend over their tillers with little fox faces,
> Grin like dollars through their fur,
> And their meat-eating sails fly down and
>   fold upon your shore.

America is no Atlantis; the child's vision remains unheeded; commerce is rampant; the imagination deadened; the "barque of Gethsemani" the only safe enclosure. The monk, the poet, the spiritual child, cannot be bought. In the early years of Merton's monastic life Gethsemani stood as a sure sign of the dignity of the individual over mass society. In time Merton came to fear the abbey's penchant for functioning like a juggernaut crushing in its slow advance all outcroppings of independent judgement. But in the forties and early fifties Merton was satisfied that Gethsemani was the place to be — as monk and as poet.

He knew that first and foremost the poet is an individualist intent on the solitary task of redeeming language and meaning. He observed in his *Secular Journal*:

> The logic of the poet — that is, the logic of language or the experience itself — develops the way a living organism grows: it spreads out towards what it loves, and is heliotropic, like a plant. A tree grows out into a free form, an organic form. It is never ideal, only free; never typical, always individual.[16]

This was not the only time Merton was to liken monks to trees; the image is a leitmotif running through his prose and poetry, essays and correspondence. He understood that "in the night of our technological barbarism, monks must be as trees — which exist silently in the dark and by their vital presence purify the air." The logic of the monk, like that of the poet, is not arbitrary nor indeed is it immediately comprehensible, for it is the logic of vision, provocative and yet faithful to its own inner law. The logic of vision is strikingly and unalterably individual — eclectic, amorphous, esoteric, temerarious — it is elusive, and abundant with conviction. It is my contention that no better way existed for Merton to approach this type of free and visionary poet than by emulating Blake. Merton read in Blake's art a testament to the human spirit's capacity to survive in the closeting atmosphere of Rationalist civilization, of the empirical Western mind. He saw in Blake's vision an imagination at work that was creative, free, and divine.

Out of the ruins of the Fall — the displaced sensibility, the disordered spirit — the poet as *maker*, in the person of Blake, constructed a private mythology whereby he sought to heal the breach, to repair the division. Blake's task became Merton's. He began to develop his own poetic–theological myth culminating in the sophisticated but incomplete structure of *Geography of Lograire*. Blake fought to recover innocence and accepted the Fall as a given. The senses were imprisoned; they must be liberated. Merton saw the scar of the Fall in language and he came to understand the poet's role as nothing less than the restitution of the word: the restoration of its sacredness, and its liberation from the uses of deception, slick rhetoric, and ideological manipulation to become once more the quiet servant of truth.

In *A Man in the Divided Sea*, Merton's theory of the dissociation of language from its transcendent source receives an early if somewhat crude expression. He uses John the Baptist as the prototype of the monk-poet, the "voice in the wilderness," the seeker who tries to re-establish communication between word and Word by repairing the legacy of Babel: "Name Him and vanish, like a proclamation" ("St. John the Baptist"). As herald of the Word, precursor of the Logos, and dweller in the desert, this "first Cistercian and the greatest Trappist" came to serve very much the same function for Merton as Rintrah did for Blake. Rintrah, as Blake says, "comprehends all the Prophetic Characters" — Jeremiah, Elijah, John the Baptist, etc.

In Merton's "Prophet" from *Thirty Poems* (1944) the speaker meets "a traveller from the holy desert" who has in some unique sense "seen the rays of our sun." The traveller is privy to some special knowledge, a knowledge characterized by the sun's rays,

> those shining, choiring rays,
> Telling the time when our woods' Saint Savior's
> promise

will "disarm the Lent" with fulfillment. The gnostic tone of the poem and its numinous images accord well with the Blakean conception of the artist as one who knows that, as Blake says in his *Annotations to "Poems" by William Wordsworth*, "one power alone makes a Poet: Imagination, The Divine Vision." Merton writes of Blake that

> the man of imagination, the artist, because of the "virtue" of his art, sees more than his eyes present to him. He does not rely like Urizen entirely on the evidence of his sense, accepting nothing else at all. Urizen is always blind and in chains, and is trying constantly to impose that blindness on the whole world.[17]

The prophet is an artist who sees without spiritual hindrance, subterfuge, or Baconian certitude. John the Baptist represents for Merton not only the hortatory and visionary dimensions of the poetic charism, but just as important, he symbolizes the purity of poetic consciousness, an unprejudiced receptivity to impression, a *tabula rasa*, innocent, pristine, and vulnerable, upon which can be sketched experience and insight. In sho rt, John the Baptist/Rintrah symbolizes a spiritual and creative condition that is a "desert testimony." The generosity and faith that the Baptist represents in the face of history and his unhindered imagination constitute the

> secret tents,
> The sacred, unimaginable tabernacles
> Burning upon the hills of our desire.
>   ("St. John's Night," *Figures for an Apocalypse* [1947])

John heralds the arrival of the Word/word; he represents the ideal condition in which the Word/word may be enfleshed/written; he is the night that allows the light to shine. The Baptist continues to live for Merton in such figures as St. Jerome, St. Paul the Hermit, and St. Anthony Abbot who, "knowing no way of withstanding the weight of His language" ("Two Desert Fathers," *Figures for an Apocalypse*) which rends asunder like bolts from heaven the "darkness of our classic intellection," have in the cauterizing silence of the desert "died to the world of concept." In such a way, the imagination is loosed from the Hellenic bonds that tie it to chronology, logic, and matter. In such a way only can the suzerainty of Urizen be shattered:

> Because our minds, lovers of map and line
> Charting the way to heaven with a pack of compasses,
> Plotting to catch our Christ between some
>   numbered parallels,
> Trick us with too much logic. . . .

Freed in the desert from the tyranny of the mind, the imagination stands open to create, unencumbered by the rationalism of Bacon or Locke. At the same time the desert frees us from the tyranny of the senses, ensuring the "lion-light" — the soul, the imagination — the possibility of unhampered creativity. The desert/Gethsemani is the schooling ground for the imagination and the novitiate for the contemplative sensibility; it is the place where "thought lies slaughtered in the broken doors." Merton returned to the Baptist in a later poem, "The Quickening of St. John the Baptist" (*The Tears of the Blind Lions*), in which he succeeded in bringing together in a remarkable fusion a number of the themes that had occupied him in the years since his conversion: the poet as apocalyptic; the monk as desert-dweller; the Baptist as prototype of the Christian hermit; the Virgin Mary as the source and/or condition of the imaginative act.

In the first stanza the speaker asks why the "Virgin of Nazareth" has fled the world of ordinary domestic experience, the world of the city:

Why do you fly those markets,
Those suburban gardens,
The trumpets of the jealous lilies,
Leaving them all, lovely among the lemon trees?

In the first verse of the second stanza the speaker reveals the terrible uniqueness of the Virgin's flight to her sister Elizabeth: "You have trusted no town / With the news behind your eyes." The "news behind your eyes" is the knowledge that comes of spiritual and not physical vision. It is news perceived in the dark, sealed, and "waiting to be born" like the Baptist. The eyes are aglow with a "knowledge" that cannot yet be seen. The eyes are like windows through which one can see only with faith. And for the Baptist the window through which he saw the Word was "Our Lady, full of Christ." In the womb of Elizabeth the young John was quickened by faith when the Virgin, with "eyes as grey as doves," alighted upon the house of Zechariah "like the peace of a new world." He saw without eyes; he "could not see a thing" and yet he was transfixed with a vision of God:

How did you see her in the eyeless dark?
What secret syllable
Woke your young faith to the mad truth
That an unborn baby could be washed in the
    Spirit of God?
Oh burning joy!

The womb of the Virgin is the imaginative faculty waiting to be quickened by some "secret syllable" and it is also the church, in whom are the "hidden children," the contemplatives, "Planted in the night of contemplation, / Sealed in the dark and waiting to be born." As the womb of Elizabeth represents the hermitage of the Baptist, so "those who by vow lie buried in the cloister or the hermitage" are in the womb of mother church. From the moment of quickening to the moment of final witness the monks see in the Baptist the model of contemplative and prophetic vocation. Like the preacher of the desert the monks are "exiles in the far end of solitude, living as listeners," relentlessly pursuing "the world's gain in an unthinkable experience." Their existence is marginal, their values peripheral in the eyes of an agnostic world; and yet "like sentinels upon the world's frontier" they wait and listen for the "first far drums of Christ the Conqueror." Like the Baptist and the poet the monks cannot see a thing; and yet with the eye of faith, the eye of imagination,

We wake and know the Virgin Presence
Receive her Christ into our night
With stabs of an intelligence as white as
    lightning.

Gethsemani, described as a barque and a womb in the 1940s, by the mid-fifties has become a barn and the lyrical poet with a taste for theology has now become the lyrical poet with a taste for mysticism.

In "Elegy for the Monastery Barn" from his 1957 collection of poems, *The Strange Islands*, Merton used the traditional mystical language of fire in a poem of rustic reality. As his friend and mentor Mark Van Doren observed:

> All is real; nothing is made up; this, we instantly believe, is the true content of the subject, which like any other subject starts on earth and gets in its own natural way to heaven.[18]

Like an old woman "announcing the hour of her death," the monastery barn dresses in the blazing finery of the flame:

> So now, one summer day's end,
> At suppertime, when wheels are still,
> The long barn suddenly puts on the traitor, beauty,
> And hails us with a dangerous cry,
> For: "Look!" she calls to the country,
> "Look how fast I dress myself in fire!"

Enveloped in fire the barn "will not have us near her." Alone and magnificent, her death by fire sears the witnesses of her terrible beauty:

> Terribly,
> Sweet Christ, how terribly her beauty burns
> us now!

But there is more to the barn than her final resplendence; there is that which precedes the flames, solitude and peace:

> Who felt the silence, there,
> The long hushed gallery
> Clean and resigned and waiting for the fire?

Robed in fire, consumed now in flames with fire feeding fire, the ghosts of those who once inhabited the barn — the "fifty invisible cattle" — return to accept their destiny: "Here is their meaning found. Here is their end."

Totally ablaze, the barn is "laved in the flame as in a Sacrament" and all are admonished to

> Fly from the silence
> Of this creature sanctified by fire!

Like Moses who was addressed by Yahweh in a burning bush and who covered his face, afraid to gaze upon the face of God, the poet declares:

> Let no man stay inside to look upon the Lord!
> Let no man wait within and see the Holy
> One sitting in the presence of disaster
> Thinking upon this barn His gentle doom!

The monastery barn is a metaphor both for the individual soul and for the monastery community. Like the soul, the barn burns when it has reached its maturity. The fire represents the "first-last hour of joy"; the culmination of the mystic's yearning for transcendence; the perfect image of the unified state, the highest state of the mystic's growth in prayer and love of the Ineffable.

But this death by fire, this beatific transformation, is not gratuitous. Years of silence and solitude, of spiritual persever- ance and monastic obedience, preceded it:

> The long, hushed gallery
> Clean and resigned and waiting for the fire.

The terrible beauty of the barn's end is the terrible beauty of its beginning. The soul has arrived only to discover it has never departed. Like the deceased cattle who have gathered to dis- cover in the barn's burning the "little minute of their destiny," the good deeds and virtuous thoughts of the mystic return to witness "their first-last hour of joy." In the burning of the barn/soul/monastery the transfiguration occurs before the faithful. The "creature sanctified by fire" is one of the elect, in whom the privileged onlookers fear to see the Holy One, the *mysterium tremendum*, "laved in the flame as in a Sacrament." In the mystical fire of Christian tradition the apocalyptic fire of Blakean inspiration finds a partial parallel. Although ortho- dox Christian thinking would have difficulty with the Blakean tenet that "the notion that man has a body distinct from his soul is to be expunged," many mystics, including medieval figures like Julian of Norwich, would certainly have no problem accepting Blake's assertion that "if the doors of perception were cleansed every thing would appear to man as it is, infinite." So it is with Merton; the walls of the barn are the "doors of perception":

> The brilliant walls are holy
> In their first-last hour of joy

and all is made holy in the sanctifying fire. As the classicist Norman O. Brown states:

The true body is the body burnt up, the spiritual body. The unity is not organic-natural unity, but the unity of fire. . . . The apocalyptic fire burns up the reality of the material world. In the baptism of water we are buried with Christ; in the baptism of fire we are conformed to the body of his glory.[19]

The fire of judgement — the apocalyptic fire of the Hebrew prophets — and Blake's apocalyptic fire of cleansing are both present in Merton's poetry, the former in his earlier and more devotional verse, and the latter in his later mystical verse. It would seem that Merton had succeeded in exorcizing the spirit of the industrial age from his memory; after all, the footsteps of commerce and technology ended at the door to the Gethsemani novitiate. Or so Merton would allow himself and his readers to believe. The reality was otherwise.

Merton knew that the abbey under Abbot Fox was slowly being transformed into a business centre, the monks into regimented labourers. Fruitcake was edging out spirituality; cheese was the manna of the new age:

> I think that we would never freeze
> Such lively assets as our cheese:
>
> — — — — — — —
>
> Poems are nought but warmed-up breeze,
> *Dollars* are made by Trappist Cheese. ("CHEE$E")

If Merton saw in Fox's expanding dairy empire a comparatively benevolent sign of the intrusion of commerce into the Gethsemani landscape, he saw Fort Knox as a symbol of commerce's malevolent encroachment on monastic values. In "The Guns of Fort Knox" from *The Strange Islands*, the Antichrist deceives the dead by summoning them forth from their graves with the promise of Judgement. Fort Knox, storehouse

for U.S. gold bullion, is located within a few miles of the Abbey
of Gethsemani and when it fires its guns they can be heard and
felt within a good radius of the fort, including the monastic
gardens:

> Guns at the camp (I hear them suddenly)
> Guns make the little house jump.

The guns shatter the privilege of cloister and stir the dead:

> They'll hear these guns tonight
> Tomorrow or some other time.
> They'll wake. They'll rise
> Through the stunned rocks, form
> Regiments and do death's work once more.

It is not the monks who will rise from the dead, but the "slain
generation," the miners and workers who have known the cost
of thankless labour, for they are slain in their dignity and in
their hope, waiting only to do "death's work once more" in the
bowels of the earth. The poet exhorts the guns to cease their
pounding because "this is not / The right resurrection." He
advises the guns to let the "slain generation" lie in peace, to

> Shake no more
> (But leave the locks secure)
> Hell's door.

Fort Knox is the symbol of American success, the false millennium that offers the reign not of God but of Mammon, the
Antichrist that will deceive many and call for the "armies of
the dead" for a false Judgement. The guns are the *tuba mirum*
summoning the slain to account.

Fort Knox is the altar of affluence; it protects and secures its possessions by generating fear. Gethsemani, by contrast, offers hospitality to the stranger, attracts the wanderer and the dispossessed, and places its trust in the "quiet Christ." Fort Knox knows only the language of intimidation and exclusion. The poverty and vulnerability of Gethsemani stand in judgement on the walled fortress, the shrine of American materialism.

Once again the monks of Gethsemani are like trees planted in an enclosure, "sentinels upon the world's frontier." The monk/tree is untouched by the presence of the Antichrist:

> Trees
> Must also feel the guns they do not want
> Even in their core.
> As each charge bumps the shocked earth
> They shudder from the root.

The monk must withstand the barrage of Fort Knox/Antichrist, the disruptive sounds and quakes that seek to supplant him. Rooted in his faith and vocation the monk/tree knows that to bend is to die.

"The Guns of Fort Knox" and "Elegy for a Monastery Barn" were published with Merton's one and only foray into playwriting: *The Tower of Babel*. It is the most elaborate treatment of his "myth-dream" to date (1957) and represents a sophisticated improvement on his earlier fragmentary effort, "Tower of Babel" in *Early Poems (1940–1942)*. Subtitled "A Morality," it is preceded by three epigraphs, each of which succinctly states one of the themes of the play: the fragmentation of language (Genesis 11: 1–9); the conflict between the heavenly city and the earthly city (St. Augustine, *The City of God*, xiv, 28); and the destruction of Babylon (Apocalypse 18: 21, 23–24). In the tradition of the medieval morality play, abstractions such as Falsehood and Propaganda are invested with dramatic personalities and the struggle for the individual is fought between the powers of the Tower and the powers of the Child. The use of the classical chorus as both actor and commentator, and the obvious indebtedness to T.S. Eliot in versification, are the more outstanding of the structural features of the play. Divided into two parts with two scenes for each, the dramatic momentum of the play consists in the dialectic between the supporters of the Leader and the supporters of the Word.

In the first scene, "the building of the tower," the reader is introduced to the two figures who remain on stage throughout the play, Thomas and Raphael. True to their names, Thomas is the doubter and Raphael the healer. Both are witnesses to the construction of the Tower; Thomas queries whether they should assist the builders and Raphael warns that

> If we learn their language
> We will no longer understand
> What is being said.

Eager to build, and motivated by veneration for the Leader, the builders profess their unqualified trust in the Tower and in the Leader:

> I believe in our common language
> Therefore I will serve the Leader.

The Chorus mirrors the enthusiasm of the builders:

> Great Babylon, grow,
> Great Babylon, touch the stars.

Thomas is rather easily persuaded that the Tower is worthy of faith and the builders themselves believers, but Raphael warns that the faith of the builders is misplaced, and their unity of voice false, because "they have only united in their / common, though hidden, desire to fail." Determined to weld the populace into a common front, the disparate tribes into a common purpose, the Leader addresses the assembled in a manner suggestive of a true twentieth-century demagogue. His name, after all, is legion — Caudillo, Poglavnic, Führer, Duce:

> Already I see that the skies are as full of words as they are of stars. Each word becomes an instrument of war. Words of the clocks and devils. Words of the wheels and machines. Steel words stronger than flesh or spirit. Secret words that divide the essences of things. Last of all, the one word which strikes at the heart of creation, and dissolves it into its original nothingness. Give me possession of this one word, and I will forget every other.

The gathered, the chorus, willingly give the leader his one word: "Fear! Fear!" It is the same word that is spoken, according to American poet Archibald MacLeish in his pre-World War II verse play *The Fall of the City*,

> In the day of confusion of reason when
>   all is delusion:
> In the day of the tyrants of tongues when
>   the truth is for hire:
> In the day of deceit when ends meet.[20]

It is in times such as these that people turn to their gods. Suddenly, following upon the Leader's diatribe, a powerful tempest levels the Tower and there is incredulity and panic everywhere. Thomas proclaims Babylon's end but Raphael is the wiser for he knows "it is Babylon's beginning."

Scene two is "The Trial," at which the authorities look for the perennial scapegoat for the disaster. Language is accused of treachery but prematurely acquitted. The Leader states that words are the "ultimate reality," and that it is silence that should be called to render an account. However, it is observed that there are three kinds of language: truth, falsehood, and propaganda; and each in turn is brought to the stand. Truth is denounced as an enemy of the "Mammoth State" and there are many who clamour for Truth's death. Merton's "Mammoth State" is not unlike the "personified State" of Carl Gustav Jung, a state or reality that has assumed incalculable authority and power over the destiny of individuals. A renegade authority that has arrogated to itself the power of the word and severed the word's link with transcendence, the State uses the word as a mechanism of control. Jung argues that we see this happen when

> belief in the word becomes credulity, and the word itself an infernal slogan capable of any deception. With credulity come propaganda and advertising to dupe the citizen with political jobbery and compromises, and the lie reaches proportions never known before in the history of the world. Thus, the word, originally announcing the unity of all . . . has in our day become the source of suspicion and distrust of all against all.[21]

Truth's death is not required. A philosopher establishes to the satisfaction of the Leader that Truth, verily, does not exist, that nothing has real being, and that "seeming is existing."

Next, Propaganda is called and skilfully avoids responsibility for the Tower's destruction by imputing guilt to diverse organizations and individuals. For this feat of side-stepping, the Leader decorates Propaganda with the "order of the Tower" and solemnly decrees that henceforth Propaganda "shall possess exclusive freedom of speech and worship in every part of the world."

Finally, Falsehood is called to account, and in so doing proceeds to define the essence of the Tower in such a way that the direct dependence of the Tower on the creative power of Falsehood is made explicit; "The tower is not a building but an influence, a mentality, an invisible power."

With Truth denied, Propaganda and Falsehood acquitted, the rapacious mob crucifies what remains: Silence.

And so ends Part One.

Part Two, "The City of God," opens with Thomas and Raphael musing aloud on the disappearance of Babylon. They are cautioned by a Prophet, however, not to believe their eyes alone, for the city lives. Babylon is ubiquitous:

> The city under the sand
> Lives everywhere. It is not a buried city.
> The westward ships will soon discover
> The old city, on another continent
> Young and new. The southward ships
> Will find that the city was never destroyed.
> The northward place soon sees the sun
> Shine on the towers of the same Babylon.

Lamenting the disunity that plagues humanity, the Prophet asks, "When will the pieces be brought together again, and receive the divine image?" Aware that humanity's spiritual and linguistic disarray are inextricably bound by a common source and a common hope, the Prophet sees in the impoverishment of language a sign of dissension and war. Only by the word shall the word be healed and only in silence shall the din of division be quieted. By means of the Word a new city will

come into being; Babylon, the "earthly city," will give way to
Jerusalem, the "heavenly city":

> As a symbol is destroyed to give
> place to a reality, so the shadow of
> Babylon will be destroyed to give place
> to the light which it might have contained.

In the concluding scene of the play, "The Exiles," Raphael
speaks to the Chorus, inquiring where they are going, and they
answer that they know not where they came from nor where
they may be going. They are without leadership, with no one
to liberate them from a history of meaningless labour:

> Who will stop the giant wheel
> Who will break the strict machine
> Who will save us from the mill?

These exiles are pilgrims perpetually in search of "another
country," with "no word to wash our wounded minds." The
Prophet responds to their despair by announcing the presence
of the Word that lives within, and Thomas, who has now
ceased to doubt, tells them that they must cast aside the
words that are devoid of meaning, recover words no longer
used, and restore new meaning to those words that have lan-
guished under the combined tyranny of utility and expedience.
Raphael, in turn, speaks of the human city as an "inverted
reflection of another city," and warns the exiles that they must
not confound truth with appearance, the eternal with the
impermanent.

Suddenly the clangour of arms can be heard and the news of
Babylon's destruction is received from a voice crying in the
distance:

Babylon the great is fallen, is fallen
And is become the house of emptiness
And is carried away by the night birds.
The kings have seen her, drowning in the sea.

The rule of Babylon is shattered by the "one Word uttered in silence." This Word was given to the desert dwellers, the pure of heart, the Blakean visionaries, who see what the Prophet sees: "The Word who would not speak when He was wounded."

The play concludes with the dramatis personae saying as one that

He alone can break the seal
And tell the conquerors His name.
ADORATE DOMINUM!

The confusion of tongues, the universal cacophony of a species divided against itself is stilled by the "Verbum sanctum."

The Tower of Babel is about the betrayal of language and the consequences of that betrayal. By the word we are sorely afflicted! Words have become the paid hirelings, the mercenaries of ambition, lust, greed, and all other manifestations of Power's will; they are the sacraments of the dead, the spawn of the Tower. For the First Exile:

The words of this land
Are interminable signals of their own emptiness
Signs without meaning.

As they manipulate meaning so are they manipulated by the Leader; words have become slaves of distortion and servants of deceit. But it was not always so: "Ah, yes, I have heard in the past that words can be true." The word must be cleansed. As we are made whole by the Word, so words are made whole by the poet. But before we can listen to the Word our words must speak the truth, and it is the poet above all who must instruct us in the art of listening to Truth's voice — silence.

Because language served power and is now powerless, it has forgotten history and disavowed destiny. It is uprooted and aimless; it is Babel. As the root of Babylon it wages war against silence. As the Leader rails,

> Words, then, are the ultimate reality!
> Let there never again be silence. For if there
> be silence, our history will instantly be
> unmade, and if we stop talking we will
> cease to exist.

The poet is the listener par excellence, whose craft is silence and whose words prayer. The poet knows that Babble-On will not easily be undone and that the primary responsibility is to renew the power of the word so that the Word may no longer be resisted. The poet must counter the persuasive logic of the Professor who argues that words

> . . . belong by right to the political process.
> Doing, making, destroying. Or rather
> Being done, being made, being destroyed.

In the midst of Babylon lies Jerusalem, in the heart of chaos lies form, and in the centre of confusion, vision.

The only answer to the geography of Babylon is the geography of Jerusalem, or of Lograire, as Merton would later argue. Babylon is the central symbol of disarray and Jerusalem/Lograire the central symbol of unity; Babel is the tower of pride and the cross the tower of humility; Nimrod is the prototype of totalitarian rule and Jesus the sign of God's favour.

In the heart of the "Babylonian captivity," however, one can have a foretaste of freedom. As the Prophet says:

> Those who have taken peace upon their tongue
> Have eaten heaven:
> They have made heaven in the midst of us,
> Jerusalem in Babylon.

Faced with the symbol of the Tower as the sign of disunity, Merton looked for the principle of unity and found it eventually in the concept of the "myth-dream," the total body of ideas drawn from our experience, sensual, intellectual, and spiritual. The Tower of Babel brought division. Where, in what, lay the possibility of unity? Where could be found unity in diversity, oneness in multiplicity? How could Merton devise a mythic structure that could preserve both the fluid and the stationary, the many and the one? He found it in the "myth-dream," a notion he explored copiously in a taped conference he gave in 1968 on cargo cults, a conference which was subsequently abbreviated and published as "Cargo Cults and the South Pacific" several years after his death. His interest in "cargo theology" would find its supreme expression in *The Geography of Lograire*. The "myth-dream" was broader and more inclusive as a theological concept than as an anthropological one:

> It is important not to escape from all the myth-dreams into a realm of pure logic but, on the contrary, to be able to move from one myth-dream to another and at the same time *to be aware of a transcendent common myth-dream which is basic to the entire human race.*[22]

The "transcendent common myth-dream" is the Fall, foundational for both Blakean and orthodox Christian mythology.

The reparation or the undoing of the Fall is Merton's own myth-dream, which he owes to both previous sources, but which bears his own unique stamp.

There are both positive and negative myth-dreams, and it is the poet's duty to awaken humanity to the hope proffered by the former and to the deception masquerading as truth in the latter. Like Blake, Merton bewailed the servile adulation of reason in Western culture — "Bring out number, weight, and measure" — abstract speculation for its own sake, and the predilection for generalizing principles; and also like Blake, he deplored the melancholy legacy of Bacon, Locke, and Newton with its desecration of imagination and innocence.

Merton warned of the negative myth-dream endemic to Western society, "that everything we do has to be logical and scientific."[23] He found the antidote to this poison in the positive myth-dream of the historical maturity of humanity, which would be accomplished by a moral and spiritual reciprocity amongst all peoples, primitive and sophisticated, Christian and non-Christian — the new geography.

Merton knew that the only effective answer to the divisive legacy of Babel is a spiritual commonality, and that the only effective answer to the fragmentation of language is the recovery of the word's integrity. The negative myth-dream that is Babel, Merton insists, determines our culture: it embodies not only our wilful skewering of language but also our collective obsession with the mastery of matter, our conviction that the *cogito, ergo sum* of Descartes is the only acceptable metaphysical statement, and our belief that what cannot be circumscribed by Urizen is a delusion, or at best, suspect. Merton's positive myth-dream — the reparation of the Fall — involves the restitution of silence and the recovery of intelligible communication. Individuals isolated by pride devour words with an anxious need for meaning; barraged with a multitude of voices, humankind yearns for the simple eloquence of silence. Merton sees the possibility of Babel's redress in the humility that allows the word to be heard. In this he is like his contemporary W.H. Auden, who wrote in his essay "The Protestant Mystics" that the

> Curse of Babel is not the diversity of tongues — diversity is essential to life — but the pride of each of us which makes us think that those who make different verbal noises from our own are incapable of human speech so that discourse with them is out of the question, a pride which, since the speech of no two persons is identical — language is not algebra — must inevitably lead to the conclusion that the gift of human speech is reserved for oneself alone. It is due to this curse that, as Sir William Osler said, "Half of us are blind, few of us feel, and we are all deaf."[24]

The wailing of the Babylonians does not go unheard by the monk or the poet. By restoring faith in the common substratum of humanity's transcendent destiny, by vanquishing the caricature of God in the Hebrew scriptures, a being that Blake calls "Nobodaddy," by casting off the overlordship of Abstraction, by reuniting (in Marshall McLuhan's language) the "disordered sensorium," and by alerting humankind to its divine nature, the poet can "assist once again at the marriage of heaven and hell." Merton sees the repair of the Fall in the final contest between the Blakean "Contraries":

> Without Contraries is no progression.
> Attraction and Repulsion, Reason and Energy,
> Love and Hate, are necessary to Human existence.
>
> (Blake, *The Marriage of Heaven and Hell*)

And indeed they are necessary for human redemption. The negative myth-dreams must be at war with the positive, scientific understanding with imaginative, technological knowledge with the archaic wisdom of "primitive" peoples and dead cultures, and the transcendent with the immanent, if there is to be progression/salvation. Humanity must not forget that Jerusalem can be found in Babylon, in the very midst of our common life.

From the Old Testament city of power and demonic association, Babylon has now acquired a Blakean significance. Merton's Babylon is Blake's Rahab, the Great Whore and enslaver of the senses, the enemy of the poet and of inspiration, the Antichrist who threatens the Lamb. Faithful imposer of Urizen's laws, Rahab is ever busy with "webs of torture," with

> Mantles of despair, girdles of bitter
>   compunction, shoes of indolence,
> Veils of ignorance covering from head
>   to feet with a cold web. (*The Four Zoas*)

In the time of judgement Rahab/Antichrist/Babylon will confront the "Universal Humanity," and the final conflict will begin, Jerusalem arising from Babylon's undoing:

> Rahab beholds the Lamb of God.
> She smites with her knife of flint. She
>   destroys her own work
> Times upon times, thinking to destroy
>   the Lamb blessed for Ever. (*The Four Zoas*)

The broad outlines of the reparation have been drawn in *The Tower of Babel* but the final picture will not appear until ten years later with *The Geography of Lograire*. In between these two works, the "political" Merton emerged.

There is something precious, rarefied, and academic about *The Tower of Babel*. Its concerns are finely phrased, its imagery rather derivative, and there is a tone of quaint theatricality about it all. The play is an experiment in dramatic verse for the religiously committed, more a *divertissement* than a call to arms. The Merton of the mid-1950s was a safe writer; his mounting anxiety over an atrophying monasticism and the self-destructive inclinations of a Cold-War world were largely confined to his restricted journals and private correspondence. But by 1960 he would leave the intellectual and spiritual cocoon and speak directly to the world. The new Merton was still the monk of Gethsemani, but he had become a citizen of the world that barely twenty years earlier he had abandoned in disgust.

In *Conjectures of a Guilty Bystander*, a diary Merton began in 1956 and completed for publication in 1965, he wrote about the poet George Oppen and in doing so he revealed the shift in his own thinking:

> . . . the poet knows another and more real world, the world not of lies and stale air in the subway, but of life. The world of life is itself manifest in words, but is not a world of words. What matters is not the words but the life. If we listen particularly to the world's speech about itself we will be lied to and deceived, but not if we listen to life itself in its humility, frailty, silence, tenacity.[25]

The conviction that "what matters is not the words but the life" became one of the radical beliefs he adopted in his newly launched campaign against the death-wielding society of the nuclear age. He had come to admit that as a poet and monk, he was a "guilty bystander." The kind of theoretical exercises that had engaged his attention for many years — the relationship of poetry to contemplation, the politics of silence, the recovery of the pure monastic charism — no longer consumed him. They were eclipsed by the moral and political crises of the age; he could no longer, and would no longer, deny his implicated status as a citizen of the world. What was of cardinal importance from 1960 on was not the question of the tension between art and mysticism but rather that of the primacy of life in a death-creating environment. In three statements, two of which appeared in the early sixties, Merton outlined his argument for a new, non-partisan but highly political poetics.

In "Message to Poets," Merton addressed a literary conference in Mexico City in 1964, inviting them simply to

> obey life, and the Spirit of Life that calls us to be poets, and we shall harvest many new fruits for which the world hungers — fruits of hope that have never been seen before. With these fruits we shall calm the resentments and the rage of man.[26]

Caught in the vortex of violence and repression, traduced by bureaucrats, judged dangerous by ruling technocrats, and vilified by the rationalists as unproductive dreamers, poets are "children of the Unknown" and "ministers of silence" whose madness will be the salvation of the world:

> In the Republic of Plato there was already no place for poets and musicians, still less for dervishes and monks. As for the technological Platos who think they now run the world we live in, they imagine they can tempt us with banalities and abstractions. But we can elude them merely by stepping into the Heraklitean river which is never crossed twice. . . . No one can enter the river wearing the garments of public and collective ideas. He must feel the water on his skin. He must know that immediacy is for . . . the innocent.[27]

Merton counters the cunning of the technocrat with the poet's ingrained and unpurchasable innocence. This innocence is not naïveté in the face of Machiavellian ministrations, nor is it indifference to the "mystifications of bureaucracy, commerce, and the police state"; rather it is both the naked openness of the poet's mind to any and every impression, and the spiritual vulnerability that alone can ensure the freedom of the individual.

The uncontrived openness to life celebrated by Blake in *Songs of Innocence* is the essential innocence of the poet: unpredictable, without fear, inured to the blandishments of the propagandist and advertiser whose language is fraught with deception, the poet declares unequivocally for life:

> There is only life in all its unpredictability and all its freedom. All magic is a ruthless venture in manipulation, a vicious circle, a self-fulfilling prophecy.[28]

Like his Blake, Merton repudiates the comfortable rationalism of his time, the easy manipulation of truth to serve private ends, the natural atheism that denies the divinity of creation, and science's contempt for prophecy. The vocation of the prophet is for Merton inextricably linked with his Blakean conception of the poet as a silent-speaking visionary. The genuine prophet rejects the curse of "word-magic," that

> impurity of language and of spirit in which words, deliberately reduced to unintelligibility, appeal mindlessly to the vulnerable will. Let us parody and deride this magic with other variants of the unintelligible, if we want to. But it is better to prophesy than to deride. To prophesy is not to predict, but to seize upon reality in its moment of highest expectation and tension toward the new.[29]

The poet/prophet is called to "seize upon reality in its moment of highest expectation" in the way Blake seized upon eternity:

To see a World in a Grain of Sand
And a Heaven in a Wild Flower,
Hold Infinity in the palm of your hand
And Eternity in an hour.
              (Blake, "Auguries of Innocence")

To prophesy is not to calculate; it is to perceive. It is to see
with the eye of Imagination, the Spiritual and not the Cor-
poreal Eye, as Blake put it. To see in this way one must love
what one sees, for all that is exists in the human imagination
and "everything that lives is holy." So say Blake and Merton.
The poet/monk/dervish is called to dance in the water of life,
called to proclaim the holiness of matter.

In "Prologo," a 1965 prose poem dedicated to Venezuelan
poet Ludovico Silva, Merton speaks with vicious irony about
the poets who are condemned to life, who

> have been chosen inexorably by the injustice which is called
> life and which refuses to obey the laws which must align all
> equal and alike in the rich experience of finality which is
> death.

The poet is a witness to life in the valley of death and must
as a consequence evade society's efforts to neutralize him, to
demand that he speak with brio and optimism when he knows
that the words he must speak are a sign of contradiction and
that ultimately the

> Cross is the exclamation that nobody understands, and it is
> also the prototype of torture as "speech." But Christ said
> nothing, except ritual words and quotations that were pure
> and full of silence. They had no political implications, they
> defined nothing, they uttered no program. They abolished
> all programs: *consummatum est*.[30]

The poet must be political without being political; a herald of the Kingdom of Life in the very midst of the Kingdom of Death, while all the others in society

> are embalmed in the vast whispering perfumed cybernetic silence of the millennium of death (Death the millionaire, Death the dictator, Death the engineer).

The poet must remain ever vigilant, careful never to be seduced by the social identity, the social construct, of "artist." As Merton writes in his 1965 essay "Answers on Art and Freedom," the artist has,

> whether he likes it or not, inherited the combined functions of hermit, pilgrim, prophet, priest, shaman, sorcerer, sooth-sayer, alchemist and bonze. How can such a man be free? How can he really "find himself" if he plays a role that society has predetermined for him? The freedom of the artist is to be sought precisely in the choice of his *work* and not in the choice of the role as "artist" which society asks him to play, for reasons that will always remain very mysterious.[31]

One could just as easily substitute "monk" for "artist" in this essay to get a good reading on Merton's adamant refusal to be reduced to a label — a marketable commodity, known, predictable, and reliable. Such is the dulling of prophecy. By contrast, Merton called on poets and all monks, marginal figures who dwell in Blake's "Realms of day," to "dance in the clarity of perfect contradiction." In his poetic essay "Atlas and the Fatman," first published in *Behavior of Titans* (1961) and reprinted in *Raids on the Unspeakable*, he recalls Blake's discovery that one can see "Heaven in a Wild Flower":

Every plant that stands in the light of the sun is a saint and an outlaw. Every tree that brings forth blossoms without the command of man is powerful in the sight of God. Every star that man has not counted is a world of sanity and perfection. Every blade of grass is an angel singing in a shower of glory.[32]

It is to remind humankind that "every blade of grass is an angel" and that the spirit-enslaving technocracies of the world conspire against human liberty, that Merton's understanding of·the role of the poet acquires a pronounced political, even if antipolitical, tone. It is time for his emblems of political fury, his poetic soundings on the political issues of moment.

To understand Merton's response to the threat to human dignity posed by modernity, particularly in its U.S. context, we need to appreciate something of the larger American tradition that informed his sensibility. He was a Blakean visionary but he was also, as the literary scholar Ross Labrie points out, a child of American romanticism, a figure who

throughout his career, as an essayist and diarist specifically, was a romantic, in that he argued that through institution-alization, and through technology, which he saw as an off-shoot of institutionalization, we have lost sight of the glory of the human being. He thought that by retreating into the monastery, avoiding the commotion of the twentieth-century world, he could recover his sense of the value and beauty of human beings. In this he is very akin to Thoreau who thought that an individual mind and soul was greater than the whole of the government of the United States. Although Thoreau and his fellow romantic Emerson were inclined to leave formal religion behind in order to gain a sense of the true unity and universality of humankind,

Merton allowed a place for formal religion. In fact, in Merton's understanding of Catholicism, he emphasized the catholicity of Catholicism, the fact that there is something catholic about the world itself. He also emphasized, and in this he was directly like Thoreau, the need to oppose *any* encroachment upon individual human consciousness, any and all efforts by society to efface the individual. In case after case he took on all antagonists who seek to diminish the sacredness, the dignity of the individual, even if these antagonists, always institutional, included his own church or even his own monastery.

To recover the glory of the human being and to protect the individual in Mammoth Society are titanic tasks, but Merton was determined, with the apocalyptic energy and visionary urgency of a latter-day William Blake, to take them on and to develop for the late twentieth century a strategy of spiritual and intellectual coping. To do this effectively he needed to identify those specific areas that constituted the greatest threat to human wholeness. He found these emblems of political fury to be: technology, war, and racism.

Merton speaks of technology in terms that first seek to desacralize it, for many have turned it into a surrogate religion, complete with priestly castes, codes of conduct, channels of divine authority, and a working jargon that connotes cosmic benedictions and offers of grace and salvation.

When it comes to taking sides, I am not with the *Beati* who are openmouthed in awe at the "New Holiness" of a technological cosmos in which man condescends to be God's collaborator and to improve everything for Him. Not that technology is by itself impious or unholy. It is simply neutral and there is no greater nonsense than taking it for an ultimate value. It is *there*; and our love and compassion for other men is now framed and scaffolded by it. Then what?

We gain nothing by surrendering to technology as if it were a ritual, a worship, a liturgy, or talking of our liturgy as if it were an expression of the sacred values supposedly now revealed in technological power. Where impiety begins is in the hypostatizing of mechanical power as something to do with the incarnation as its fulfillment, as its Epiphany.[33]

What Merton most deplores is not technology per se but the mentality, the philosophy that undergirds Western culture's idolatrous subservience to it. It is technologism that is the threat, and technologism is Urizen. Humanity is prepared to, as Blake phrased it, "bring out number, weight and measure in a year of dearth" and to serve unthinkingly in the "Mills of Satan & Beelzeboul." The rule of technology is the rule of Urizen, subtle, insinuating, comprehensive, and insidious. It is also total.

It is by means of technology that man the person, the subject of qualified and perfectible freedom, becomes *quantified*, that is, becomes part of a mass — mass man — whose only function is to enter anonymously into the process of production and consumption. He becomes on one side an implement, a "hand," or better, a "bio-physical link" between machines: on the one side he is a mouth, a digestive system and an anus, something *through which* pass the products of his technological world, leaving a transient and meaningless sense of enjoyment. The effect of a totally emancipated technology is the regression of man to a climate of moral infancy, in total dependence not on "mother nature" (such a dependence could be partly tolerable and human) but on the pseudonature of technology, which has replaced nature by a closed system of mechanisms with no purpose but that of keeping themselves going.[34]

The most demonic expression of technology's capacity to effect human regression "to a climate of moral infancy" is the Adolf Eichmann affair. Spirited away by the Israeli Mossad from his hideout in Argentina in 1960 and tried for his crimes in the Holy Land, Eichmann and his trial, judgement, and execution captured the imagination of the world. Hannah Arendt, the philosopher and journalist who covered the trial for the American press, particularly the *New Yorker*, succeeded through her reportage and commentary in rousing passions, accusations, recriminations, and a bout of soul-searching not seen since the Nuremburg trials. Merton was transfixed by the trial and its coverage; the Eichmann affair became an obsession and he wrote about it and its consequences in poem, diary entry, and essay. In Eichmann totalitarianism and technologism came together in one frightful, satanic symbiosis.

Eichmann was the quintessentially sane man who represented the crisis of the liberal conscience and the impotence of a humane tradition in the face of the unspeakable savageries of the Reich. At his trial, the moral bankruptcy of Nazi Germany was condemned, but the European belief in the rule of Reason and the morality of high culture was also judged and found wanting. George Steiner underscores this scandalous fact with unnerving precision:

> Contrary to the "Scythian" fantasies of nineteenth century apocalyptic fables, barbarism did come from the European heartland. Though in parodistic and ultimately negating forms, political bestiality did take on certain of the conventions, idiom and external values of high culture. . . . Mined

by *ennui* and the aesthetics of violence, a fair proportion of the intelligentsia and of the institutions of European civilization — letters, the academy, the performing arts — met inhumanity with varying degrees of inhumanity. Nothing in the next-door world of Dachau impinged on the great winter cycle of Beethoven chamber music played in Munich. No canvases came off the museum walls as the butchers strolled past, guide-book in hand.[35]

In Eichmann, Thomas Merton saw the immaculate German officer who was also a symbol of the corruption of obedience, the sterility of the Kantian conception of duty, and the wedding of technology with death. In "parodistic and ultimately negating" form, Merton wrote a poem that he describes, in a letter to his Portuguese translator, the Brazilian nun M. Emmanuel de Souza e Silva, as a "very lugubrious poem about Auschwitz . . . a florilegium of statements from official documents and other declarations, for the most part. That makes it even more terrible."[36] This 1961 Swiftian prose poem, "Chant to Be Used in Processions Around a Site with Furnaces," is an emblem of the totalitarianism that follows upon the death of private conscience and the triumph of the Mammoth Society. It is Eichmann's story told anonymously, for it could be any one of a number of officers of whom Eichmann is the type. The terror is compounded.

The poem is a dramatic monologue. The speaker, an unnamed commandant of a concentration camp, justifies his life's work — implementing the Final Solution — *after* he has been executed. Defending himself, he protests that

> In my day we worked hard we saw what we did our self-sacrifice was conscientious and complete our work was faultless and detailed

There is no compunction, no suggestion even of doubt as the commandant works diligently to improve operations:

> I was the commander I made improvements and
> installed a guaranteed system taking account of hum-
> an weakness I purified and I remained decent
>
> How I commanded

The speaker is proud of what he has accomplished because he knows that he cannot be faulted as an officer — "All the while I had obeyed perfectly" — and his final justification is the unsettling accusation against those who witness his execution:

> You smile at my career but you would do as I did if
> you knew yourself and dared

The moral vacuity of the commandant is accompanied by an extraordinary rectitude of manner and conviction revealing the gaping insufficiency of an abstract morality. The Eichmann affair, Merton writes in his journal,

> shows the breakdown of forensic concepts of morality and
> demands an existential respect for the human reality of each
> situation. Without this respect, principles will never regain
> their meaning in concrete life.[37]

The affair also revealed the inhumanity of an individual who represents the ideal incarnation of rationality, unaffected by feeling and conscience: the perfect automaton for the new millennium. Eichmann is *the* technological person, sane, efficient, loyal, and for Merton a harbinger of death. In his bitterly ironic essay, "A Devout Meditation in Memory of

Adolf Eichmann," written in response to the Arendt *New Yorker* pieces of 1963, Merton addresses the issue of Eichmann's mad sanity.

> The sanity of Eichmann is disturbing. We equate sanity with a sense of justice, with humaneness, with prudence, with the capacity to love and understand other people. We rely on the sane people of the world to preserve it from barbarism, madness, destruction. And now it begins to dawn on us that it is precisely the *sane* ones who are the most dangerous. . . . The whole concept of sanity in a society where spiritual values have lost their meaning is itself meaningless.[38]

In the hands of Eichmann and those commandants who saw in his military code of honour the model for the Reich's servants, technology became death's most productive associate. Throughout "Chant to Be Used in Processions Around a Site with Furnaces" the speaker catalogues the number of refinements which he recommended to the manufacturers of the death instruments:

> Another improvement I made was I built the chambers for two thousand invitations at a time the naked votaries were disinfected with Zyklon B

and

> For putting them into a test fragrance I suggested an express elevator operated by the latest cylinder it was guaranteed

The operations were made palatable with the complicity of language, the correspondence between the military and industrial authorities denuding language of any moral significance:

"For transporting the customers we suggest using
light carts on wheels a drawing is submitted"

By debasing language the authorities veil the monstrous
truth of their transportation business; they contribute in this
way to the moral evacuation of humanity, clothing their sinister intentions in a language of lies. "Chant" is pure parody.
But is it? Merton wonders — for the

> double-talk of totalism and propaganda is probably not
> intentionally ironic. But it is so systematically dedicated to
> an ambiguous concept of reality that no parody could equal
> the macabre horror of its humor. There is nothing left but
> to quote the actual words of these men.[39]

Technology's link with sanity and death established, Merton's next emblem of political fury, war, is more menacing
than ever. As we have already seen with *My Argument with
the Gestapo*, Merton abominated war, and even though he
avoided the draft by entering the monastery, he was far from
successful in keeping the consequences of war outside the
Abbey's gate. His brother's death in 1943 pierced the monastic
sheath, reminding him that the conflicts of the world could
enter quite effortlessly the vulnerable enclosure in the knobs
and bottoms of Kentucky that had become his home. Since
Hiroshima we all live in the shadow of destruction.

As early as the 1940s Merton's anger at Catholic indifference
to the consequences of total war and to the ethical soft line
taken by the official moralists was in sharp evidence. Having received a letter from New Directions publisher James
Laughlin telling him that the U.S. had invented an "atomic
cloud" that could erase whole cities from the map, he noted in
his diary that Catholic silence if not passivity was "one of the
reasons why the wars are getting to be as bad as they are now."

Eventually, he would write about this atomic cloud with Swift-ian acidity in his 1962 prose poem *Original Child Bomb*, subtitled "points for meditation to be scratched on the walls of a cave." Comprising forty-one sections, it is a dispassionate narrative of the salient events that led up to President Truman's decision to use the atomic bomb on Hiroshima and Nagasaki, the military and political considerations that determined its use on Japan, and the battle plan that saw the implementation of the master strategy that would end the war in the Pacific. The language is succinct, taut, clinical, devoid of polemical fury or any moralistic sentiment. As there is no place for morality in the decisions of the state there need be none in the historical record of a momentous occasion. However, the voice of the moralist may be best discovered in the unpredictable cadences of irony and not in the orotund swells of exhortation:

> In the year 1945 an Original Child was born. The name Original Child was given to it by the Japanese people, who recognized that it was the first of its kind.

The horror is understated, and to the degree that it *is* understated the reader can gauge its full measure. The poem simulates the detachment and methodical accuracy of a military brief and avoids any direct reference to the philosophical questions that attach to each and every decision that affects the future of humanity. Only the concluding section raises any doubt about the effects of the atomic bomb in other than a military light:

> As to the Original Child that was now born, President Truman summed up the philosophy of the situation in a few words. "We found the bomb," he said, "and we used it."

Since that summer many other bombs have been "found." What is going to happen? At the time of writing, after a season of brisk speculation, men seem to be fatigued by the whole question.

The tone is disquieting, the discrepancy between the heinousness of the deed and the restrained recounting exacerbating the mood of dread and capturing in reasoned discourse the sheer lunacy of a world governed not by the wise but by the warrior. In a letter written to the Honourable Shinzo Hamai, mayor of Hiroshima, Merton makes explicit what is implied in *Original Child Bomb*:

We are all walking backwards towards a precipice. We know the precipice is there, but we assert that we are all the while going forward. This is because the world in its madness is guided by military men, who are the blindest of the blind.[40]

Surrounded by the spectre of mass death, of obliteration, humankind prefers not to see the precipice toward which it is headed. Merton was resolved to help it see, and to that end he found himself drawn more and more to the peace movement. Shortly after sending "Chant to Be Used . . ." to *The Catholic Worker* for publication in 1961 he had his first contact with the young peace activist who would later emerge as a trusted confidant, close friend, and sympathetic biographer: James Forest. Although Forest's high profile and radical pacifist tactics placed him somewhat outside the more detached mode of resistance found in the monastery, he saw in Merton from the beginning a soul brother.

To understand Merton's involvement in the peace issue you need to appreciate something of how Merton reacted to things in general. His usual way of responding to something or someone was first of all to fall in love. The latest book was always the best book. Two days later it was a book seriously flawed or even to be approached with great caution or the most threatening work that had wonderful strengths and weaknesses. This is how he responded initially to the peace movement. At the beginning he was aware that the movement and its concerns was something desperately needed not only in the Roman Catholic community specifically but in the Christian community generally. He could see that the work we were doing was both necessary and wonderful. And the closer he got to it, the more intimate his involvement became, the more aware he became of its flaws. When you examine his correspondence with peace activists, people like me, Dan Berrigan, Jim Douglass, etc., you see him becoming more and more critical and yet supportive, providing helpful insights, alerting us to the problems and dangers in the movement as well as advice or direction on matters concerning our individual spiritual needs. We needed to be conscious of the fact that the direction in which our society at large was heading was destructive and that our movement was firmly situated in this very same society — we weren't living on the moon — we were shaped by the same attitudes, the same contempt, one could find in society. Merton saw very clearly our capacity to become myopic, closed in, and self-isolating.

Merton's role in the peace movement was more than simply providing a social critique of searing honesty. He took on the public forces committed to the war industry, the supporters keen or tepid about nuclear arms, patriotic bishops and unthinking politicians, and Catholic moralists awash in a sea of deadly caution. His writings became increasingly suspect, powerful figures in the ecclesiastical world opposed his peace publications, no less powerful figures in the political world pressed for his silencing, and Merton found himself, like Dan Berrigan, facing church sanctions. Berrigan's superiors succumbed to pressure by the influential Cardinal Archbishop of New York, Francis Spellman, and he was sent into exile for his pains as a peace activist. For Merton, as Berrigan recalls,

> his fate was as swift as a guillotine. The knife came down on him very clean and very fast. The censors of the order were in no mood to tolerate his peace writings. There was a conventional and frozen idea at the top of the order that saw Merton engaged in activities that compromised the monastic vocation. It was as simple as that. Monks were supposed to be on their knees; they were supposed to be indifferent to the course of the world; all decisions were to be made for them and not by them. It was actually a kind of passivity that was blasphemous to a man of Merton's temperament. The suppression of his peace writings was a type of martyrdom for him. But as we know the suppression was by no means a complete silencing. There were the Cold War Letters.

Even with the publication in 1963 of Pope John XXIII's peace encyclical, *Pacem in Terris*, Merton was to be disappointed in his hope that the ban would be lifted. The authorities were unbending. He confides bitterly to his diary:

> Letter from the [Abbot] General came today categorically denying my request to publish *Peace in the Post-Christian Era* now that the Encyclical has said what I was saying myself! At the back of his mind obviously is an adamant connection that France should have the bomb and use it if

necessary. He says that the Encyclical has changed nothing
in the right of a nation to arm itself with nuclear weapons
for self-defense, and speaks only of "aggressive war." I
suppose the letter was composed by his secretary, Père
Clement: it reflects his obtuseness. . . . this is the Order in
which I am. But I do not have to be obsessed with its
unrealities.[41]

Merton persisted with his peace interests, but they created
difficulties for him both inside the monastery and outside its
walls. For instance, as Berrigan relates:

Roger Laporte of the Catholic Worker movement immo-
lated himself in November of 1965 on the steps of the
Pentagon. I was under the strictest orders to keep quiet
about the whole thing. However, it was bruited about in
Catholic circles that Laporte's death was a suicide and this
rankled me. When the stricken young folk at *The Catholic
Worker* asked me to preside at a memorial service for Roger
and speak about his death, I could not refuse. I said that talk
of his suicide was nonsense and that I refused to attach a
label to his death that would taint his memory. Meanwhile,
Merton sent a telegram to those of us in the Catholic Peace
Fellowship, which incidentally he helped to found, announcing his resignation in high, and not just ordinary,
dudgeon. It was a typical response from the woods. I mean,
he had no knowledge of the circumstances, was responding
to some sensational story without knowing all the particu-
lars. But, in fairness, once he was apprised of all the facts,
he withdrew his request to withdraw from the Fellowship.

In the Canadian Broadcasting Corporation's *Man Alive* television program on Merton ("Monk on the Run"), Roy Bonisteel

interviewed Gordon Zahn, a sociologist and pacifist, who argued that Merton's greatest contribution to the peace movement was to be found in his very credibility.

> Merton made the peace movement respectable. During the Second World War and after the war people like Dorothy Day and I, conscientious objectors, were written off for the most part as a lunatic fringe. And then suddenly in the early 1960s this great spiritual writer and contemplative comes out and denounces nuclear war, and this shocked many people. After all, here was someone *respectable* in the peace movement. He then drew more and more people into the movement, into the great Catholic peace conspiracy, a movement already peopled with the likes of the Berrigan brothers, Tom Cornell, Jim Forest, etc. In fact, the new, credible phase of Catholic peace activities may have begun with a retreat Merton gave at Gethsemani in 1964 on the spiritual roots of protest. Indeed, with the exception of just a few of the highly select group who attended, within a short time all served prison terms for various non-violent protest activities. Merton fomented, challenged, made respectable, but he also made clear his dissatisfaction with more aggressive tactics of resistance, like draft card burnings and some military plant raids, because they tended to make fearful people more fearful and because they suggested for many observers an escalation into violence. For the peace movement, that would be an escalation into self-contradiction.

For Zahn, Berrigan, and Forest, in addition to countless others, Merton's involvement in peace issues was welcome news. But for Merton, this involvement meant more than a bystander's conversion to action, it was a means, his means, of atonement. On September 8, 1963, he recorded a conversation he held on his peace writings with the pre-eminent Catholic moralist of his day, the German Redemptorist Bernard Häring, who had expressly come to see Merton at Gethsemani in order to talk about his peace writings:

> He thought it was important for this to continue and said that he would speak to the General about it. He said I should be writing about peace to make reparation for St. Bernard's preaching of crusades — and that if a monk could preach a crusade then a monk could certainly be allowed to write about peace. Needless to say I agree.[42]

There is a sweet irony in Häring's observation that Merton could not have missed: Bernard of Clairvaux (d. 1143), scholar, preacher, mystic, and saint, was perhaps the greatest Cistercian of all. Merton had written on him extensively, argued vigorously for the re-insertion of Bernard's insights into contemporary monasticism, and made the case again and again that his life and teachings, along with those of St. Benedict (d. 547), are fundamental in western monasticism. Now, heeding Häring's advice, he found himself, champion of St. Bernard, making amends for the Abbot of Clairvaux's dangerous zeal and crusading fever. Bernard's passionate exhortations to crush the Cathar heresy in the south of France resulted in a bloody crusade. Merton could only appreciate the delicious symmetry suggested by Häring's remarks.

The censors began to soften, and by 1967 the issue of censorship, certainly as it pertained to Merton, had in effect been "suspended, if not repealed." The peace monk could write with impunity.

But the third issue — race — would demand its own fight, on its own terms. Merton's interest in the difficulties of racial prejudice and disharmony actually predates his arrival at Gethsemani and his social awakening of the sixties. In his post-conversion phase in the late thirties Merton had been drawn to work at Friendship House in Harlem by the Baroness Catherine de Hueck Doherty. In this "huge, dark, steaming slum" he had found the dulling of all senses, the death of the spirit.

> What has not been devoured, in your dark furnace, Harlem, by marijuana, by gin, by insanity, hysteria, syphilis. . . . Harlem is, in a sense, what God thinks of Hollywood. And Hollywood is all Harlem has, in its despair, to grasp at, by way of a surrogate for heaven.
> The most terrible thing about it all is that there is not a Negro in the whole place who does not realize, somewhere in the depths of his nature, that the culture of the white men is not worth the dirt in Harlem's gutters.[43]

Although he would choose the monastic vocation over the apostolic labours of Friendship House as his life commitment, his experiences at Harlem never left him and he was haunted by the horrors there for years to come. His friendships with Dr. Martin Luther King, James Baldwin, the novelist and essayist, and with Eldridge Cleaver, the activist whose autobiographical *Soul on Ice* paid homage to Brother Merton, attest to the esteem and the confidence he enjoyed amongst the leaders of the racial struggle. It was King's doctrine of non-violence that most appealed to Merton, for in it he saw Mohandas Gandhi's struggle for a free India revisited. As the drama of civil rights resistance played itself out, the denouement could be safely predicted. But, as he reflected during a conference with his fellow monks following the assassination of King in Memphis in 1968, things might have been otherwise:

> The question of the death of Martin Luther King is closer to home than you realize. Some mutual friends of King's and mine in Atlanta discussed with him the possibility of his

coming to Gethsemani for a retreat by way of preparation for the March on Washington. My Quaker friend in Atlanta wrote me and said, and I quote: "If Martin had taken a period at Gethsemani he might have had the wisdom and repose to stay out of Memphis in the first place and it was a mistake to go there. He had done no preparation and came in cold to a hot situation where the young militants had him just where they wanted him." So, it was a kind of crucial and providential thing that he might have come here and if he had come here he wouldn't have gone to Memphis and if he hadn't gone to Memphis he wouldn't have got killed. One of the things that you have to understand is that this whole race situation right now is much more complicated than it looks because there is a big division between the Negro people themselves. Most of the Negro people do not want this violence but you have a lot of young kids who are very mad and very fanatical and some of them are members of certain movements and others are not, but they are pushing the violence. Actually, King was caught between these two groups in Memphis and this made it tough because he was really trying desperately to keep the whole thing non-violent.[44]

King never made it to Gethsemani. But John Howard Griffin, author of the groundbreaking *Black Like Me*, did. Merton came to rely on Griffin as a source of up-to-date information on the politics of racism, the anguish gripping black America, the tension and sacrifices to be found in black leadership, and the beacons of hope in a darkening landscape. In early 1963 Griffin visited Merton at Gethsemani and they spoke of many things — their shared friendship with Jacques Maritain, music, aboriginal peoples, etc. — and Griffin spoke of Clyde Kennard. Merton was transfixed.

John Howard Griffin was here at the end of last week. Spoke of Clyde Kennard, the Negro who suffered unbelievable cruelties and injustices for trying quietly to register at Mississippi State University. (Not the U. of Miss, where the case is very public.) Framed by the police, put in a forced labor gang, although he was supposed to be hospitalized with stomach cancer. Somehow they got him out of Miss. He is dying in a Chicago hospital. It is a dreadful story, and bodes evil.[45]

Griffin's telling of the Kennard tragedy — he personally promised the dying Kennard to "speak of it in every lecture" — attests to his belief that this black martyr's death was, as Maritain himself described it, "among the most significant events of our age." Merton agreed.

But he found the evil of racism elsewhere as well, particularly in the city of Birmingham, Alabama, where black children were set upon by police dogs, hosed, and mocked by a white mob. He responded to the incident by writing a suitably vicious parody of the "Little Red Riding Hood" fairy tale titled "And the Children of Birmingham," published in *Saturday Review* in August of 1963:

And the children of Birmingham
Walked into the story
Of Grandma's pointed teeth
("Better to love you with")

"Grandma" is the Law, "man's best friend." More important, she represents the intransigence of established prejudice, made secure by statute and convention. As the child protesters, the children of Birmingham, approach the police phalanx, "the singing wall,"

Fire and water
Poured over everyone:
"Hymns were extreme,
So there would be no pardon!"

Disguised as a benevolent grandmother, the Law is in fact a
wolf eager to devour those unsuspecting citizens who expect
too much of her impartiality. Protesting the injustice of a racist
legal system, the children discover for themselves the ferocity
of the law once it is threatened:

And the children of Birmingham
Walked into the fury
Of Grandma's hug:
Her friendly cells
("Better to love you with")
Her friendly officers
And "dooms of love."

The singular courage of these children impressed Merton not
only because politically

. . . what the children did that time
Gave their town
A name to be remembered

but because theologically they are the sign of the *kairos* or
"providential hour" and witness to truth:

The Negro children of Birmingham, who walked calmly
up to the police dogs that lunged at them with a fury capable of tearing their small bodies to pieces, were not only
confronting the truth in an exalted moment of faith, a

providential *kairos*. They were also, in their simplicity, bearing heroic Christian witness to the truth, for they were exposing their bodies to death in order to show God and man that they believed in the just rights of their people, knew that those rights had been unjustly, shamefully and systematically violated, and realized that the violation called for expiation and redemptive protest, because it was an offense against God and His truth.[46]

Outraged by the sad toll racism took on both blacks and whites, the consequent diminution of America's humanity, and the prospect of unending civil strife, Merton sought more and more ways by which to identify himself with the sufferings of the blacks. In a letter written to a young black opera singer barely five months before his own death Merton drew more than a few extravagant comparisons between his life and the plight of America's blacks:

> I happen to be able to understand something of the rejection and frustration of black people because I am first of all an orphan and second a Trappist. As an orphan, I went through the business of being passed around from family to family, and being a "ward," and an "object of charitable concern," etc. etc. I know how inhuman and frustrating that can be — being treated as a thing and not as a person. And reacting against it with dreams that were sometimes shattered in a most inhuman way, through nobody's fault, just because they were dreams. As a Trappist, I can say that I lived for twenty-five years in a situation in which I had NO human and civil rights whatever.[47]

Even allowing for Merton's penchant for hyperbole and righteous indignation, the comparison of the American black's plight with that of a Trappist is a bit much. Still, Merton at his best achieved a degree of empathy with the black community that very few white leaders could equal and this earned him an unmatched degree of trust amongst blacks.

The ravages of technologism, the menace of nuclear catastrophe, and the deep social scars of racism were Merton's three emblems of political fury, the signs of Urizen's lordship. In prose and in poetry he wrote against the cruel subjection of all the faculties and all the senses to the rule of Urizen; he wrote against the facile proliferation of lies; he wrote against the sundering of the commonweal. The sixties unleashed Merton. He found himself engaged in an all-out assault on the social and political systems that bear the mark of the Beast — Urizen. He knew that the route to human authenticity was lonely, full of risk, a pilgrim's terror. But he also knew that the meaningful rebirth of society could only be achieved when the dominance of Single Vision was ended, the common origin and essential dignity of all humanity fully respected, and Spiritual Imagination restored to its rightful place. It was time now to write his own epics showing the pilgrim's way forward out of, as another bold Christian artist, John Bunyan, would have it, the Slough of Despond. It was time for *Cables to the Ace*.

In 1967 New Directions published *Cables to the Ace or Familiar Liturgies of Misunderstanding*, a work many years in the making. At the same time one poem and many poems, it is divided into eighty-eight sections, or "cables," with both a prologue and an epilogue. Parts of it had been published in various journals before being woven together in the larger structure of this epic work.

Cables carries Merton's Blakean imperative — the reconstitution by vision of humankind's wholeness or spiritual unity — to its final stages. In Blake's poetry the vision is worked out in his prophetic books, with the Apocalypse, Jerusalem, and the final reintegration through Jesus or the Spiritual Imagination. In *Cables* Merton resolved to "assist once again at the marriage of heaven and hell" (Cable 1); he continues the Blakean dream: "These words were once heard, uttered by a lonely, disembodied voice, seemingly in a cloud" (9).

Just before the book's publication Merton spoke of it in less than flattering terms in a letter to a fellow poet:

> Maybe you will feel it does not communicate: it is imprecise, noisy, crude, full of vulgarity, making faces, criticizing and so on . . .[48]

He feared that it would be misunderstood, that he was less than capable of realizing the next step in the unfolding of his myth-dream: the reparation of the Fall. There is no doubt that *Cables* is a daring undertaking. It is a kaleidoscope of sixty pages of poetic experimentation and raises the "problem of word" to a new level of intensity.

> Since language has become a medium in which we are totally immersed, there is no longer any need to say anything. The saying says itself all around us. No one need attend. Listening is obsolete. So is silence. Each one travels alone in a small blue capsule of indignation. (Some of the better informed have declared war on language.) (3)

There is an air of desperation about this poem precisely because it is written with a sense of urgency. It is electric in form and imagery: "electric jungle," "their imitable wire," "expert lights," all contributing to the mad congestion of "the blue electric palaces of polar night." (34) The poem's irony is oppressive, communication and mobility are everywhere but no one hears and language has become static in the world of "the monogag" and "the telefake." The world of immediate intimacy is a world of "dull energies in the dust of collapsing walls" (44). It is not the garden of paradise but the wasteland of apocalypse. We have been deceived by language and the "Great Meaning," loving the inevitable, each having "his appointed vector / In the mathematical takeoff" (52).

In *Cables* form *is* content; it does not contain or transmit a message, it simply *is* a message. The title of the poem itself suggests the identification of the means of transmission with the content transmitted, for a cable is both the electrical apparatus by which the message is channelled and the message or cablegram itself. The medium is the message. For neither Marshall McLuhan nor Merton, however, are electric communication and its creation, the "global village," any panacea:

> Some may say that the electric world
> Is a suspicious village
> Or better a jungle where all the howls
> Are banal
> NO! The electric jungle is a village,
> Where howling is not suspicious
> Without it we would be afraid
> That fear was usual (14)

The unity that is created by electronic immediacy is not a communion of vital entities, a participation in the Mystical Body of Christ, or the "marriage of heaven and hell." It is a false unity, force-fed and not spontaneous, reductionist and not expansive. It is a homogenizing unity that ultimately seeks the elimination of opposites, a project equally anathema to Blake, Merton, and the Taoist sage Chuang Tzu, a favourite of Merton's.

Of Chuang, a thinker whom he found "profoundly original and sane," Merton wrote that the

> key to Chuang Tzu's thought is the complementarity of opposites and this can be seen only when one grasps the central "pivot" of Tao which passes squarely through both "Yes" and "No," "I" and "Not-I." Life is a continual development. All beings are in a state of flux. Chuang Tzu would have agreed with Herakleitos.[49]

The "complementarity of opposites," the "Yin-yang palace of opposites," and the "marriage of heaven and hell" represent for Merton a metaphysical and psychological unity that is humane and holistic, a unity which he referred to as "final integration," a state of

> transcultural maturity far beyond mere social adjustment, which always implies partiality and compromise. The man who is "fully born" has an entirely "inner experience of life." He apprehends his life fully and wholly from an inner ground that is at once more universal than the empirical ego and yet entirely his own. He is in a certain sense "cosmic" and "universal man". . . . He accepts not only his own community, his own society, his own friends, his own culture, but all mankind. . . . He is fully "Catholic" in the best sense of the word. He has a unified vision and experience of the one truth shining out in all its various manifestations, some clearer than others, some more definite and more certain than others. He does not set these partial views up in opposition to each other, but unifies them in a dialectic or an insight of complementarity. With this view of life he is able to bring perspective, liberty and spontaneity into the lives of others.[50]

The unity known as "final integration" stands in judgement on that mass conformism that masquerades as unity but is no more than an "electric jungle." It is, by another name, Four-Fold Vision.

Cables underscores humankind's desperate need for redemptive unity precisely because it highlights the dissensions that pervade human society, dissensions that are often the result of an egocentrism nourished by the media and the technocratic overlords. The medium is indeed the message; the form of the poem is the statement.

Cables is a mosaic of messages of reassurance, of good fortune, which, once decoded, reveals the compelling credibility of skilful dissembling. In the Prologue Merton makes explicit his implicit contempt of the advertiser, the master scribbler of our consumerist society:

> My attitudes are common and my ironies are no less
> usual than the bright pages of your favorite magazine.
> The soaps, the smells, the liquors, the insurance, the
> third, dull, gin-soaked cheer: what more do you want,
> Rabble?

By detailing the lies that have been our common diet, the poem obliges the reader to accept the implications of this ironic feedback. The cables are "familiar liturgies of misunderstanding" and it is the reader's moral and intellectual duty to reject the tyranny of lies, by ceasing to misunderstand. This is best done by appreciating the intention of antipoetry, a genre that Merton defines as "a deliberate ironic feedback of cliché":

> Marcuse has shown how mass culture tends to be an anti-
> culture — to stifle creative work by the sheer volume of
> what is "produced," or reproduced. In which case, poetry,

for example, must start with an awareness of this contradiction and *use* it — as antipoetry — which freely draws on
the material of superabundant nonsense at its disposal. One
no longer has to parody, it is enough to quote — and feed back
quotations into the mass consumption of pseudoculture.[51]

Failure to accept the implications of this ironic feedback
could result in a sentence of mass death, a possibility Merton
considers in the Epilogue, where the uncommon juxtaposition of apocalyptic sentiment with an outrageously parodied
advertising jargon shows not only an adept handling of "superabundant nonsense" but an intensity of purpose by no means
subdued in the poet's mature years:

> The name of the day is Doom. But first a word from our
> sponsor and his lasting gorgeous lovelorn satisfactions.
> Never mind the bugle Miss Daisy. For a dollar ninety-nine
> you will have immortal longings here on the front porch.
> You will become as slim and lovely as our own hypnotic
> phlogiston toothpaste enriched with armpit deodorant. All
> you have to do is dance a little and you will attract the
> infinite toy attentions of the élite.

The "élite" are the architects of our universal ruin, the
technocrats and engineers who design the instruments of
our doom. But their most effective weapon is language, for
language is power and the advertisers/politicians/engineers
combine their respective energies to ensure that language does
their bidding:

> Let choirs of educated men compose
> Their shaken elements and present academies
>   of electronic renown
> With better languages. Knowing health

And marital status first of all they must
  provide
Automatic spelling devices or moneymaking
Conundrums to program
The next ice-age from end-to-end
In mournful proverbs

Let such choirs intone
More deep insulted shades
That mime the arts of diction
Four-footed metaphors must then parade
Firm resolution or superb command
Of the wrong innuendo (16)

In an earlier work, the viciously sarcastic "A Letter to Pablo
Antonio Cuadra Concerning Giants" that appeared first in
Spanish in the spring of 1962 in *Sur* and then in English a year
later in *Emblems of a Season of Fury*, Merton distinguished
between two modern adversaries in biblical dress: Gog, the lover
of power, and Magog, the servant of money. Read the U.S.S.R.
and the U.S.A. respectively. Merton asks:

Are they not perhaps spectres without essence, emanations
from the terrified and puny hearts of politicians, policemen
and millionaires?

In the figure of Caliban in *Cables* we have just such an
emanation from the "puny hearts" of technocrats and adver-
tisers, a savage spectre prepared to wreak havoc on his masters:

"You taught me language and my profit on't
Is, I know how to curse. The red plague rid you
For learning me your language!" (Caliban) (6)

In Shakespeare's *The Tempest* Caliban is so eager for vengeance on his master Prospero that he is easily made use of by Stephano the butler and Trinculo the jester in their plot to dispose of Prospero. Caliban cautions the co-conspirators to

Remember
First to possess his books; for without them
He's but a sot, as I am, nor hath not
One spirit to command.

To use the terms of Blake and Merton: Caliban, having learned Prospero's language, seeks the power it bestows at the same time as he repudiates its source, the Logos/Word/Jesus and his emanation Wisdom/Spirit/Urthona. Humanity, more especially in the guise of technocrat and engineer, seeks the power of Prospero but brings only confusion and division, the bequest of Caliban and the curse of Babel:

Twelve smoky gates flame with mass demonstrations.
Power of Caliban. Mitres of blood and salt. Buildings
  as well-run machines with eyes and teeth (Bosch).
Love the inevitable! Hate alone is perfectly secure in its
  reasons.
Over the door of Hell is written: *"Therefore!"* (22)

The consequence of Caliban's treason is apocalypse, the avenging arm of truth laying waste the legions of deception, among whose ranks can be found as the host Urizen/Descartes, whose formidable *"Therefore"* is the greeting of Hell. The supreme inadequacy of Reason to guarantee our survival points only too clearly at humankind's misplaced faith, ready acceptance of material reality, and outright denial of spiritual reality. For Merton, the true heir to the legacy of Bacon, Locke, and

Newton is contemporary humanity, which has created in full biblical splendour the concluding drama of salvation history, a "waste heaven of deadly rays," and a "cataclysm of designs." The apocalypse is the consummate "brilliant intuition of an engineer." Abstraction/Urizen has firmly ensnared humankind, and the Cartesian *cogito* secures our continued isolation. We stand entranced while Urizen works our enslavement:

> Look! The Engineer! He thinks he has caught something! He wrestles with it in mid-air! (51)

The false and deadly wisdom of the engineer is the wisdom of Eichmann. It is a scientific knowledge that is efficient, mathematical, objective, and quantitative. It is the wisdom of Abstraction, with its generalizing principles, its hospitality to technological conceptions, its denial of inspiration, and its anti-spiritual "Philosophy of the Five Senses." It is the wisdom known as *scientia* — speculative, systematic, cognitive. It is the French philosopher Gabriel Marcel's "philosophy which . . . is a hatred of wisdom." It is Urizen!

There is another wisdom, however, known as *sapientia*, which goes beyond cognition and intuition to become a mystical connaturality without ceasing at the same time to be a practical *via sapientia*. This sapiential mode of life provides Merton with the only reasonable corrective, the only workable inoculation against what Albert Camus calls our "plague of cerebration," that scourge of Urizen, which haunts our culture and our time. In a penetratingly insightful article on William Faulkner, Merton observes that the "wisdom" approach to humanity

> seeks to apprehend man's value and destiny in their global and even ultimate significance. Since fragmentation and objectivity do not suffice for this and since quantitative

analysis will not serve, either, sapiential thought resorts to poetic myth and to religious and archetypal symbol. . . . Sapiential awareness deepens our communion with the concrete: It is not an initiation into a world of abstractions and ideals. . . . Sapiential thinking has, as another of its characteristics, the capacity to bridge the cognitive gap between our minds and the realm of the transcendent and the unknown, so that without "understanding" what lies beyond the limit of human vision, we nevertheless enter into an intuitive affinity with it.[52]

Sapience/Divine Wisdom/Four-Fold Vision is the dream of life; Abstraction/Scientific Wisdom/Urizen is the dream of death. I do not wish to suggest that Merton saw *only* the handiwork of the Antichrist in the technological accomplishments of our time. He saw, rather, the danger of scientific wisdom in the creation of Eichmann, in the tyranny of a rationalism that gauges human worth by measure and number, and in the undisputed hegemony of mathematical reasoning at the expense of the imagination.

The emanation of the scientist and the engineer hovers over a cowering humanity as a perpetual sign of the power of apparently value-free rationalizations. Against the power and presumed superiority of our Urizenic masters, Merton claims for the spirit, for *sapientia*, the simplicity of the "children of Birmingham." But the Blakean innocence of the "children of Birmingham" is insufficient to combat the legacy of Bacon, Locke, and Newton; it is essential that the Blakean Four-Fold Vision inform the contemporary spiritual witness:

Now I a fourfold vision see,
And a fourfold vision is given to me;
'Tis fourfold in my supreme delight

And threefold in soft Beulah's night
And twofold Always. May God us keep
From Single Vision & Newton's sleep.
                    ("Letter to Thomas Butts," 22 November 1802)

Merton found his modern Blakean witness and ideal contemplative artist in the Russian writer Boris Pasternak. They corresponded in French during the time following the Soviet government's refusal to grant permission for Pasternak to re-enter Russia, were he to leave in order to receive the Nobel Prize for Literature. The author of *Doctor Zhivago* stands, Merton argues,

> first of all for the great spiritual values that are under attack in our materialistic world. He stands for the freedom and nobility of the individual person, for man the image of God, for man in whom God dwells. For Pasternak, the person is and must always remain prior to the collectivity. He stands for courageous, independent loyalty to his own conscience, and for the refusal to compromise with slogans and rationalizations imposed by compulsion. Pasternak is fighting for man's true freedom, his true creativity, against the false and empty humanism of the Marxists — for whom man does not yet truly exist. Over against the technological jargon and the empty scientism of modern man, Pasternak sets creative symbolism, the power of imagination and of intuition, the glory of liturgy and the fire of contemplation. But he does so in new words, in a new way. He speaks for all that is sanest and most permanently vital in religious and cultural tradition, but with the voice of a man of our own time.[53]

Resolved to escape the tyranny of "Single Vision & Newton's sleep" and to speak, like Pasternak, for that which is "most permanently vital" in our common heritage, Merton turned inward to replenish his parched soul.

But first of all, he needed to heal his heart.

4

LUVAH:
The Lover

MERTON DEPLORED the public perception that the monk was a special kind of human being, somehow gratefully free of those ordinary and meddlesome features of life like sexual temptation, pettiness, ambition, acquisitiveness, etc. Nothing could be further from the truth, but he knew that he had himself contributed to that very perception in some of his earlier writings with their ethereal tone and pious certainties. The notion that the monk was in some way a rarefied creature, sanctified and other-worldly, distressed him acutely once he discovered or, better, rediscovered his body. In a letter written two years before his death to Clayton Eshelman, an American poet, Merton reacted vigorously to the idea that the monk can be found "living detached on a special lane":

This business of chastity is much more complex than that. First of all, it is not a question of negatively scouring out all sexual desire, though many do this or try to. Properly it should be a long hard job of sublimation: and doubtless few of us completely succeed. In any case I have never led or advocated a totally disincarnate life. I was in love before entering the monastery and I have also been in love since (though pretty hampered by the restrictions!) and in the end I have come to a position where I refuse to generalize, and above all I know that I don't have the "Big Answers" (who has?).[1]

The year he wrote this letter to Eshelman — 1966 — was a watershed year for Merton; it was the year in which he fell wildly in love with a young nurse. It was to be "a time of gruesome yet beautiful alienation," a time when the two lovers were to "spin in space like empty capsules." It would prove the single greatest challenge to his continuing identity as a monk.

In one sense, of course, Merton was never out of love. As he observed autobiographically in *Cables to the Ace*:

> I am sustained
> By ravens only and by the fancies
> Of female benefactors. (74)

This rather coy reference to his hybrid status as part romantic solitary and part hermit-scholar belies the deeper truth that Merton was "sustained" in more ways than one by "female benefactors." But the largesse, intellectual sympathy, and spiritual solidarity that he received from his women friends were not enough. As Jim Forest rightly observes,

> I think that Merton's attitude toward women changed near the end of his life in a most surprising way. Mind you, he was living in an all male environment and the only contact

he had with women since he entered the monastery in 1941 was the occasional, the very occasional, visits that were allowed. At least this was so up to the mid-sixties. In fact, the major part of the monastery, the cloistered area, was literally off limits to women and you could face automatic excommunication if you violated the laws of enclosure. This severe restriction to the access of women has created a problem for many clerics and monks — and Merton was both — although this exclusively male and isolated "state" could be a reason for drawing some men to the monastic life. But not Merton. Integrating women into his life was a long and difficult process that took some startling turns. There was, for instance, his intense correspondence with Rosemary Radford Ruether, his "dream women" Proverb and the Chinese Princess, the women writers and editors who were an essential part of his life, and then, of course, the domestic and familial role played by the Hammers and the O'Callaghans. He simply could not exclude women from his life.

But the question of how to include them is soon supplanted by the more delicate question: how could a contemplative, a world-famous monk-writer, become a self-designated "priest who has a woman"? Befuddled, dispirited, and yet strangely defiant, Merton poignantly notes in a diary entry made on the Feast of the Body of Christ (Corpus Christi), June 9, 1966:

> Concelebration early. I stood there among all the others, soberly aware of myself as a priest who has a woman. True, we have done nothing drastically wrong — though in the eyes of many our lovemaking is still wrong even though it stops short of complete sex. Before God I think we have been conscientious and have kept our love good. Yet is it

reasonable for me to be writing her love poems — even a song?[2]

Merton's quandary is monasticism's dilemma. The solution lies in Four-Fold Vision. Enter Blake's Luvah. Variously described as the principle of sexual energy, the senses, the heart, the emotions, Luvah represents the antithesis of Urizenic mastery. The heart must be heard, and for too long Merton's emotions, his sexual yearnings, his need for affectivity, had been sublimated, shelved, and denied. As a consequence, he was far from the complete monk. His need for integration — the healthy conjoining of instinct, heart, reason and spirit — was defined in the most dramatic terms at the beginning. John Howard Griffin recalls:

At the end of the first year of his life, Merton was baptized even though this was probably the father's doing only because his mother didn't want any spurious religious influences brought to bear until he was of an age to decide for himself. Ruth has been considered rather coldly by those people who only know her through her son's writings. However, her diaries show a profound love and a profound concern for Thomas, and a certain discomfort because he was not doing, say, what an eighteen-month or two-year old child should be doing. Merton was a remarkably rapid learner but he didn't care anything about toys. He cared about images, about the music his father played, for Owen was an accomplished pianist, and he very quickly learned words.

Tom received the first big shattering shock of his life when his mother disappeared and no one really let him know anything about it. His father handed him a letter which his mother had written from Bellevue Hospital. Ruth had terminal cancer of the stomach and had kept this information from Tom because she believed that nothing unpleasant or morbid should be known by children. His reaction to the letter, he later said, was not of childish grief but of profound adult sorrow and misery, in the sense that "my mother was informing me by mail that she was about to die and would never see me again."[3]

The early and devastating loss of his mother crippled Merton emotionally in ways he could only fully appreciate in his mature years. His mother was too untimely ripped from him and he spent years searching for the warmth he had only partially glimpsed in her stoic and undemonstrative persona. The death of Owen ten years later orphaned him; he now had only his brother, John Paul, and his maternal grandparents as his immediate family. In time they would be plucked from him, but none with such enervating effect as John Paul. Although they had been reared largely apart, in the years since Tom's entry at Gethsemani they had become closer. In fact, they had begun to enjoy a hitherto nonexistent fraternal intimacy. But it would not last long. It was late in coming; and Tom was haunted by the casual cruelty he had often displayed toward his brother in the early years.

John Paul had joined the Royal Canadian Air Force prior to the U.S. declaration of war in 1941. On a bombing raid to Mannheim in April of 1943 his plane was shot down in the North Sea and the pilot and John Paul were killed. But his brother first lingered in anguish for hours. Merton wrote:

He was very badly hurt; maybe his neck was broken. He lay in the bottom of the dinghy in delirium.

He was terribly thirsty. He kept asking for water. But they didn't have any. The water tank had broken in the crash, and the water was all gone.

It did not last too long. He had three hours of it, and then he died. Something of the three hours of the thirst of Christ Who loved him, and died for him many centuries ago, and had been offered again that very day, too, on many altars.[4]

He was buried at sea. It was Friday, April 16, the Feast of Our Lady of Sorrows. The depth of Merton's loss is captured in his exquisite elegy, "For My Brother: Reported Missing in Action, 1943":

Sweet brother, if I do not sleep
My eyes are flowers for your tomb;
And if I cannot eat my bread,
My fasts shall live like willows where you died.
If in the heat I find no water for my thirst,
My thirst shall turn to springs for you, poor traveller.

Where, in what desolate and smokey country,
Lies your poor body, lost and dead?
And in what landscape of disaster
Has your unhappy spirit lost its road?

Come, in my labor find a resting place
And in my sorrows lay your head,
Or rather take my life and blood
And buy yourself a better bed —
Or take my breath and take my death
And buy yourself a better rest.

When all the men of war are shot
And flags have fallen into dust,
Your cross and mine shall tell men still
Christ died on each, for both of us.

For in the wreckage of your April Christ lies slain,
And Christ weeps in the ruins of my spring:
The money of Whose tears shall fall
Into your weak and friendless hand,
And buy you back to your own land:

The silence of Whose tears shall fall
Like bells upon your alien tomb.
Hear them and come: they call you home.

This elegy has a maturity of feeling and style shaped as much
by the discipline of mourning as by Merton's deep feeling for
the eloquence of music. Mark Van Doren identified this poem
for special comment in his introduction to a collection of
Merton's poetry:

There must be a music that absorbs them [the figures of the
poem] and relates them, and gives them in the end a power
for which we cannot assign a cause. We can say that the very
intensity of the poet's fear that he will fail is somehow the
reason for his success; we can guess that inarticulate grief
manages here, simply because it must, to become articulate
after all; but it is truer to say that in such a poem sadness sings
— a low note, in perfect pitch, that carries around the world.[5]

This moving lament for his brother is sustained by a violence
of paradox that speaks with the purity of deep grief:

If in the heat I find no water for my thirst,
My thirst shall turn to springs for you, poor traveller.

For Merton, as long as his brother is missing, does not sleep
and his "eyes are flowers for your tomb," and his fasts are

"willows where you died." The elegy reads like a summons, a
call to return: a merciful Yahweh speaking through the psalm-
ist to a lost tribe, a loving shepherd to a lost sheep, a man to
his younger brother:

> Come, in my labor find a resting place
> And in my sorrows lay your head.

In a stanza that echoes the rich parallelism of the psalms the
poet offers his life for the "unhappy spirit" that has "lost its
road":

> Or rather take my life and blood
> And buy yourself a better bed —
> Or take my breath and take my death
> And buy yourself a better rest.

This is the language of *kenosis*, of unconditional and self-
emptying love, of total generosity. Forsaken "in what landscape
of disaster," abandoned "in what desolate smokey country"
lies the soul-less body of the brother? In a passage of considerable force Merton juxtaposes T.S. Eliot's "cruellest month"
with the resurrection, desolation with revivified hope:

> For in the wreckage of your April Christ lies slain,
> And Christ weeps in the ruins of my spring.

Once bought and paid for, the brother will be redeemed by
Christ with his tears turned currency so that he may buy him
back to his own land. These tears "shall fall like bells" in
silence, calling home the weary traveller. In the silence of his
cell, his "alien tomb," he may know the love that speaks with
his brother's tears, and the price paid by his brother's offering.

The elegy moves from a note of disconsolate sorrow, through one of anguished questioning, followed by one of gentle imploring, to one of quiet hope and prayerful resolve. It is a gradual but assured ascent from the pain of loss to the joy of hope; an ascent which Merton described in an early poem, "The City's Spring," where "Though jealous March, in marble skies / Prisoned our April Saturdays," the Easter rain will "bring sweet songs and strawberries."

John Paul's death left Tom numb. He could only speak through his poetry. Something of the affection he felt for the brother he too little knew has been recounted by his former abbot, James Fox, who remembers his own introduction to his famous charge while in conference with his brother. Merton, the novice, bounced into the room and had to be asked to wait outside:

> The novice did this most graciously. However, his most expressive eyes pleaded with me, saying, "Please don't be too long. He's my brother — he's leaving soon for the War — I may never see him again." And so it was.[6]

John Paul died in a distant place, sealed off, inaccessible — as Ruth, their mother, had done many years before. The terrible repetition of Merton's first loss was only partially ameliorated by the support and prayers of his Gethsemani home. The emotional emptiness around him had widened.

Merton needed to find emotional surrogates in a contemplative setting and it is not surprising that he would find some form of affective, if still largely spiritualized, bond in his invocation of that most pedestrian and yet sublime of mystics, Thérèse Martin, St. Thérèse de Lisieux. A French Carmelite who died at the age of twenty-four of tuberculosis in 1897, Thérèse was the youngest of five sisters, all of whom became nuns. She entered the Carmelite monastery in Lisieux at the age of fifteen and took the name Thérèse of the Child Jesus and the Holy Face. Her autobiography underscored her conviction that extraordinary spiritual heroism or sanctity is available to all in the ordinary matter of our lives. Her profound simplicity, her utter trust in the limitless generosity of grace, and her uncompromising joy in the face of relentless physical suffering combined to make her the most popular saint since Francis of Assisi. Although Merton found aspects of her cult scandalous, the "molasses-art and gorgonzola angels" in particular, he was attracted by her unsentimental and heroic spirituality, in which he found a quality of innocence like that in Blake's images of childhood. Upon receiving a first-class relic of St. Thérèse from a nun friend at Marquette University, he wrote in his journals that

> I have it over my heart and it gives me great comfort. I have no doubt that now my whole life is going to be completely transformed and that at last I shall do something to please our dearest Lord. Here I have this seed of miracles resting at the center of my physical life. It fills me with deep recollection. Here what was once part of her now is, her soul's gaze will still be fixed, and she will be offering me all day to God. She will sing with me and penetrate my prayer and lead me along in contemplation and protect me. I think she has been sent to me, not because I am worthy or have done anything good that might seem to deserve it, but because I have perhaps been going backwards, or am in danger of doing so fast, and she has been sent to keep pushing me forward as well as to remind me of the pact that I once made with her and to remind me to stop all this monkey business and begin to behave.[7]

He repeatedly invoked her help in making him a Trappist. She understood something of the difficulties involved in seeking admission to an order, especially a cloistered order. She would appreciate his dilemma. He implored her to help him overcome the obstacles that stood in the way — his lecherous past, which had kept him from becoming a Franciscan friar, his pending draft, his crushing feelings of inferiority — and he, in turn, would aspire to be as heroic a Trappist as she was a Carmelite. He would, in fact, become *her* Trappist. There is a mushy and even mawkish quality to some of Merton's devotion to the cult of St. Thérèse, but he also saw, beyond the dreadful piety that encased her and the saccharin veneration that turned her into the most popular saint in Catholicism, something of the diaphanous, the luminous in her holy submissiveness; he saw something of the divine rebel in the obedient nun.

The appeal of the cult of the Little Flower, as St. Thérèse was often called, was universal. It is not surprising that Merton succumbed to her saintly charms. Although he decried the abuses of her cult, the cheap romanticizing of her sufferings, and the proliferation of appalling religious art under her patronage, he nonetheless saw in her stubborn persistence and holy resolve a depth of character he sought to emulate in his own vocation struggle.

The other figure who came to represent for him the supreme model of Trappist holiness was the Blessed Virgin Mary. Merton's devotion to Mary makes institutional sense in that she was the patron of all Cistercians. Indeed, each Cistercian used the initial M in his monastic name — for instance, Merton's name in religion was M. Louis, M for Mary and Louis for St. Louis of France. But she also represented for him the feminine face of God and served as the model of all monks and poets in her grateful *fiat*, allowing the Word into history, idea into form.

In a poem written in the 1940s, "Aubade — The Annunciation," the Virgin waits in the dead of March when "on the brown, bare furrows / The winter wind still croons as dumb as pain." She is like the earth at dawn and nature on the threshold of spring, for the fullness of light. The monk and the poet, like the Virgin, are in a state of perpetual readiness. In them the soul and the imagination are the womb in which they will recreate the moment of Incarnation. They will assist in the enfleshment of word, making incarnate idea and vision. When inspiration comes in the early morning, barely seen, "when the dim light, at Lauds, comes strike her window," then it is that "thoughts hide in the height like hawks" and all stand motionless until the name is spoken "like a meteor falling."

The window of imagination, the window of the soul, in the quiet of perfected discipline, waits to receive the light of creation. As the Virgin waits for the "speech of an angel" and the poet for the voice of inspiration, the monk, the silent sentinel, witnesses the ongoing reality of the Incarnation. The monk continues the work of the Virgin and renders complete the work of the poet.

The terrifying splendour and transforming refulgence of the Incarnation is best depicted in another poem of the 1940s, "The Blessed Virgin Mary Compared to a Window." The Virgin, like a window, is "slain in the strong rays of the bridegroom sun." Mary's will is as "simple as a window," and she longs for dawn so that she may "die by transubstantiation into light." Transformed by the Beloved, the light, "my lover, steals my life in secret" and only the frame of the window is visible as "the geometry of my cross." Once the Virgin has "become the substance of my lover," once she has become impregnated by the Holy Spirit, she reflects the light of her "newborn Morning" so that the monks in their rooms and humankind in their "tombs, / Or vaults of night" will be filled "with the clarity of living Heaven."

The window both receives and transmits the light, and Mary dying "by brightness and the Holy Spirit" becomes the image

of deliverance and intercession. It is through her that the "sun
rejoices in your jail, my kneeling Christian," and it is because
of her and her unique destiny that

> you shall see the sun, my Son, my Substance,
> Come to convince the world of the day's end, and
>   of the night

The window's light is humankind's light filtered through
Mary, the approachable intermediary, who "knows no shame
of original dust" and whose love is as "simple as a window."
The transparency of the Virgin's love for "my other son," and
the translucence of the Son's love which shines "with the rays
of God's Jerusalem" are visible in the enclosed frame, the small
receptacle of unutterable brilliance. Through the window one
can behold the redemptive act and by the window die in the
love "of the bridegroom sun." The Virgin is a window whereby
"it is my life to die, like glass, by light." As a windowpane
Mary "longed all night (when I was visible) for dawn my
death," knowing that with the daylight, with the sun/Christ
the windowpane disappears, dies "by transubstantiation into
light." Mary is an image of the God-bearing person/pane becoming neither a barrier nor a prism but a totally transparent,
invisible/humble channel of the light.

Mary is also a stained-glass window on which is pictured a
life of total surrender to the Other's will. The image of the
Virgin as a window paints a portrait of perfection, for by being
"obedient, sinless glass" and by loving "all things that need
my lover's life," Mary has become a mirror of perfection, a
window overlooking eternity.

Merton is not unique in using the image of the windowpane
when speaking of the soul illumined by God's grace. St. John
of the Cross had done so in his *The Ascent of Mount Carmel*

and the seventeenth-century Metaphysical poets — Donne, Herbert, Crashaw, etc. — with their taste for unconventional imagery and elaborate conceits did likewise. But for Merton, tropes and symbols aside, the Blessed Virgin Mary performed the additional function of grounding his spirituality in the affective order. The early loss of his mother, in particular, made him vulnerable to bouts of unsatisfied emotional craving, of a deeper emptiness, of feeling unloved and alone. The Blessed Virgin Mary secured him, if only temporarily.

It wasn't an easy fight, sublimating his sexual needs, integrating his "free" past into his "disciplined" present. In his private journal entry of August 14, 1948, while on a visit to Louisville, he noted that although he felt quite alienated from the world and its activities, he "did not necessarily feel out of sympathy with the people who were walking around." He then observed that "without any conscious effort being necessary" he avoided commenting on anyone, "including women, except two." Ingenuously, he notes that one of them was a

> wild-looking jane in a black dress with much lipstick — I thought of her all of a sudden when I was taking the discipline yesterday morning and hoped she didn't happen to be in the way of needing some vicarious penance.[8]

Clearly Merton had not mastered full "custody of the eyes"; and not insignificantly, the "wild-looking jane" resurfaced when he was taking the "discipline" (an instrument of penance like a manual scourge to be applied with moderation to tame the flesh). The custom of the discipline has fallen out of use and the later Merton would very likely have spoken of the incident with his tongue in his cheek, but the Merton of the 1940s was intensely earnest in his desire to eradicate any and all entrapments of an amorous or libidinous nature. The censors thought likewise. When the public version of this journal appeared to critical and popular acclaim in 1953 as *The Sign of Jonas*, the above passage with its reminder of monkish weakness was excised. Either that, or Merton himself edited it out in the first draft. Such themes harked back to the old Adam, when all that mattered now was the new Adam, safe, redeemed and whole. Or so he and his superiors thought.

The 1950s were years of mounting inner turbulence for Merton. Increasingly restive, in search of a hermit regime, unhappy with his public persona and its straitjacketing of his thoughts, in flight from his emotions, and plagued with poor health, Merton was ripe for a breakdown of serious dimensions. Invited to attend a course in psychiatry for religious at the Benedictine Abbey of St. John's in Collegeville, Minnesota, to be conducted by the eminent convert-psychiatrist Gregory Zilboorg, Merton was given permission by James Fox to go. It was 1956, and as Monica Furlong notes in *Merton: A Biography*, the icon of Gethsemani "teetered on the edge of breakdown."

Zilboorg was fascinated by Merton long before he met him. In fact, Merton was persuaded that Zilboorg connived to get him to Collegeville. He pulled no punches when "diagnosing" Merton, labelled him a Wall Street promoter, a gadfly to his superiors, a potential "semi-psychotic" quack, megalomaniacal and narcissistic, and consumed with self-aggrandizement. While enduring this steady barrage of searing analysis, Merton wryly comments on "how much he looks like Stalin." Still, he listened and was grateful. Zilboorg may have lacked tact and nuance but he did provide Merton with some acute insights into his behaviour. He allowed him to see what happens when the self is dangerously divided:

Another thing he said — "It is not intelligence you lack, but affectivity" — meaning it is there but I never let it get out

— so that when the situation calls for it I either intellectual-ize — verbalize — or else go into a depression.[9]

Merton needed to listen to the affective side. Time was running out. The unconscious was repairing the imbalance, if only he would attend. His dreams disclosed the cry of his heart. In late February of 1958 he had a dream in which he, standing on the porch of his grandparents' house in Douglaston, is "embraced with determined and virginal passion by a young Jewish girl." She clings to him and he likes it. She tells him that she is called Proverb and he speaks of the name's signifi-cance and beauty, but she appears unimpressed. When he awakes, he begins to intellectualize the experience and then, possibly remembering Zilboorg's admonishment, he simply accepts it without explanation. "It was a charming dream."

But it was more than charming. It haunted him. In a letter to Boris Pasternak, he spoke of the dream and went on to identify Proverb with all the people he had recently seen on a Louisville street, "her extraordinary beauty and purity and shyness" shining through them all. To Pasternak he confessed that now

> you are initiated into the scandalous secret of a monk who is in love with a girl, and a Jew at that! One cannot expect much from monks these days. The heroic asceticism of the past is no more.[10]

But the decade-long crisis, with its aridity of soul and emo-tional dislocation, was not over. On the Feast of St. John, December 27, 1958, Merton remarked with dark foreboding:

> The end of a year — and the beginning of a very grave year of struggle, Christ, may I not go under!
>
> I understand now Hopkins' last sonnets. Does religious life do this to everyone sensitive?[11]

Comparing his misery to the black desolation conveyed in Hopkins' sonnets of terror betrays Merton's love of self-dramatization, admittedly, but it also tells us that as year folds into year escape into the light seems less and less likely. But Merton is nothing if not resilient and his scorching chats with Zilboorg seem to have had some therapeutic effect. The affective side, particularly when it involved women, got increasing attention in his diaries and letters, as early even as 1959. He was thrilled, for instance, when poet Stephen Spender's wife, Natasha, "blew in with a girl from the Coast, Margot Dennis." Their day together does not follow the monastic horarium or schedule. At first they are "very decorous and intelligent," talking about music, Freud, Zen, Carmelite mystics, etc., and then they go "down a notch," walk to St. Bernard's Lake, eat sandwiches and fruitcake and talk about monasteries, bishops, Mexico and other things. And then they go to Dom Frederic's Lake and Merton forgets what they talked about. It is easy to see why:

> Margot, once dipped into the water, became completely transformed into a Naiad-like creature, smiling a primitive smile through hanging wet hair.[12]

Merton chose to neutralize the experience. He recalled the events of the day in such a way as to place emphasis on what it revealed of his needs — for conversation, for female company, for fun. "Utterly starved" for the kind of intelligent banter he had with Natasha and Margot, he noted ruefully that "no woman can resist that hunger I am sure." They might be able to, but the celebrity of Gethsemani was discovering, however gradually, that *he* could not.

Later in 1959 he identified Emily Dickinson as his "own flesh and blood," a kind of "quiet rebel" who was a fierce defender of the integrity and independence of the spirit and who had little time for "catchwords and formalities." The Desert Fathers must now make room for a fighting nineteenth-century American rebel poet, whose appeal for Merton resided in part in her extraterritoriality, her capacity to resist being owned and named by her contemporaries. To know Emily Dickinson was "like hugging an angel." Merton fell in love with her blessed elusiveness, her inexhaustible mystery.

By 1961 Merton was beginning to confide more and more frankly his misgivings over the constricting monastic view of virginity and chastity, which he felt emptied them of real meaning. On the surface, he had been reading Erich Fromm, but he had also been looking inward.

> It is certainly true that man is most human, and proves his humanity, by the quality of his relationship with woman. . . . Here in the monastery with our chastity, we are ideally supposed to go further, in this dimension of humanism and love. This is one of the keys to our problems: how can one go further than that to which one has not yet attained?
>
> Not that virginity cannot be deeply and purely human. But it has to be spiritual and positive. And this spiritual character of chastity and virginity is *not* found in alienation. It is *not* found in sentimentality, in a "thought" of pure love for Jesus.[13]

And then in 1964, "Proverb" returned, this time in the guise of a Chinese princess. Merton marvelled and puzzled over this "lovely and familiar archetypal person," who haunted him in and out of his dreams. Proverb/Princess was fresh, unattainable, youthful, on the horizon but tantalizingly beyond grasp. She loved him and he felt great consolation in the knowledge.

The language he had used to describe Mary, the Virgin Mother of God, and Thérèse, the mystic Carmelite of Lisieux, was now superseded by a language with a markedly more Jungian timbre. The Catholic devotional discourse of the pre–Second Vatican Council was replaced by a psychoanalytical jargon typical of the mid-sixties. The Blessed Virgin Mary was out and the Chinese Princess was in.

By 1965 Merton was more candid still. Gone were the Jungian archetypes; instead he spoke of his selfishness, his inability to love, his poor self-esteem, his failure to realize that the girls he flirted and cavorted with had loved him, at least for a time. It is a cold night on January 30th, the vigil of his fiftieth birthday, and he mentally reviews his past. He notices one unsuppressible constant:

> So one thing on my mind is sex, as something I did not use maturely and well, something I gave up without having come to terms with it. That is hardly worth thinking about now — twenty-five years nearly since my last adultery, in the blinding, demoralizing summer heat of Virginia.[14]

By now Merton had become increasingly occupied with thinking and writing about his sexuality. His diary entries on the subject are neither coy nor elliptical, but direct and unnervingly honest in their expressions of regret, shame, and longing. He revisits his past and scours the amorous landscape for opportunities missed or abused. He tries to makes sense of the sexual quagmire of his past and juxtaposes the sordid with the pure in a romantic's desperate effort to recover something of innocent love. In a diary entry redolent of nostalgia, Merton remembered and reconfigured impressions from the past, returning to the England of his youth and a time when he met the sister of his old school chum, Andrew Winser, and to the New York of his Columbia days, when he dated Virginia Burton.

> The other day (St. John Baptist perhaps) after my Mass I suddenly thought of Ann Winser, Andrew's little sister. She was about twelve or thirteen when I used to visit him on the Isle of Wight, in that quiet rectory at Brooke. She was the quietest thing on it, dark and secret child. One does not fall in love with a child of thirteen, and I hardly remember even thinking about her. Yet the other day I realized that I had never forgotten her and with a sort of Burnt Norton feeling about the part of the garden I never went to, and that if I had taken another turn in the road I might have ended up married to Ann. Actually, I think she is a symbol of the true (quiet) woman I never really came to terms [with] in the world, and because of this there remains an incompleteness that cannot be remedied. The years in which I chased whores or made whores out of my girlfriends (no, that is too strong and also silly, besides there were plenty that I was too shy to sleep with) did nothing to make sense of my life — on the contrary. When I came to the monastery, Ginny Burton was the symbol of the girl I ought to have fallen in love with but didn't (and she remains the image of one I really did love with a love of companionship not of passion).[15]

Not insignificantly Merton penned these musings at the same time as he was reading psychiatrist Karl Stern's seminal study, *Flight from Woman*. The Montreal-based convert had as important an influence in Catholic circles in the sixties as Gregory Zilboorg had had in the fifties. Merton read Stern with rapt attention and recommended him to several of his regular correspondents. He struck a chord.

But there is a rationalizing tone, an etherealization of the subject matter, in Merton's diary entry on Winser and Burton. He could deal with them as *types*, as distant and safe memories: romanticizing the past is one thing, and not particularly threatening at that, but facing the unarticulated sexual emptiness of the present is a different matter entirely. Within barely two months of writing the Winser/Burton piece, he came back to the underlying meaning of it all in a blunt entry of August 17, 1965, stripping away the nostalgia and Jungian games and dealing forthrightly with the implications of love and "tragic chastity." He spoke about his love for his old friend, editor and agent Naomi Burton Stone, and tried to understand the implications, for a monk, of this love. What Stone provided was

> . . . the warmth that cannot come from a man, and that is so essential. Psychologically, my doubt is based in this giant, stupid rift in my life, the *refusal* of woman which is a fault in my chastity. . . . But I am learning to accept this love (of Naomi, for instance) even if it means admitting a certain loss. (Chastity is in fact my most radical poverty, and my un-poverty in accumulating things is a desperate and useless expedient to cover this irreparable loss which I have not fully accepted. . . .) The tragic chastity which suddenly realizes itself to be mere loss and fears that death has won — that one is sterile, useless, hateful.[16]

If he was somewhat diffident in admitting his affection for Naomi, or at least the depth and implications of that affection, he was downright bold in confessing his poorly sublimated feelings towards her in his Christmas diary entry of the same year:

> I had a curious, somewhat sexual dream about Naomi, which says something of my ambivalence toward her perhaps

and my sense of her ambivalence toward me. In a way I guess we love each other, and we are both so complicated — and so devout, maybe (or she is anyway) that it gets funny, and is very inhibited, or rather not. I feel it and bear it as another bloody nuisance, like my psychosomatic sickness.[17]

Although peppered with qualifiers — "perhaps," "I guess" — the passage demonstrates Merton's increasing difficulty in camouflaging his sexual urges, as he realized that his dreams were becoming less and less archetypal and ethereal and more and more graphic and visceral. Less Jung and more Freud.

Throughout his life Merton needed women. Earlier, his pattern had been to behave like a roué, and later, of course, like an ascetic. Either way, it was a "flight," and it was time for him to face the consequences. Luvah, the heart, must have her way. The psychosomatic illnesses that plagued him throughout most of his monastic life were the clearest bodily sign of his inner division. It was time for radical healing.

It was not that Merton avoided women. Quite the contrary. He cultivated and valued long and stimulating relationships with women wherein they exercised variously the roles of confidante, sister, adviser, and soulmate, but not lover. Appropriate, considering his vocational vows. But incomplete.

The list of Merton's women friends — friendships nurtured by meticulous and honest correspondence — is illustrative of his wide range of interests; the friends were Roman Catholic as well as drawn from other faiths and traditions; consecrated religious, and lay women; professional scholars and writers both established and unknown. The list is stunning in its length and variety, but it is possible to identify several women to whom he had a special attachment and who played, singly and collectively, a critical role in the shaping and maturing of the often female-shy monk of Gethsemani. The list includes Raissa Maritain, poet and mystic; Angela Collins, Carmelite prioress; Mary Luke Tobin, former Superior-General of the Sisters of Loretto; Hildegard Goss-Mayr, peace activist; June Yungblut, civil rights activist; Etta Gullick, spiritual writer; Thérèse Lentfoehr, poet and professor; Nora Chadwick, scholar and expert on monasticism; Rosemary Radford Ruether, theologian and writer; Joan Baez, composer and folk singer; and many others. He had friends galore, but something was missing. Something had to give.

And then, in March of 1966 (a year that was to prove for him both an *annus horribilis* and an *annus mirabilis*), he encountered the young nurse in a Louisville hospital who would be known simply as "M." in Christine Bochen's edited volume of Merton's restricted journals covering January 1966–October 1967. She would change his life utterly. He would become, in his own words, "a priest who has a woman." But the phrase, even applied by Merton to his own situation, seriously misrepresents the beauty and destructive potential of a relationship that became the passion of his life. Daniel Berrigan places the affair in context while avoiding the self-dramatization Merton was prone to:

When I learned about this woman in his life, I was surprised and I blinked a few times, and all that, and I think it took me maybe a few days after my visit with him to realize that this was the next phase, the next chapter in this very public life. But I knew that he was not going to lead a double life, that he was not going to be surreptitious or tawdry. In fact, he was open with his confessor, his abbot, and eventually the whole community. He worked with his confessor in an honest effort to see it through to the right end.

I felt personally a great deal for M., even though I never

met her. I knew that she must be a woman of great quality because they were obviously and deeply in love and I knew Merton to be a man of great quality. But I also knew in my bones that once the episode was over she would go on to marriage and that, thank God, in the grand scheme of things no harm would be done to her or to him.

Berrigan's sanguine view was not shared by everyone, but there is no doubt that the "nurse thing" was a watershed experience for both of the principals.

It began innocuously enough in March of 1966 when Merton was admitted once again to hospital, this time for back surgery at St. Joseph's in Louisville. The neurosurgeon, Thomas M. Marshall, performed an anterior cervical fusion in order to correct Merton's cervical spondylosis. Merton was astonished to discover that he could now lie on his back without pain. As Mott points out, though, Merton's delight in his improved condition was offset by his impatience and edginess when confined to a bed and subjected to hospital routine. That changed, however, on March 31, six days after the operation, when a young student nurse appeared in his room and announced that she was his nurse and it was time for a sponge bath. She had the advantage of knowing who her famous patient was and had been instructed by her supervisor to respect Merton's solitude. Still, she was vivacious and talkative and after some initial wariness on Merton's part he found himself drawn to her. She was Proverb, the Chinese Princess, Virginia Burton — she was flesh, blood, presence, and charm. He was smitten.

When he returned to Gethsemani during Holy Week in April he found it more difficult than he had anticipated to acclimate himself to his familiar monastic regimen. She didn't leave his thoughts. What might have been a simple and safe sentimental attachment was obviously more. He hungered to hear from her; she was never far from his thoughts. He had, in fact, encouraged the continuing contact when he wrote her a letter while still in hospital telling her that he needed friendship and that she could write to him at the monastery and that she could ensure that it was for his eyes only by identifying the correspondence as "Conscience Matter." Merton had no intention of depriving their relationship of the oxygen it needed. He phoned the hospital before his post-surgical checkup scheduled for April 26, had her paged, and asked her to meet him.

This was more than an infatuation. On April 25 he writes:

> The basic fact is that she does love me — she does need from me a certain kind of love that will support her and help her believe in herself and get free from some destructive patterns and attachments that are likely to wreck her. Her love arouses in me at once an overwhelming gratitude and the impulse to fling my whole self into her arms, and also panic, doubt, fear of being deceived and hurt (as I lay awake half the night tormented by the thought of the guy she is probably sleeping with!).[18]

Following his meeting with the orthopedics specialist, William C. Mitchell, Merton had a rendezvous with M. They were both scared. They had little time together — they were "chaperoned" by Merton's psychologist friend, Jim Wygal, but the monastic authorities were not informed and they were both nervous about what it all meant. But clearly, it wasn't over; it had barely begun.

There was a cataract of telephone calls, a deluge of letters, the carefully arranged and innocent-looking meetings, friends intriguing, and the mounting unease felt by the principals and co-conspirators. The frisson of budding and illicit love brought a goodly measure of Catholic guilt with it, and Merton knew that there would be a toll to pay. But no guilt or unease could diminish the intense pleasure of the fifth and seventh of May, which he would name the "Paradise Feasts."

On May 5, Merton and M. dined with his friends James Laughlin and Nicanor Parra at the Louisville Airport, and then

> M. and I had a little while alone and went off by ourselves and found a quiet corner, sat on the grass out of sight and loved each other to ecstasy. It was beautiful, awesomely so, to love so much and to be loved, and to be able to say it all completely without fear and without observation (not that we sexually consummated it).[19]

This was followed with a picnic of May 7, Derby Day, at Dom Frederic's Lake with Jack Ford (a professor of philosophy and an old friend), his wife Gladys, and Merton's diocesan priest friend, John Loftus. They all ate and drank convivially but there was a dimension of discomfort felt by all save the lovers. M. and Merton went off for a couple of hours to some moss by a little creek Merton was fond of, "talked and loved and opened our hearts to each other." Although "not as ecstatic as the evening at the airport," there was a sweetness and depth about their time together that touched Merton to the core.

The "Paradise Feasts" revealed to Merton the unsettling fact that in both of them there were

> deep capacities for love, especially in her. I have never seen so much simple, spontaneous, total love. And I realize that the deepest capacities for human love in me have never been tapped, that I too can love with an awful completeness. Responding to her has opened up the depths of my life in ways I can't begin to understand or analyze now.[20]

But the time "to understand or analyze" could not be put off forever. Decisions had to be made; lives could not be put on hold for much longer. But that time was not May.

In many ways Merton spoke most eloquently and honestly about his love for M. in poetry rather than in prose, although, as was his custom, he chronicled the "affair" in his journal. But he was always the poet, and out of his love for M. would come eighteen love poems which he sent to his publisher for safekeeping using the code name "Menendez File." Menendez, Laughlin explained in a letter to the Abbot of Gethsemani, was the chef of the Alta Lodge where he (Laughlin) had been staying during a skiing holiday, and he and Merton had playfully borrowed his name, indulging the poet-monk's taste for tricks and ploys. Merton insisted that the poems not be published until after his death, as they were, in a limited edition of a few hundred, by New Directions in 1985.

In prose it was a "gorgeous game," a "beautiful thing," but in poetry Merton let love and speech soar:

No one sees your eyes first open
Only the dim light
which is now perhaps at this moment changed
Into the light you look at
And the day that is known to you
Knows the moment of your return
From the rivers of night
From that nowhere
That ocean of sightless quiet
Inviolate unknowing where your heart
Slept for me
For me restored itself to life and to the love
By which alone I stay alive
For whose essential and direct messages
I am waiting now pacing up and down

In this messy, lonely place
Waiting once again to live
And at war with my own heart
Because I cannot be there
To see your eyes reveal you
Opening not only to the light of my day
But to my own eyes and waiting heart.

("Aubade on a Cloudy Morning")

Tortured by the knowledge that he could not be there when the sun first wakened her, Merton also lived in fear that his monastic superiors would discover their love. He wasn't yet ready to speak to the community of his feelings and their implications. The clandestine phone calls made in the cellarer's office to M. could not remain forever undetected. The longing so movingly evoked in the poem was exacerbated not only by the difference in age — approximately thirty years divided them — but also, and far more, by the conditions attached to their respective vocations. Merton the monk and M. the student nurse both led regulated lives; their activities were monitored to ensure that they conformed to the accepted "rules" of their respective institutions. Clear restrictions were attached to their contact with the external world; there was a curfew. But for M. these would pass once her nursing training was completed. For Merton, it was a life commitment.

Even as he wrote his love poems to M. he knew that this situation could not last, that he was fooling himself if he thought no life-changing decision was on the horizon. Marriage seemed unthinkable; he knew that he faced excommunication for his *fuga cum muliere* (flight with a woman), allegations of apostasy, the dread prospect of being hounded by monastic and curial officials. And yet he persisted in his love for M., pushing as far as he could, always the frontier person — venturesome, radical, and reckless. And on Ascension Day, May 19, the adventure peaked.

M. was driven to Gethsemani by another nurse, who dropped her off and promised to come back in the late afternoon to pick her up for the return trip to Louisville. Merton and M. went off into the woods at the foot of Vineyard Knobs, found a secluded place, picnicked on herring, ham and sauterne, read poems, talked of themselves, and "mostly made love and love and love for five hours." Not your regular monastic outing. In the full flush of passion, Merton's description of the day is as explicit as he ever gets:

> [T]he grave thing is — this solemn and beautiful thing — that we are doing what lovers perhaps rarely do today — we are moving slowly toward a complete physical ripening of love, a leisurely preparation of our whole being, like the maturing of apples in the sun — and I suddenly realized I had never permitted this before — had always in my youth been in a hurry, and thought about it too much and tried to precipitate everything before its time. No wonder I was unhappy. . . . I feel that somehow my sexuality has been made real and decent again after years of rather frantic suppression (for though I thought I had it all truly controlled, this was an illusion). I feel less sick, I feel human, I am grateful for her love which is so totally mine. All the beauty of it comes from this that we are *not* just playing, we belong totally to each other's love (except for the vow that prevents the last complete surrender).[21]

This is passion writ large, a young lovers' feast, careless, intense, complete (or almost so). Merton's diary reads like a highly charged youth's rapturous record of erotic bliss, precociously eloquent but unreflective. Merton's "ripening" left him spinning in an emotional whirlwind, indifferent to the "adult" world outside his feelings. It was as if he had returned to his adolescence with a vengeance, to do right this time what went awry the first time. But such a reading ultimately diminishes the genuine love that clearly existed between Merton and M. and reduces his passion to suppressed libido, which is too convenient, and too Freudian. Merton's capacity to love was not reducible to reawakened genital excitation. And he knew it.

A week after the Ascension Day revel, on the Vigil of Pentecost, Merton mused guiltily:

> Too much stirring up of sex. What strikes me most of all is the wastefulness of spiritual energy that all this gets me into. I believe deeply in our love and I know that the spiritual upheaval is basically good and healthy, but I get all kinds of warning signals. I know not only full sexual consummation would be wrong and harmful, but also the more or less "licit" lovemaking we have indulged in.[22]

Merton's Pentecost hesitation evaporated, however, as soon as he spoke to her again by phone. He found himself once again sucked into the vortex of their love, and all else was relegated to the periphery. For an internationally famous monk and socially sought-after hermit, this was problematic. He had numerous writing obligations — publishing deadlines to meet and a large correspondence to be maintained — and there was of course his spiritual life. The strains generated by the contradictions tearing at both his self-image and his public persona were increasing. It was more and more difficult to keep them at bay. The chalice he now drank from brought him love and pain in equal measure:

> This love of ours — very joyous today, very sure of itself, triumphantly articulate — is still an immense reservoir of

anguish, especially for me. But I don't care. Now I can accept the anguish, the risk, the awful insecurity, even the guilt (though we are doing nothing radically wrong, i.e., not sinning). . . . We are far beyond the point where I used to get off the bus in all my old love affairs. I am in much deeper than ever I was before. (In the light of M.'s love I realize for the first time how deeply I was loved back in those days by girls whose names I have even forgotten.)[23]

What Merton discovered in his love for M. was a way to bring closure to the inadequacies of the past; his love was curative and humanizing; their affair healed the wounds of his early life. His love for M., he wrote, helped him see the limitations of theology and the law as well as the dangers inherent in pontificating on the existential questions of life, those questions that are concrete rather than abstract, visceral rather than academic. He came to understand, in a way that he had not appreciated before, that

Theology is sometimes sickness
A broken neck of questions
A helpless doubt
In an electric bed ("Untitled Poem")

A theology that has a platonic thrust to it, that prefers abstraction to incarnated reality, that harbours a deep, if covert, loathing of the body, is a theology, a spirituality, stamped with the mark of Urizen. A disembodied love is a partial love, etherealized, safe, but without that plenitude that distinguishes true, generous, and full love from its pale approximation. Merton's love for the Blessed Virgin Mary and for Thérèse of Lisieux and for his many female friends and correspondents remained genuine, uncompromised by his love for M. But what his love for M. succeeded in doing was both liberating and threatening. His capacity for love, limited as it was to the platonic and other-worldly, had prevented him from achieving that level of psychosexual maturation essential for a fully integrated spirituality. Luvah, the Heart, has its reasons that Urizen, the Intellect, does not and cannot know.

> Danger of "platonic love" — concentration on the "essence of love" or on the "essence of woman" — whereas what love demands is to find *the actuality of love and of woman* in this concrete, existing woman who gives herself to me as she is; to love *her* womanliness and be conquered by it in order to give her what she asks out of her deepest heart. But M. does not ask sex: she asks a love that fully respects her in her wholeness as person (this does *not* exclude sex by any means, but in our case circumstances do — what is important is the union of which sex is only a sign). I have to stop making sex a problem in this (torment, wanting it so badly and knowing it has to remain impossible, fear of going into it in some messy dishonest way!).[24]

Merton's struggle to make sense of his feelings for M. often reads like a classic case of Freudian rationalization. His erotic stirrings troubled him at the same time as they added a rich dimension to his dormant affectivity. Perhaps Zilboorg was right after all, although he would have been disappointed at the "object" of Merton's resurrected affections. Still, in spite of the rationalizing, Merton understood that his love for M., for all its imperfections, its interrupted passion, its adolescent giddiness, its cavalier disregard for the demands of the "real" and the "proper," had irreversibly changed him, and for the better.

It was June that brought everything to a head. One of the monks had listened in on one of his calls to M., and had reported the matter to Dom James. Merton realized that choosing the right time was not an option. It had been decided for him. Rather than wait nervously for the inevitable abbatial summons, Merton chose to act quickly, and on his own initiative told Dom James about the phone calls. Fox was both "kind and understanding" but insisted on a "complete break." He wanted to write to M. and hinted that Merton was perhaps *too* lonely in the hermitage, and should return to the abbey and sleep in the infirmary. Merton said a firm no to both requests. Some concessions were made, however, and Merton was allowed to meet with various ecumenical and interfaith groups. Undoubtedly Fox thought that with some continuing human company, Merton might be less vulnerable to emotional and amorous crises in his hermitage. The old distrust ran deep.

Three days after his confrontation with the abbot, Merton began a record of his love entitled "A Midsummer Diary for M." He wrote this 23,000-word diary in a week. It is a hybrid work and reflects the many pressures — interior and exterior — that Merton felt at work on his life. Part journal, part confession, part apologia, and part love letter, it is paradoxically both luminous and opaque, direct and convoluted, self-referential and other-oriented. There is a great deal of discussion about Camus, the absurd, false solitude, "the tyranny of diagnosis," the fine distinction between *realizing* and *knowing*, and the role of lucidity and compassion in human affairs.

But it is really about his troubled soul, the Gordian knot that is his relationship with M., the need to bring irresolution to an end, to decide on a course of action that involves not only his "salvation" but that of M. as well. As Merton knows: after the "great wave" of love subsides, there is the "stark expanse of mud-flats." The beginning of love, the time when no decisions are necessary, was over, and it was not enough to say, "If God has brought her into my life and if God has willed our love, then it is more His affair than ours."[25]

That wouldn't do, and Merton knew it. In an entry of June 21, he unambiguously affirmed the priority of his monastic commitment, but still puzzled over the relation that existed between his love for M. and his solitude. The very next day he wrote of this love as something much larger than "just an episode," as something that is a "profound event,"

> which will have entered deeply into my heart to alter and transform my whole climate of thought and experience: for in her I now realize I had found something, someone, that I had been looking for all my life. . . . What we have found in each other will not be lost: yet it will not be truly possessed either. . . . I know that someday she must love another, because it would be inhuman to expect such a deprivation in anyone's life. As for me, I am supposed to be lonely and live alone and sleep alone, so I have no problem and no complaint. It is merely what I have chosen and the choice is ratified over and over each day. Even though I so vividly remember her body and long for her love.[26]

Merton knew that their separation would be exquisitely painful:

> How desolate love seems
> Now that even our sobs
> Are silent. ("Evening: Long Distance Call")

And he knew that their star-crossed love could never admit of any kind of satisfactory temporal resolution. He candidly declared to his diary that their love could not alter the simple fact that he was no longer an "unknown kid," who could do what he liked with impunity. Countless numbers of people wanted him, needed him, to be the monk and solitary his books professed him to be; he knew that there were many who lived the contemplative life vicariously through him. His vocation was not a matter only of wearing a religious habit and living in a monastery. He was a public person; he had made himself a public person. His life as a monk was

> a gift that has been given to me not for myself but for everyone, even including M. I cannot let it be squandered and dissipated foolishly. It would be criminal to do so. In the end I would ruin her along with myself.[27]

By late June he felt that he fully understood what the consequences of his abandoning his vocation as a monk-writer would be, for himself and for M. It was out of the question. He shared with M. not only the "Midsummer Diary" but a later record of their love, "Retrospect," which was written in July and subsequently placed into the hands of J. Laughlin. M. was in no doubt about Merton's personal view of their love and its implications. She knew his intimate thoughts. Neither of them prevaricated or indulged in fantasy about the future — which both ensured their connectedness with the real world and compounded their pain.

In his private journal, with lacerating honesty, Merton wrote of his fear that he could be "enslaved to the need for her body." He submitted his motives to the most exacting scrutiny:

> I suppose really what my nature, in its hunger, really secretly planned was to have her as a kind of mistress while I continued to live as a hermit. Could anything be more dishonest?[28]

Presumably he did *not* share this entry with M., but he most likely shared his distrust of his motives with her at some point, in spite of the fact that he never doubted the authenticity of their love. If he was, at the theoretical level at least, persuaded that the relationship, though not the love, must come to an end, he was still unprepared to act. By August, Merton's discomfiture was exacerbated by his serio-comic encounter with Abbot Fox. The abbot lectured him, "not unkindly, but with the great moral superiority he now enjoys," and there was a fair bit of sharpness in their seemingly playful banter. The abbot joked that he might write a book himself about how to get hermits into heaven; Merton seethed; the abbot gloated; it was Fox's turn to chalk one up. But then, as Merton was leaving the office, he could not resist a final thrust:

> "When the baby is born you can be its godfather!" A slight shadow crossed his face and he laughed with less enthusiasm. Was I really kidding? We are a pair of damned cats.[29]

Abbot Fox was not really amused and Father Merton far less glib than his remarks might suggest. They were studying each other cautiously and both were conscious of the large stakes involved should there be a serious miscalculation. Merton procrastinated, wavered, ruminated with Camusian intensity, and trembled. The Fox waited.

And then on September 8th, Merton made a decision: ". . . to live in solitude for the rest of my life." He made this commitment on paper and it was witnessed by his abbot. But the end wasn't yet in sight. M. and Merton continued to have contact, although on a less frequent basis. Gradually the intensity ebbed, and when he found himself in St. Anthony's Hospital in the fall, with the opportunity of occasional visits with her, he knew that for the first time since April the affair had become less passionate and he could breathe easier. But in spite of his decision to remain firm in his vows, Merton's love for M. continued to prey on him and he explored various options, if only to reject them immediately. He tortured himself with his obsessive need to revisit the love that could only too clearly speak its name.

By mid-November, irrespective of his fleeting vacillations, Merton decided that the

> objective fact of my vows, [is] more than a juridical obligation. It has deep personal and spiritual roots. I cannot be true to myself if I am not true to so deep a commitment.[30]

The commitment to his vows took precedence over his love for M. The love story was not over, but it would now unfold on a different plane. By May 11, 1967, slightly over a year after the affair began, Merton would write that he had no intention of preventing the eventual publication of his record of their love, at least in so far as this pertained to the Restricted Journals. But he stated his wish that it not be published until twenty-five years after his death. He could not have anticipated how close he was to his death, nor that many of the players would still be alive when the journal was published in its complete form in 1997, and earlier in paraphrased and fragmentary form in 1983 with *Follow the Ecstasy*. He was determined, with his customary candour,

> to be completely open, both about my mistakes and about my effort to make sense out of my life. The affair with M. is an important part of it — and shows my limitations as well as a side of me that is — well, it needs to be known too, for it is part of me. My need for love, my loneliness, my inner division, the struggle in which solitude is at once a problem and a "solution." And perhaps not a perfect solution either.

However, I think a lot of merely foolish stuff can be destroyed: most of the love letters are in this category. They were merely garrulous outpourings of feeling, and this is usually not magnificent, only routine sentiment. The true feeling is no doubt in some of the poems.[31]

There is no doubt that the prose entries and letters written during the course of the affair, expressing and exploring his love for M., were often marred by an inadequacy of language that is unexpected in a poet and wordsmith of Merton's accomplishment. His prose suffered from strained sentimentalization, an easy reliance on clichéd phrasing, bathos and self-evident rationalization. Merton's feelings for M. were genuine and his agonizing efforts to make sense of his riven life were honest if confused, but the real depth of feeling is only truly conveyed in the eighteen poems born of his love and desperation:

How can I sleep exhausted
Torn out my dear school
To lie alone thinking of one day's lesson
Love's new geography and form
Love's new map and clear highway
Where there is no other traffic
Where we both now know
We ride without a block
And without any rival. ("Six Night Letters—IV")

Through his affair with M., Merton came to understand "Love's new geography and form" and he came to realize that Luvah/Heart/Emotion has its critical place in the monastic scheme of things. To be a fully integrated monk he had to be a fully integrated human being, to accept his emotional emptiness and his yearning for reciprocated love; he had to move beyond sublimation, abstraction, and platonic love to a concrete, particular, and incarnate love.

Merton's chronicle of his love for M. reveals him at his most vulnerable. It is not surprising that at one point in the heat of the affair he had a dream about another girl, not M., as well as another student nurse who had come to see him briefly in hospital. In the midst of all this, he writes, he saw a

> tangle of dark briars and light roses. My attention singles out one beautiful pink rose, which becomes luminous, and I am much aware of the silky texture of the petals. My Mother's face appears behind the roses, which vanish.[32]

An orthodox Freudian analyst would make much of this, as indeed would a Jungian, but suffice it to say that Merton's quest for the feminine, his recovery of the affective side of his personality, his resuscitation of that buried and hurt love entombed with his mother, and his resolve to face the sexual waywardness of the past through an honest erotic encounter in the present attest to his progress toward "Four-Fold Vision."

The last of the Four Zoas is Urthona — Wisdom. For Merton, it was time for the final integration.

URTHONA:
The Wise One

IN HIS 1995 MEMOIR, *A Blue Boy in a Black Dress*, the Canadian fiction writer and critic T.F. Rigelhof publicly acknowledged the sanity-saving role Merton played in his turbulent struggle for religious meaning. Disappointed with institutional religion, and with the spiritual emptiness proffered by the priestly ministry he was studying to enter, Rigelhof looked to Merton for guidance. He wanted

> most of all to learn from Tom Merton how to see the difference between things that concentrated me on a search for my true self and things that distorted and destroyed my authentic sense of my self, to know which rules to follow and which to break in living a non-materialistic life.[1]

Rigelhof, like many of his contemporaries, turned to Merton precisely because he offers something of that wholeness that cannot be circumscribed by any one tradition or culture; Merton conveys, in his writings and through his personal journey to integration, an authentically searching spirituality that will not be compromised by fidelity to structures. As Rigelhof notes:

> Merton somehow achieved a wonderful sense of the plenitude of creation and of the spirit. He understood the richness involved in being human and he knew that no one person or culture could represent humanity in its fullness. I suppose this truly catholic sensibility is the secret to his great friendships with so many diverse people. To my mind this is the side of Merton that remains alive to me even now so many years after his death, this extraordinary capacity to connect with other human lives.

Merton's pilgrimage became public property during his own lifetime; he wanted it so.

In the late 1960s, the stage was set for the final instalment, the final quadrant, the fourth Zoa: Urthona, or Wisdom. The meaning of wisdom for Merton was fluid, evolving over time, a mature and ripe dimension of life that cannot be hurried, scheduled or programmed. He thought about wisdom a great deal in its many configurations and if finally he was to embody wisdom, become Urthona, it was a natural progression of many years' seasoning.

The first extended and major treatment of the theme of wisdom can be found in his lengthy prose-poem "Hagia Sophia" (Holy Wisdom) published in 1962, the product of a correspondence he had with his close friend Victor Hammer. A typographer, bookbinder, and calligrapher, in addition to his teaching duties in lettering, drawing, and painting, Hammer was the consummate artist and craftsman. On one occasion when Merton was visiting Victor and his wife, Carolyn, Hammer showed his guest a triptych he had been working on.

The central panel showed a woman crowning a young boy and Merton asked aloud who the woman was. Hammer had initially conceived of the woman and the young boy as a Madonna and Child, but no longer knew who she was. Merton then responded, "I know who she is. I have always known her. She is Hagia Sophia."

In a letter dated May 2, 1959, Hammer invited Merton to come and bless the triptych and explain in greater detail what he meant by Hagia Sophia. This latter request Merton met in a twofold manner: in a letter dated May 14th, and in the prose poem of the same name.

The poem is an eloquent meditation on and celebration of wisdom. It is divided into four sections — "Dawn," "Early Morning," "High Morning," "Sunset" — and it is modelled on the monastic Office of Praise: Lauds, Prime, Terce, Compline. Of dawn, or the Hour of Lauds, Merton writes:

> There is in all things an inexhaustible sweetness and purity, a silence that is a fount of action and joy. It rises up in wordless gentleness and flows out to me from the unseen roots of all created being, welcoming me tenderly, saluting me with indescribable humility. This is at once my own being, my own nature, and the Gift of my Creator's Thought and Art within me, speaking as Hagia Sophia, speaking as my sister, Wisdom.

It is in the dawn, the moment of pristine innocence, the moment of prelapsarian joy, the sweet point or *point vierge*, that one may happen on Hagia Sophia. In *Conjectures of a Guilty Bystander*, in a passage about the "first chirps of the waking day birds," Merton observes that they

> speak to Him, not with fluent song, but with an awakening question that is their dawn state, their state at the "point

vierge". . . . All wisdom seeks to collect and manifest itself at that blind sweet point. Man's wisdom does not succeed, for we are all fallen into self-mastery and cannot ask permission of anyone. We face our mornings as men of undaunted purpose. . . . For the birds there is not a time that they tell, but the virgin point between darkness and light, between non-being and being. . . . Here is an unspeakable secret: paradise is all around us and we do not understand. It is wide open. The sword is taken away, but we do not know it. . . . "Wisdom," cries the dawn deacon [the bird] but we do not attend.[2]

Merton corresponded with Louis Massignon, the distinguished Islamicist, and it was from him that he first heard the term *point vierge*, which means "the center of the soul, where despair corners the heart of the outsider." It is not only the sweet point but the enlightened awareness at the juncture of despair. Wisdom represents the voice of creation and the voice of unity, the summons to being and the sound of judgement. In the dawn state one can recognize

the first morning of the world (when Adam, at the sweet voice of Wisdom woke from nonentity and knew her), and . . . the Last Morning of the world when all the fragments of Adam will return from death at the voice of Hagia Sophia.

In part two of the poem, "Early Morning," the poet records that in our human efforts to awaken to the wisdom that speaks at the *point vierge*, we long to leave the blindness of our fallen state and rediscover our innocence:

The heavenly lights rejoice in the going forth of one man to make a new world in the morning, because he has come out of the confused primordial dark night into consciousness.

He has expressed the clear silence of Sophia in his own heart. He has become eternal.

When one is truly innocent one is truly eternal, finding "the impeccable pure simplicity of One consciousness in all and through all."

In the third part of the poem, "High Morning," Wisdom is spoken of as the divinity in all things and as the power of mercy in us,

the yielding and tender counterpart of the power,
justice and creative dynamism of the Father.

Hagia Sophia is both plenitude and nothingness:

God as all, and God reduced to Nothing:
inexhaustible nothingness.

In "Sunset," the concluding part, Hagia Sophia is directly identified with the Blessed Virgin Mary, whose consent to enflesh divinity guaranteed the offer of salvation to a recalcitrant creation and who is traditionally titled *Sedes Sapientiae* (Seat of Wisdom):

God enters into His creation. Through her wise answer, through her obedient understanding, through the sweet yielding consent of Sophia God enters without publicity into the city of rapacious men.

The speaker of the poem tells us at the beginning that he is in a hospital, lying asleep, and that it is the second of July, the Feast of the Visitation, "A Feast of Wisdom." Sophia comes to him in his sleep as Philosophy came to Boethius and Beatrice to Dante and Gabriel to Mary, a consolation and a dream, a vision and a longing. In a diary entry of the same day in 1960, Merton wrote of dreaming in a very quiet hospital when he was awakened by the "soft voice of the nurse." He asks:

> Who is more little than the helpless man, asleep in bed, having entrusted himself gladly to sleep and to night? Him the gentle voice will awake, all that is sweet in woman will awaken him. Not for conquest and pleasure, but for the far deeper wisdom of love and joy and communion.[3]

This recorded experience forms the context of the poem; the speaker and Merton are one and the same. Merton appreciates the unfathomable riches, the "invisible fecundity" of all things, revealed by Sophia. The sleeper, however — as all who sleep a temporal sleep must — *awakens* to the night having *dreamt* in the light:

> The shadows fall. The stars appear. The birds begin to sleep. Night embraces the silent half of the earth. A vagrant, a destitute wanderer with dusty feet, finds his way down a new road. A homeless God, lost in the night, without papers, without identification, without even a number, a frail expendable exile lies down in desolation under the sweet stars of the world and entrusts Himself to sleep.

As long as the speaker/sleeper/Merton dreams of Wisdom he comes out of the confused primordial dark night into consciousness, into the light of his dream, the luminosity of Wisdom.

In the tradition of the Early Church Fathers and the Neo-Platonists, Merton writes of Wisdom not as a particular quality but as a unique *manifestation* of the triune God. Wisdom is an image or emanation of the Godhead and not some disembodied divine attribute. Wisdom also assists in the repair of creation in the same way that the Virgin assists Christ in the Incarnation. And equally Wisdom will assist the poet in the task of repairing the word.

Hagia Sophia is Urthona, the *point vierge* of our being, the Virgin/window, and the Jungian anima. As Urthona, dethroned by Urizen, Wisdom seeks the co-operation of Art or Los in Blake's mythology, in order "to preserve some kind of harmony and order and intelligibility in the created world." As the virgin point of our being, Wisdom, Merton notes, is

> a point of pure truth, a point or spark which belongs entirely to God . . . which is inaccessible to the fantasies of our own mind or the brutalities of our own will. This little point of nothingness and of absolute poverty is the pure glory of God in us. It is so to speak His name written in us. . . . It is like a pure diamond, blazing with the invisible light of heaven. It is in everybody, and if we could see it we would see these billions of points of light coming together in the face and blaze of a sun that would make all the darkness and cruelty of life vanish completely. . . . I have no program for this seeing. It is only given. But the gate of heaven is everywhere.[4]

As the Virgin/window, Wisdom is the pane through which pour the rays, the grace of Christ the Daystar; Wisdom is "His manifestation in radiant splendor."

This is all rather rich language, full of superlatives and reverence, filled to over-brimming with sublime notions and exalted sentiments. "Hagia Sophia" is Merton the rhapsodic scribe with a taste for high mysticism; but there is another Merton, flesh-defined, achingly eager for the feminine touch, longing for that gentle voice that will awaken him to "all that is sweet in woman." In retrospect, it could not have been lost on Merton that his 1960 dream about lying in a hospital and coming to consciousness to the soothing sounds of a female nurse would in part be realized in 1966. Hagia Sophia, meet M. But is this incident just déjà vu, or is it something that has both psychological and spiritual significance?

Sophia cannot be M., since Merton had yet to meet her when he wrote the poem, but there is much more to Wisdom than theological rapture. In his lifelong work of integration Merton understood that all the dimensions of mature and holy living must be respected. To be wise is to be whole. The episode with M. would underscore the dangers inherent in suppressing the affective side of his life and he was eager to break the cycle of emotional deprivation and negative self-denial. Real asceticism was built on a healthy acceptance of the body and not on a fearful denial of it.

To acquire wisdom or holiness or integration was a life's project that increasingly forced Merton to examine the tools of his trade. Those tools — silence, contemplation, universal empathy — would be applied with a new exactitude and with a vigorous self-critique. Merton emerged from his love for M. with a deeper comprehension of his wounded personality and with a new resolve to penetrate deeper to the heart of his monkhood.

The first tool, silence, held many meanings for Merton. It was a *mode of protest* against the abuse of language in our propaganda-mad twentieth century. Merton was not alone in his attack on the calculated misuse of the word. W.H. Auden's post-war observation that

> All words like peace and love,
> All sane affirmative speech,
> Had been soiled, profaned, debased
> To a horrid mechanical speech
> ("To Reinhold and Ursula Niebuhr," *Nones, 1847–1950*)

has been echoed again and again by poet and critic alike. In her groundbreaking essay, "The Aesthetics of Silence," American writer Susan Sontag argues that silence as protest is a "radical critique of consciousness," a "strategy for the transvaluation of art" and a "program of perceptual and cultural therapy." There comes a time when, in Sontag's words, language itself must be "employed to check language, to express muteness." In order "to express muteness" language must resort to either *absence* or *parody*. The absence of language can take one of two forms: either the articulate pause of a Samuel Beckett or the non-linearity of a Harold Pinter. Merton opted for parody: with either the Swiftian satire of *Original Child Bomb* or the antipoetry of *Cables to the Ace*.

From the very beginning of his monastic life in 1941 Merton had agonized over the decision of whether to still his pen in order better to serve the calling of his religious vocation, or continue to write, conscious of having chosen the lesser path. A later development of this dilemma took the form outlined by George Steiner in "Silence and the Poet":

> To a writer who feels that the condition of language is in question, that the word may be losing something of its humane genius, two essential courses are available: he may seek to render his own idiom representative of the general crisis, to convey through it the precariousness and vulnerability of the communicative act; or he may choose the suicidal rhetoric of silence. . . . Precisely because it is the signature of his humanity, because it is that which makes a man a being of striving unrest, the word should have no natural life, no neutral sanctuary, in the places and season of bestiality. Silence is an alternative. When the words in the city are full of savagery and lies, nothing speaks louder than the unwritten poem.[5]

Although consecrated to silence in a way secular writers like Steiner and Sontag are not, Merton found the election of silence as a literary protest to be ultimately a self-defeating tactic. The absence of words, the stilling of the clamour, is necessary if the Word, the numinous, the "hidden wholeness" is to be heard. But he also knew that the poet must speak, that the wordsmith

> must discover new words reborn
> out of an old time
> Like new seed from an old harvest. (*The Tower of Babel*)

In other words, the literally "silent poem" is in the end unacceptable. But the silence of the poet, for Merton, is an extension of the very silence that is his life, a silence that is beginning and end, advent and apocalypse, a silence he spoke about in his essay "Ecumenism and Renewal":

> The monastic life (when it is true to its own charism) is pervaded with the sense of the definitive that comes to those who, in silence, refrain from the futility of articulation. Yet also what must be grasped are the provisional needs to be articulated in honest and undogmatic speech. The two go together. The monastic dialectic of silence and language underlines the deeper dialectic of eschatology and incarnation.[6]

Besides being a *mode of protest*, silence is also an *objective spiritual condition* or *ontology*. In silence the soul is replenished, the imagination rendered supple, the emotions quiescent, and the ego disciplined. The quintessential person of silence, however, is not the cenobite or the monk who lives in a community, but the anchorite or solitary whose silence is not only an interior disposition but an accompanying physical fact. The solitary is alone with silence. Mute, the solitary waits upon the unspoken utterance in order that the stilled voice may be made ready to speak. As Merton wrote in his 1960 article "The Solitary Life":

> there are not a few who are beginning to feel the futility of adding more words to the constant flood of language that pours meaninglessly over everybody, everywhere, from morning to night. For language to have meaning, there must be intervals of silence somewhere, to divide word from word and utterance from utterance.[7]

What for many writers would be a metaphorical retreat from the word was for Merton his *modus vivendi*, not merely a temporary condition but a foretaste of that ideal perfect state of unconditional absorption by the Transcendent to which all ascetics and mystics aspire. The irony that continued to plague Merton throughout his monastic life was that this very same spiritual ontology, this silence, did not demand the cessation of words nor even their diminution, but their reconstitution by means of myth and parody as vehicles of meaning and redemption. Words hounded Merton even in his hermit's cottage from 1965 onwards. However, unlike an earlier figure of the desert, Simeon of Stylites, who perched himself on top of a pole for many years to avoid temptation and whose salvation depended on his strength to resist the temptations that lured him from his resolve, Merton depended for his salvation as poet and monk on his ability to *submit* to his temptation to use words in an anarchic and often absurd manner, thus paradoxically reclaiming words by disowning their meaning. By reconstituting language the poet recovers for the word what critic Norman O. Brown calls the "subterranean original meaning," a meaning infused for Merton with the spiritual significance of the Incarnate Word.

In addition to understanding silence as a *mode of protest* and as a *spiritual ontology*, Merton also saw silence as a *phenomenology of liberation*, a liberation both perceptual and spiritual. On this point we can hear the voice of Blake once again. Merton knew that in the silent life God is seen as the "ground of being," the ineffable matrix of radiant and "hidden wholeness" that the soul longs to see. Whereas theologians in the West have generally spoken of the transcendent God, there have been not a few mystics in the same tradition who have sought to know God by the immanentist approach, and such a one was Blake. In his paintings and in his poetry Blake's esoteric genius unseated the Enlightenment god and replaced him with a god at the heart of created reality, and not on its periphery, for all is suffused with holiness. In silence, Merton writes in "Contemplation in a World of Action,"

> the "doors of perception" are opened and all life takes on a completely new meaning: the real sense of our own existence, which is normally veiled and distorted by the routine distractions of an alienated life, is now revealed in a central intuition. What was lost and dispersed in the relative meaninglessness and triviality of purposeless behavior . . . is brought together in fully integrated conscious significance.[8]

As a *phenomenology of liberation* silence alerts the conventional imagination to the inner dynamism of things. Silence revitalizes both perceptually and spiritually and frees the intellect from benighted ideas, the senses from staid commonplaces and the soul from spiritless habits.

Silence revitalizes perceptually! Complementary to Blake's poetry are Blake's accompanying drawings or translated visions which, to George Steiner's mind, allow for "new inter-actions of typography and syntax, of language and space, of graphic means and verbal codes." Similarly Merton, in his own quest for a "dynamic suggestion of new meanings," exper-imented in his later poetry both syntactically with his anti-poetry and typographically with his semiotic and concrete poems. Of the "signatures" or "calligraphies" — Rorschach-like illustrations or abstract markings — which accompanied his prose collection *Raids on the Unspeakable*, he had this to say in "Signatures: Notes on the Author's Drawings":

> No need to categorize these marks. It is better if they remain unidentified vestiges, signatures of someone who is not around. If these drawings are able to persist in a certain autonomy and fidelity, they may continue to awaken possi-bilities, consonances; they may dimly help to alter one's perceptions.[9]

Like Blake, Merton saw his drawings or signs "transcending all logical interpretation," their raison d'être as "summonses to awareness."

Silence revitalizes spiritually! As a form of liberation, silence is invested with a Blakean significance that is teleological in meaning, for silence is the source and perfection of language, with the final word spoken in silence. Like the twentieth-century Swiss philosopher Max Picard, Merton knew that the "word leads the human silence to the silence of God." In silence the word is made whole and the Word heard, perception and intuition are perfected, and human destiny unfolded. Silence is both *anticipation* and *consummation*, advent and apocalypse, source and end; it is the ultimate language, the root of language, the memory and fulfilment of language. As Picard notes: "It is as though the human word were sustained by the absolute word."

If silence is the first tool of the trade, contemplation is the second, and its importance to Merton cannot be doubted: his very vocation was contemplative. Initially the life of a monk necessitates not only a withdrawal from the world but a concomitant spurning of the world's claim on his sympathies. Such a world-hating attitude can easily lead the monk to see the contemplative calling as the most exalted of human endeavours with its very clear and righteous repudiation of the allurements of all that flesh can offer. And then some.

Although in his early life as a monk Merton shared this view, it never had a complete hold on him. Eventually, after years of meditation and spiritual growth, he came to see the contemplative life as a *dependence* on God, a dependence organized in such a way that God is both the nexus and the guiding spirit of the individual's life. It is possible, Merton concluded, to be a contemplative outside the cloister.

> What is called the contemplative life is really a life arranged in such a way that a person can more easily and more simply and more naturally live in an awareness of direct dependence on God — almost with the sense of realizing consciously, at every moment, how much we depend on Him; and receive from Him directly everything that comes to us as a pure gift; and experience, taste in our hearts, the love of God in this gift, the delicacy and the personal attention of God to us in His merciful love, which St. Thérèse de Lisieux brought out so beautifully.[10]

This is the first of three meanings Merton attached to contemplation: the spiritual/vocational. But contemplation in its second meaning for Merton is nothing less than the remaining guarantor of human freedom. The free person, the genuine contemplative, is in harmony with the order of creation, undeceived by public whim, alert to the real threats to civilized society. With his contemporary, the French Catholic existentialist Gabriel Marcel, Merton would agree that

> a civilization in which technical progress is tending to emancipate itself more and more from speculative knowledge, and finally to question the traditional rights of speculative knowledge, a civilization which, one may say, finally denies the place of contemplation and shuts out the very possibility of contemplation, such a civilization, I say, sets us inevitably on the road towards a philosophy which is not so much a *love of wisdom* as a *hatred of wisdom*.[11]

Contemplation, then, seen as the guarantor of human freedom, is not just a metaphysical proposition. It is a political one as well. Indeed, for Merton contemplation became his only political article of faith. Not an ideologue by temperament and continually suspicious of all political platforms, Merton discovered in contemplation the only remaining measure that could secure human freedom in an environment of unsympathetic and destructive forces. Even in the peak years of his political awakening — the 1960s — Merton the anarchist, the subversive voice of *My Argument with the Gestapo*, was never far away. In 1968 Merton would go so far as to argue that the monk, the contemplative par excellence, is engaged in an activity not unlike that of the Marxist revolutionary. Though he stands in judgement, like the Marxist, on the alienating forces of society, the monk is loath to use those means — guerrilla warfare, kidnappings, and sabotage — that are too common a feature of revolutionary resistance. The monk seeks liberation from the restrictive and archaic structures of society in order to liberate people from their own self-oppression. As he remarked in his final public address, delivered only hours before his death, "Marxism and Monastic Perspectives,"

The monk . . . has attained, or is about to attain, or seeks to attain full realization . . . dwells in the center of society as one who has attained realization . . . knows the score . . . has come to experience the ground of his own being in such a way that he knows the secret of liberation and can somehow or other communicate this to others.[12]

It is important to note that at the time he spoke the above he preferred to speak of the contemplative/monk as one who "dwells in the center of society." No longer on the periphery, no longer the sentinel or marginal person as was the case in the 1940s and 1950s, the contemplative is now at the very heart of society as witness to freedom's possibility.

Contemplation's third meaning consists of the means of recovering silence — the final assurance of artistic and spiritual openness. Although it is often cast as art's formidable rival in the arena of perfection, contemplation is vital for artistic integrity. In the words of composer R. Murray Schafer, contemplation

would teach us how to regard silence as a positive and felicitous state in itself, as the great and beautiful backdrop over which our actions are sketched and without which they would be incomprehensible, indeed could not even exist.[13]

It is the final tool of the trade — universal empathy — that will draw both silence and contemplation together in one grand fusion in the arduous struggle for wisdom. But this universal empathy must be first sifted through the prism of Zen. Merton had first embarked on his reading of Zen in conjunction with his reading of the Early Church Fathers in the mid-1950s. Zen Buddhism would quickly become one of the passions of his life.

In his emblems of mystical fury — a series of Zen poems published in *Emblems of a Season of Fury* (1963) — he concentrated years of Zen study and exploration in a tightly disciplined and word-spare poetics. In "Song for Nobody," for instance, the speaker of the poem simply rejoices in the sheer, unconditional *givenness* of creation. Nature's beauty is non-utilitarian, and its design and meaning have no purpose other than being itself:

> A yellow flower
> (Light and spirit)
> Sings by itself
> For nobody.

The poem speaks of the awareness that is necessary if we are to truly see the *claritas* that reveals the hidden resplendence of what *is*, the perception of reality that transcends Single Vision:

> (No light, no gold, no name, no color
> And no thought:
> O wide awake!)
> A golden heaven
> Sings by itself
> A song to nobody.

In order to see, as Blake would have it, "a World in a Grain of Sand," to discover the "hidden wholeness," we must cleanse the "doors of perception" clouded by the rule of abstraction. "Song for Nobody" reads like a Zen meditation, illustrating both the incisiveness and the economy of expression of a Zen perception. In "Song for Nobody" Merton tries to crystallize in words the act of direct and uncluttered seeing, without reducing the experience to Urizenic dissection:

Instead of seeing *things* and *facts* as they are we see them as reflections and verifications of the sentences we have previously made up in our minds. We quickly forget how to simply *see* things and substitute our words and our formulas for the things themselves, manipulating facts so that we see only what conveniently fits our prejudices. Zen uses language against itself to blast out these preconceptions and to destroy the specious "reality" in our minds so that we can *see directly*. Zen is saying, as Wittgenstein said, "Don't think: Look!"[14]

Blake and Zen alike seek the dismantling of abstraction's hold on creation with its narrow vision and its constricted spirituality. The "doors of perception" are imaginative and spiritual — for Blake they are one and the same — and poetic skill and mystical intuition must align in a common campaign against the "specious 'reality'" that dominates our minds.

In "O Sweet Irrational Worship," another of the Zen poems, simplicity and sparseness of phrasing come together in an act of seemingly effortless art:

By ceasing to question the sun
I have become light,

Bird and wind.

My leaves sing.

I am earth, earth

The speaker is the undifferentiated self; he identifies with nature and does not know an identity distinct from her when he ceases to question what is, and allows what is to be. In this act of "irrational worship" a paradisal innocence is recalled:

When I had a spirit,
When I was on fire
When the valley was
Made out of fresh air
You spoke my name
In naming your Silence:
O sweet, irrational worship.

The poet longs to restore the integrity and harmony that once existed before individual consciousness or reflexive ego-awareness shattered prelapsarian unity. The poet realizes that the only way we can recover paradise is not by ratiocination or systematic inquiry but by a poetic and mystical identification or cosympathy with creation, discovering in its mystery the *irrelevance* of the "I" and the illusoriness of the empirical self:

My heart's love
Bursts with hay and flower.
I am a lake of blue air
In which my own appointed place
Field and valley
Stand reflected.

What remains hidden to reason may be known to rapture. This is the language of Zen; this is the wisdom of Zen.

There is a remarkable significance in the contiguity of two diary entries in *Conjectures of a Guilty Bystander* that demonstrate the common meaning of Blake and Zen for Merton and that find an eloquent vindication in "O Sweet Irrational Worship." In the first of these entries Merton speaks of the superiority of Blake's understanding of nature over Newton's, the superiority of an understanding that is evocative, reverential, and sublime over one that is diagnostic, familiar, and mundane. Merton states this by way of suggestion and not by way of declaration:

> Evening light. Purple caves and holes of shadow in the bosom of the hills. The little white gable of Newton's house smiles so peacefully amid the bare trees in the middle of the valley! This is the peace and luminosity that Blake loved.[15]

Of course the Kentucky Newton and Sir Isaac are separated by centuries, land, and culture, but Merton's meditation plays on the name. For Merton, Newtonians live in the very heart of nature and yet do not know it. They are blinded by a naïve literalism and a reductionist empiricism. Their contempt for the image and their deification of the concept prevent them from truly *seeing*. Dominated for centuries by what Blake calls Natural Religion, the west longs for mystery, for the irreducible sensation, and for an authentic communion with nature. The West is starved for the supernatural; it knows only the assurances of reason.

In his second entry, Merton makes clear the anti-Cartesianism of Zen and its rejection of the supremacy, indeed the very legitimacy of the "I":

> The taste for Zen in the West is in part a healthy reaction of people exasperated with the heritage of four centuries of Cartesianism: the reification of concepts, idolization of the reflexive consciousness, flight from being into verbalism, mathematics, and rationalization. Descartes made a fetish out of the mirror in which the self finds itself. Zen shatters it.[16]

Both Zen and Blake shatter the mirror, the rule of Descartes/ Urizen. The speaker's "irrational worship" proclaims the liberating vision of the wholeness of creation:

I am earth, earth

Out of my grass heart
Rises the bobwhite.

Out of my nameless weeds
His foolish worship.

This liberating vision, however, must be sought in solitude
and in the emptiness that solitude may bring. In "Song: If
You Seek" Merton outlines the essence of this emptiness and
reveals in the process the confluence of Zen and the wisdom
of the Desert Fathers, the fourth-century solitaries whose
spiritual insight and psychological perspicacity so moved Merton that he translated many of their sayings. The speaker of
"Song: If You Seek" *is* solitude:

If you seek a heavenly light
I, Solitude, am your professor!

Solitude prepares the imagination for inspiration, stills the
restless intellect, and beckons the spirit to new possibilities:

I go before you into emptiness,
Raise strange suns for your new mornings,
Opening the windows
Of your innermost apartment.

In solitude one can rediscover paradise as the Desert Fathers
and Zen masters prove. To do so, however, requires a divest-
ment of the ego so thorough as to virtually deny its reality; it
requires a levelling of the will and a subsuming of all desire
into the *one* yearning for wholeness; and it requires the realization of a spiritual vulnerability that places the seeker
wholly in the hands of the Other. In short, the seeker must

empty himself. To be emptied is to love, for the greatest act of love for the Christian is *kenosis*, the self-emptying love of the crucified Jesus. It is *this* kenotic love that every seeker of the "heavenly light" must attain if solitude is to reveal the innocence and purity of heart that is paradise:

> Follow my ways and I will lead you
> To golden-haired suns,
> Logos and music, blameless joys,
> Innocent of questions
> And beyond answers:
> For I, Solitude, am thine own self:
> I, Nothingness, am thy All.
> I, Silence, am thy Amen!

Stripped of all presupposition and reflexive awareness and completely enveloped in the Other — the Non-Object of the seeker's quest — the emptied subject recovers, in solitude, paradise.

Paradise will forever elude the seeker should it be desired, for desire presupposes an object to be possessed. Desire's fulfilment rests in the acquisition of the object desired. The logic of Zen and of the Christian mystics necessitates, however, the dispossession of desire or the death of the ego if the seeker is to be in turn possessed by paradise.

With the language of Zen, a language of extrarational meaning, contradiction, and negation, and with the language of Blake, a language of innocence, private mythology, and mystical symbol, Merton sought to unveil paradise in the undefiled vision of emptiness. Paradise, for Merton, is neither eternal nor temporal but a "Yin-yang palace of opposites in unity" as he argues in *The Way of Chuang Tzu* (1965). It is Four-Fold Vision.

Throughout these mystical poems Merton is concerned with an acquiescence of soul and mind, with a creative passivity, an openness to impression, that purifies the "doors of perception" and liberates humanity from the tyranny of the *cogito*. The poems are concerned with both an imaginative and a spiritual liberation that is Blakean in conception and Zen-like in imagery.

With the concluding poem of the mystical sequence, "Love Winter When the Plant Says Nothing," the presence of John of the Cross can be seen in harmony with Blake and Zen. This poem can be read as a summary of the themes of emptiness, paradise, and "unbracketed" perception. The plant is both the soul and the imagination. It must love the winter, a season of spiritual and creative desolation, in spite of the aridity of soul and paucity of ideas that it brings. The winter is the "dark night of the soul," the terrifying Absence that is a Presence. It is the desert filled to overflowing with emptiness,

> Secret
> Vegetal words,
> Unlettered water,
> Daily zero.

In the winter the plant is dormant, insular, and cautious. But it is also in winter that the plant may retreat into itself, realizing the wealth of its nothingness, the peace that passes understanding:

> Fire, turn inward
> To your weak fort,
> To a burly infant spot,
> A house of nothing.
> O peace, bless this mad place.

In the very caverns of the mind Silence beckons with the light of inspiration:

O Silence, golden zero
Unsetting sun.

Love winter when the plant says nothing.

The paradoxes of mystical intuition, the anti-logic aphorisms of Zen, and the tension of the Blakean Contraries, without which there is no progression, define the tenor of these mystical poems.

The emblems of mystical fury must be read in conjunction with the emblems of political fury spoken of in the chapter on Urizen, precisely because they *are* the Blakean Contraries. As Blake says in *The Marriage of Heaven and Hell*:

Attraction and Repulsion, Reason and Energy,
Love and Hate, are necessary to Human Existence.

The poems of political fury with their oppressive irony and apocalyptic temper speak of the lordship of reason, the triumph of abstraction over imagination, the confounding of the gift of personhood with the "I" of Descartes, the dethronement of *Sapientia* by *Scientia*, and the fracturing of a comprehensive vision through the tyranny of extreme realism. The poems of mystical fury with their gentle longing for peace and restoration and their irreverent paradoxes speak of the rule of the powerless, the primacy of Spiritual Imagination, the plenitude of the emptied "I," the holiness of the desert, and the unity of Four-Fold Vision.

The emblems of both political and mystical fury are concerned with rationality: its bankruptcy, its excess. Eichmann and Pasternak, Urizen and Urthona, constitute the Contraries. Zen, Merton affirms, allows us to *see* the vital need for "irrational worship" and the unreasonableness of rationality:

The point is that facts are not just plain facts. There is a dimension where the bottom drops out of the world of factuality and of the ordinary. Western industrial culture is in the curious position of having simultaneously reached the climax of an entire totalitarian rationality of organization and of complete absurdity and self-contradiction. Existentialists and a few others have noticed the absurdity. But the majority persist in seeing only the rational machinery against which no protest avails: because, after all, it is "rational," and it is "a fact." So, too, is the internal contradiction. . . .
It might be good to open our eyes and *see*.[17]

Zen enabled Merton to see; it was his means of intersection with memory, innocence and eternity. Zen allowed him to be a child again, to see with fresh eyes, and to taste the mercy of God. But in one sense, as theologian Jacques Goulet observes, Merton was always the child:

He's utterly the child. He lives intensely the present moment. For instance, his journal entries consist of many judgements about people and ideas that are full of superlatives. This particular writer is the greatest writer, this thinker the greatest thinker, or the worst. Merton is totally present to the moment at hand. There is no person past or future, just the present Merton completely in love with you, focussed on you, when he speaks to you. He's *your* friend, and when you're gone he is somebody else's. Now, it has to be admitted, for many people this is disconcerting and they dismiss him as an extremist. But when a child cries, the *whole* person cries, and when a child laughs, the *whole* person laughs. People often demand the adult in Merton and they get the child. He is too honest to be otherwise.

Take the matter of his Columbia University erotic cartoons for example, or indeed his relationship with the Louisville nurse. We all have a blueprint of someone we consider a saint, the ideal monk, a holy one, and when the idealized person no longer fits the blueprint, either we change our expectations and the blueprint is altered or we register our disappointment with the idealized figure's failure to meet our specifications. We blame Merton for not conforming to our mould. We don't allow Merton to be Merton — the perennial child, full of wonder and surprise.

Merton, the Zen child, the Blakean child, not only opened himself to everyone and to every experience with both fresh-ness and a dangerous indifference to caution, he also longed to identify promiscuously with all. This child-like predilection to imaginatively embrace all was never erased by adulthood, it was just transformed into his capacity for universal empathy. The theologian Anthony Padovano speaks of Merton as a par-adigmatic figure, a symbol of the century:

> Merton exemplified for me that rare figure who can recon-cile the antinomies, hold in harmony the contradictions of life. That sounds very speculative, so let me be specific. I think, for example, that in the nineteenth century we were very much engaged in either/or thinking. It was either authority or conscience; it was either West or East. It was either male or female. I think that in the twentieth century we have splintered those artificial boundaries, and as a consequence there is now a vague embarrassment about

being too much *anything*, whether male or female, Catholic, American, Canadian, Western, whatever. To my mind, Merton, in both his life and in his work, tried to bring all the real and apparent contradictions together, and I think he did it with effective symbolism, with a sense of drama, eventually becoming a *symbol* himself.

Merton's effort to unify, to balance the Contraries, in his life and work was his supreme Blakean task. He wanted to be genuinely catholic, excluding nothing, including all:

the more I am able to affirm others, to say "yes" to them in myself, by discovering them in myself and myself in them, the more real I am. I am fully real if my own heart says *yes to everyone*.

I will be a better Catholic, not if I can *refute* every shade of Protestantism, but if I can affirm the truth in it and still go further.

So, too, with the Muslims, the Hindus, the Buddhists, etc. This does not mean syncretism, indifferentism, the vapid and careless friendliness that accepts everything by thinking of nothing. There is much that one cannot "affirm" and "accept," but first one must say "yes" where one really can.

If I affirm myself as a Catholic merely by denying all that is Muslim, Jewish, Protestant, Hindu, Buddhist, etc., in the end I will find that there is not much left for me to affirm as a Catholic: and certainly no breath of the Spirit with which to affirm it.[18]

The struggle to unite in himself the disparate strains of feeling, culture, history, and religion was there from the beginning. His extraterritoriality came naturally: born in the south of France to an American mother and a New Zealander father;

educated in several countries; an intellectual mongrel at both Cambridge and Columbia universities; an artistic and spiritual bohemian; rooted in one religious tradition but eager to incorporate the "truth" of all; the perfect gyrovague or wandering monk, eclectic and yet fiercely traditional, the living contradiction that would unite the Contraries.

It is interesting to note the rather stark contrast between his reflections on America at the time he took out U.S. citizenship in 1951 — "Perhaps I am called upon to objectify the truth that America, for all its evil, is innocent and somehow ignorantly holy"[19] — with his February 15, 1958, journal entry wherein he has moved beyond the narrow confines of the United States to speak of America:

> Suddenly, saw, this afternoon, the meaning of my *American* destiny — one of those moments when many unrelated pieces of one's life and thought fall into place in a great unity towards which one has been growing.
>
> My destiny is indeed to be an American — not just an American of the U.S. We are only the fringe of the True America. I can never be satisfied with this only partial reality that is almost nothing at all — is so little that it is like a few words written in chalk on a blackboard, easily rubbed out. . . . My vocation is American — *to see and to understand and to have in myself the life and the roots and the belief and the destiny and the Orientation of the whole hemisphere* — as an expansion of something of God, of Christ, that the world has not yet found out — something that is only now, after hundreds of years, coming to maturity. . . . No one fragment can begin to be enough. Not Spanish colonial Catholicism, not 19th. century republicanism, not agrarian radicalism . . . not the Indianism of Mexico — but all of it, everything. To be oneself a whole

hemisphere and help the hemisphere to realize its own destiny.[20]

Five years later, in a letter dated August 1, 1963, and addressed to his former novice and fellow poet, the Nicaraguan priest and political activist Ernesto Cardenal, Merton wrote bluntly of his hope that there would come a time when "America (North, Central and South) will perhaps be the great living unity that it was meant to be and that it now is not."[21] By 1967 Merton had set out to produce a testament to this dream for American unity but it had broadened to include all the hemispheres, the greater geography, the enlarged myth-dream: his Blakean masterpiece, *The Geography of Lograire*.

Geography is the final working out of the vision, the uniting of the Four Zoas — Tharmas, Urizen, Luvah, Urthona — and the making of a new beginning even as it marked the perfect end. It was, as he said in a letter to publisher Helen Wolff, "an apocalypse of our age."

Shortly before he left on his Asian journey in the fall of 1968, Merton sent J. Laughlin the final draft of *Geography*. Though in itself a complete work it was intended to be only part of a larger work, a work that was never written. Merton wrote in the "Author's Note" that serves as a preface to the poem:

> This is a purely tentative first draft of a longer work in progress, in which there are, necessarily, many gaps.

Though designed as merely part of a pattern *Geography* emerges as the most intricate undertaking of Merton's career as a writer. It is divided into four distinct, separate cantos — South, North, East, West — each of which is further divided into sections or individual poems: eleven in the South canto; four and a prologue in the North; ten and an epigraph in the

East; and four in the West canto. There is also a general prologue to the complete poem, a prefatory note, and sundry notes on sources provided by the editor.

Geography consists of surrealistic meditations, prose poems, antipoems, found poetry, and Joycean word experiments. It is a wild, eclectic, syncretic testament to Merton's universality of vision:

> In this wide-angle mosaic of poems and dreams I have without scruple mixed what is my own experience with what is almost everybody else's.

Merton refers to *Geography* as "only a beginning of patterns" and freely admits to tampering with the sources that chronicle our common human experiences, confessing all the while that even "where more drastic editing is called for by my own dream, well, I have dreamed it." He ferreted widely, delving into esoteric tracts, the newest anthropological investigations and studies, ancient documents and standard histories, personal records and sacred scriptures. He incorporated as part of his vision the cargo cults of Melanesia, the ghost dances of U.S. natives, Arctic expeditions, and the recorded experiences of a fourteenth-century Arab traveller; he drew as well on a generous spectrum of Christian and pre-Christian sources. *Geography* is a gallimaufry, a hodgepodge of narratives, myths, legends, and histories that together create a rich, even if fragmentary, mosaic of the human endeavour, the sacred quest for ultimate meaning.

There is a problem with *Geography*, however, as there was earlier with *Cables*, which does not arise with either the lyrical poems or the shorter prose poems, and that is the ultimate insufficiency of antipoetry. In *Thomas Merton, Monk and Poet*, the biographer and critic George Woodcock pointedly highlights the difficulty:

> . . . we are forced to question Marcuse's idea of the infinite
> resources available to the anti-poet. Once we accept such
> an idea, we face the problem of how to select from the
> great mass of bad and good print that offers itself. How,
> having elected for anti-poetry and thus abdicated poetic
> discrimination, can we select what may be antipoetically
> acceptable? Inevitably, we find ourselves bound to set up
> criteria of badness in anti-poetry. And when that comes we
> are back in the old game of reserving special subjects and a
> special language — even if an anti-language — for poetry.[22]

Antipoetry has its purposes, but it also has its very clear
limitations. Merton realized the role of parody and antipoetry
had to be complemented and balanced by the role of lyrical and
Zen mystical poetry. They are "creative contraries" and constitute a poetic and tactical "marriage of heaven and hell."
Both are integral to Merton's vision, and realize in literary
form that "complementarity of opposites" or "final integration" that Merton speaks of as spiritual wholeness. Considered
in this light Merton the antipoet can face the limitations of
antipoetry without crisis because the anti-poems stand in
creative tension with their vital "contrary."

Although highly complex, recondite, and not easily accessible, *Geography* does not stand apart from the earlier verse —
not, at least, in the sense of being discontinuous with it,
because it is the culmination of all Merton's poetic efforts to
that point, making sense of seemingly unrelated works and, as
he wrote of the work of the U.S. poet Louis Zukofsky, like
"all really valid poetry," in search of a new start. As Daniel
Berrigan phrases it in his article "The Seventy Times Seventy
Seven Storey Mountain":

> Strange how grandly disparate works,
> probings, experiments, finally, after

years, stand out as reasonable, linked,
sensible; the real accomplishment can be
seen then for what it is.
The times are plain mad, a solid view.
Therefore writing has an element of
nihilism, starting over, history not
rearranged or finagled with, but a new start.[23]

Geography certainly has "an element of nihilism" about
it, as Merton attempted to clarify and compress his central
myth-dream into a structure he thought would suggest, if not
incorporate, the universality of his vision. Still, he was determined that his vision be understood as a public endeavour, a
"common participation." He comments to that end in his
"Author's Note":

A poet spends his life in repeated projects, over and over
again attempting to build or to dream the world in which
he lives. But more and more he realizes that this world is at
once his and everybody's. It cannot be purely private, any
more than it can be purely public. It cannot be fully com-
municated. It grows out of a common participation which
is nevertheless recorded in authentically personal images.

Merton's "dream [of] the world in which he lives" is his
vision of the wholeness of creation, the "marriage of heaven
and hell," and the coming of what Blake calls Universal
Humanity or Jesus. In his act of dreaming the world, the
poet-visionary seeks its restoration to creative harmony; and
though this dream is public the task is solitary:

He who sees reality in the universe may try to negate it
(West:1)

and

> IF YOU HAVE HEART FAILURE WHILE READING
> THIS THE POET IS NOT RESPONSIBLE (South: IV)

Yet his clowning reveals a heart weary with the heavy truths of one who *sees*.

In an age of Urizenic security, when Abstraction threatens Life, vision is the only alternative to absurdity and despair. The necessity of vision in a world of formulae and theories, of imagination in a world of cerebration, underscores the metaphysical truth of the "marriage of heaven and hell." This truth, known to Blake, Chuang Tzu, and Zen sages, was also the privileged possession of various ancient and now extinct societies. It is to the ancient peoples that Merton turned — the Maya, the Zapotec, the Yana — to discover a program for seeing. These people

> had inherited an archaic wisdom which did somehow protect them against the dangers of a merely superficial, wilful and cerebral existence.[24]

In an effort to understand this "archaic wisdom" and to integrate it into Western society's self-understanding before the latter's violent dissolution into disorder, Merton turned to various studies of different cultures that incarnated this wisdom, and used them in *Geography* as counterpoint to the ambition, efficiency and sterile confidence of technocratic society. The ancient "archaic wisdom" or vision represents his "reality," his "identity," his place in the scheme of things. The primitive is at the point of intersection, where phenomena and the numinous, the divine and the human, commingle without suppression or elimination. The individual is at the

crossroads established by the gods, points of communication not only between the visible and the invisible, the
obvious and the unexplained, the higher and the lower,
the strong and the helpless: but above all between complementary opposites which balanced and fulfilled each other
(fire-water, heat-cold, rain-earth, light-dark, life-death). . . .
One's identity was the intersection of chords where one
"belonged." The intersection was to be sought in terms of
a kind of musical or aesthetic and scientific synchronicity
— one fell in step with the dance of the universe, the liturgy
of the stars.[25]

In striking contrast with this *visionary* understanding is our
post-Enlightenment understanding — Cartesian, Urizenic, and
in the end, absurdist. The only way out of this dilemma is to
set aright our understanding of thought itself, and that would
require a visionary appreciation of the harmony and inter-
connectedness of creation, such as that realized for Merton in
Blake, the primitive and the child, who remains

in direct sensuous contact with what is outside him, and is
most happy when this contact is celebrated in aesthetic and
ritual joy.[26]

Merton intended *Geography*, in keeping with its Blakean
inspiration, to be a poetic and historical-anthropological treatment of the visionary mode of life and to redress the perilous
imbalance caused by the domination in Western society of the
abstractionist heritage of Bacon, Locke, and Newton.

The tyranny of mind and power in Western culture prevents
any sympathy for or understanding of an ancient's self-
affirmation. As Merton acidly remarks in his essay "The
Shoshoneans," "To be an Indian is a lifelong desultory exercise
in acting as somebody else's invention."[27]

To bring an end to this tyranny, to reclaim by means of a "geography of the word" the "geography of the Word," was Merton's central myth-dream. Like Blake, in whose *Jerusalem* the Four Zoas, the "Four Mighty Ones . . . in every man" unite, Merton dreamt that a time would come when

> every Man stood Fourfold; each Four
>   Faces had: One to the West,
> One toward the East, One to the South, One
>   to the North, the Horses Fourfold. . . .
> Awaking [Man] to Life among the flowers of
>   Beulah, rejoicing in Unity
> In the Four Senses, in the Outline, the
>   Circumference & Form, for ever.
> In forgiveness of Sins which is Self-
>   Annihilation; it is the Covenant of
> Jehovah. (*Jerusalem*)

In the unity of the Four Zoas with their mysterious harmony of tension there can be found the Universal Man/Jesus, for

> a Perfect Unity
> Cannot Exist but from the Universal
>   Brotherhood of Eden
> The Universal Man, To Whom be Glory Evermore,
>   Amen. (*Vala* or *The Four Zoas*)

The achievement, to use a distinctly un-Zen-like phrase, of "perfect unity" was closer at hand than Merton realized. Having sent *Geography* to his publisher in September 1968 with the accompanying note that he considered it "a much more significant piece of work than most of what I have done before," Merton eagerly turned his full attention to the preparations for his Asian journey.

On September 9, Merton celebrated his last Mass at Gethsemani. Brother Patrick Hart recounts the occasion:

> The day before he left for Bangkok Merton invited Brother
> Maurice Flood who took care of some of his physical needs,
> Philip Stark, a Jesuit, who was typing some of his manu-
> scripts and working on Merton's literary magazine, *Monk's
> Pond* [initiated by Merton in 1967, it was conceived as a
> four-issue publication of offbeat poetry and prose], and me,
> his secretary, up to his hermitage for his last Mass. It was
> very moving. We arrived about 6:00 or 6:30, just as day
> was breaking, and we celebrated Mass in a little hermitage
> chapel, big enough for just about three people. It was the
> Feast of the Jesuit saint Peter Claver; he said the Mass in
> English; the Gospel of the day was the Good Samaritan; and
> surprisingly, given our small number, he gave us a brief
> homily and thanked us for being Good Samaritans to him.
> It was very moving. After Mass we had breakfast at a long
> table at the front of the hermitage. We had coffee, dough-
> nuts, and a half-bottle of Mass wine. We toasted him and
> took photographs of each other. He gave us some books —
> I received *The John Howard Griffin Reader* — we joked
> about the trip, and we gave him advice on what to do and
> what to avoid: be content with beer and wine and dispense
> with the tap water. He was like a young boy off to the circus,
> full of life, full of joy.

Merton was giddy with excitement as he left for the Louisville airport, but he was also anxious about a trip that would
take him away from Gethsemani for several months. It was
one thing to complain about James Fox and his intransigence
— although the abbot who had given him permission to travel
was Fox's successor, Flavian Burns — but it was quite another

to be set free to travel extensively, with very few strings attached. Merton liked the strings; they helped to define him. He was now at liberty in a way he hadn't been for some time. The future was daunting and he was unsure of his footing. After all, 1966 had proven that he could fall madly in love. What would 1968 prove?

Prior to leaving for the East, he spent some time in Chicago, Alaska, and the West Coast before actually departing for Asia on October 15th; the major stops, as recorded in his *Asian Journal*, were: Bangkok (October 18), Calcutta (October 19–27), New Delhi (October 28–31), the Himalayas (November 1–25), Madras (November 26–28), Ceylon, now Sri Lanka (November 29–December 6), with a return visit to Bangkok (December 7–8).

As his meticulously kept journal reveals, Merton's appetite for knowledge and intellectual curiosity were insatiable; his sociable nature was given ample exercise; his experience of the interior life deepened. He met scholars, clerics, religious leaders of many faith traditions, ordinary folk, dignitaries, and elevated figures of international reputation, including the Dalai Lama, about whom he wrote after his visit:

> He is strong and alert, bigger than I expected (for some reason I thought he would be small.) A very solid, energetic, generous, and warm person, very capably trying to handle enormous problems — none of which he mentioned directly. The whole conversation was about religion and philosophy and especially ways of meditation. He said he was glad to see me, had heard a lot about me.[28]

Merton was touched by the Dalai Lama's familiarity with his work. He came to believe that there was a real spiritual bond between them, that they "were somehow very close to each other." His affection for the Dalai Lama was reciprocated.

As a result of our discussions, I got a certain feeling I was with a person who had a great desire to learn. So I thought it quite fit, appropriate, to call him a Catholic *Geshe*. This means "a scholar" or "learned one." Also I could say he was a holy man. I don't know the exact Western interpretation of this term *holy*, but from a Buddhist viewpoint a holy person is one who sincerely implements what he knows. That we call *holy*. And, despite his knowledge or his position, lives a very simple way of life and is honest, and respects other people. I found these qualities in Thomas Merton.[29]

Merton impressed more than the Dalai Lama with his spiritual integrity. His personal holiness touched not a few. And he was touched, and touched deeply, by the Ineffable. He recounts the experience in some detail in the *Asian Journal*. He was in Sri Lanka and he had visited Polonnaruwa, a ruined city of palaces and of Hindu and Buddhist temples. It is renowned for its three gigantic Buddha figures carved out of immense stones. While gazing on these colossal figures Merton had an epiphany of deep significance, presaging mortal closure:

I was suddenly, almost forcibly, jerked clean out of the habitual, half-tied vision of things, and an inner clearness, clarity, as if exploding from the rocks themselves, became evident and obvious. . . . The thing about all this is that there is no puzzle, no problem, and really no "mystery." All problems are resolved and everything is clear, simply because what matters is clear. The rock, all matter, all life, is charged with dharmakaya [the essence of all beings] . . . everything is emptiness and everything is compassion. I don't know when in my life I have ever had such a sense of beauty and spiritual validity running together in one aesthetic illumination . . . my Asian pilgrimage has come clear and purified itself. I mean, I know and I have seen what I was obscurely looking for. I don't know what else remains but I have now seen and have pierced through the surface and have got beyond the shadow and the disguise.[30]

In Polonnaruwa Merton experienced something of what Blake meant by Four-Fold Vision. Beauty, spiritual validity, and naked reality all came together for him in a powerful instance of *claritas*, of "pure seeing," of divine love. Merton *saw* what he "was obscurely looking for."

On December 10th he made his last public appearance when he gave his address, "Marxism and Monastic Perspectives," to various religious gathered at the Aide à l'Implantation Monastique conference held at Samutprakarn, just thirty-odd kilometres from downtown Bangkok. Impressed by the similarities that exist between the monk's and the Marxist's critique of inauthentic structures — social and conceptual — Merton spoke eloquently of the need for transformation. For the Christian monk, this transformation involves nothing less than a commitment to become a completely new person. The demand is total and the gift is total in the shadow of Polonnaruwa.

Merton died by accidental electrocution on the same day as this address. The world was stunned; his friends reeled in disbelief; his brother monks were desolate. At the age of fifty-three, in the prime of life, healthier than he had been for decades, emotionally and spiritually whole, he died an unpredictable and bizarre death. But there was a fearless symmetry to it, full of Blakean bravado, charged, cruel, brilliant.

It was to be in the East where he would be *possessed* by Four-Fold Vision. It *seemed* right; it *was* perfect.

He didn't discover the East; the East discovered him. Freed at last to create a new role for the monk of the West, he united in himself the traditions, as he dreamt he would, of all that seek the holy. He became the Universal Man/Jesus/Four-Fold Vision, one who sought to "contain all divided worlds."

Merton was the quintessential spiritual quester or adventurer. His life was a life in progress. As Donald Grayston notes:

> one might even call Merton a pilgrim in process. He saw himself and wrote of himself as an unfinished piece of work, as somebody on a journey. At the end of *The Seven Storey Mountain* he has that little Latin phrase that says that "it may be the end of the book, but it is not the end of the seeking." I see that as Merton's signature. This colophon in the *Mountain* remains true throughout all of his life.
>
> He started out with Scholastic answers, black and white, the Dominican colours, and finally decided that there were too many shades of gray for him to restrict himself to Scholastic theology alone. And so he offers himself as unfinished.
>
> I think that his *Asian Journal* is a good emblem of this still incomplete and still to be perfected man because it is an unfinished book. It is a book that I think was magnificently put together by its editors out of the fragments left to them by Merton — little notebooks, impressionistic entries, obscurely identified sources, etc. I think it is very appropriate that his last work was not edited by himself, as was the case with that masterpiece of twentieth-century theology: Dietrich Bonhoeffer's *Letters and Papers from Prison*. Both works, fragmentary, confessional, insightful, are unfinished and yet perfect.

In the words of his Hindu friend, the philosopher Amiya Chakravarty, one of the three editors of the *Asian Journal*:

Merton sanctified India for me as he had sanctified American life and traditions with his courage and the nobility of a universal vision. The turmoil, the conflict of several theological dogmas, the general confusion of our times yielded to the sure faith he had in . . . spiritual humanity. The meaning of religious harmony and genuine internationalism came home to me. It is true that we still live in a violent age, with serfs and slaves, with guns going off, with women still under world-wide duress. As I walked in the garden of the Gethsemani monastery in Kentucky after Thomas Merton's death, I saw the little black cross which marked the grave of this radiant and simple personality, both a priest and a man . . . whose body had been flown out to Louisville from Bangkok. He was there in the world in which we live, and he was also somewhere in a realm which we cannot reach. I felt once more the utter tenderness, the infinitude of a life lived with courage and an encompassing wholeness.[31]

Merton, the monk with "heretic blood," Blake's twentieth-century descendant, the extraterritorial quester, this very Merton, died as he had lived: electric and suffused with energy.

Notes

INTRODUCTION

1. J.S. Porter, "Silent Lamp: The Lives of Thomas Merton," *Brick: A Literary Journal*, no. 55 (Fall 1996): 12.

2. Thomas Merton, *A Vow of Conversation: Journals 1964–1965* (New York: Farrar, Straus & Giroux, 1988), 19.

3. Peter Ackroyd, *Blake* (London: Minerva, 1996), 3.

4. Merton to Czeslaw Milosz, 12 September 1959, in Thomas Merton, *The Courage for Truth: Letters to Writers*, selected and edited by Christine M. Bochen (New York: Farrar, Straus & Giroux, 1993), 64.

5. Thomas Merton, *Turning Toward the World: The Journals of Thomas Merton, Volume Four 1960–1963*, edited by Victor A. Kramer (New York: HarperCollins, 1996), 320.

6. Merton to Daniel Berrigan, in Thomas Merton, *The Hidden Ground of Love: Letters on Religious Experience and Social Concerns*, selected and edited by William H. Shannon (New York: Farrar, Straus & Giroux, 1985), 79.

7. Ibid., 157.

8. Merton to Dom Jean Leclercq, in Thomas Merton, *The School of Charity: Letters on Religious Renewal and Spiritual Direction*, selected and edited by Patrick Hart, ocso (New York: Farrar, Straus & Giroux, 1990), 337.

9. *A Vow of Conversation*, 27.

10. George Steiner, *Extraterritoriality* (New York: Atheneum, 1971), 4.

11. Merton to Victor Hammer, in Thomas Merton, *Witness to Freedom: Letters in Times of Crisis*, selected and edited by William H. Shannon (New York: Farrar, Straus & Giroux, 1994), 9.

12. *Turning Toward the World*, 6.

CHAPTER I / THE PILGRIM

1. Bruce Chatwin, quoted in "The Life and Early Death of Bruce Chatwin," by Susannah Clapp, *The New Yorker*, December 23 and 30, 1996, 98.

2. Thomas Merton, *The Seven Storey Mountain* (New York: Harcourt Brace, 1948), 3.

3. Ibid., 38.

4. Ibid., 43.

5. Michael Mott, *The Seven Mountains of Thomas Merton* (Boston: Houghton Mifflin, 1984), 40.

6. *Seven Storey Mountain*, 87.

7. Thomas Merton, *My Argument with the Gestapo* (New York: Doubleday, 1969), v.

8. Merton to James Laughlin, 8 October 1966, *Thomas Merton and James Laughlin: Selected Letters*, edited by David Cooper (New York: W.W. Norton, 1997), 301.

9. *Seven Storey Mountain*, 190–191.

10. Merton to Bob Lax, 11 August 1938, in Thomas Merton, *The Road to Joy: Letters to New and Old Friends*, selected and edited by Robert E. Daggy (New York: Farrar, Straus & Giroux, 1989), 142.

11. *Seven Storey Mountain*, 88.

12. Thomas Merton, *Run to the Mountain: The Journals of Thomas Merton, Volume One 1939–1941*, edited by Patrick Hart, ocso (New York: Harper-Collins, 1995), 218.

13. Ibid., 455–456.

14. Ibid., 467.

15. Mark Van Doren, introduction to *Selected Poems of Thomas Merton* (New York: New Directions, 1967), xvii.

16. "For My Brother: Reported Missing in Action, 1943," *Selected Poems*, 12–13.

17. *Merton By Those Who Knew Him Best*, Giroux et al., edited by Paul Wilkes (New York: Harper & Row, 1984), 21–22.

18. Ibid., 21.

19. Thomas Merton, *Introductions East & West: The Foreign Prefaces of Thomas Merton*, edited by Robert E. Daggy (Greensboro: Unicorn Press, 1981), 43.

20. Thomas Merton, *A Search for Solitude: The Journals of Thomas Merton, Volume Three 1952–1960*, edited by Lawrence S. Cunningham (New York: HarperCollins, 1996), 246–247.

21. Merton to Hans Urs von Balthasar, 7 August 1964, in Thomas Merton, *The School of Charity: Letters on Religious Renewal and Spiritual Direction*, selected and edited by Patrick Hart, ocso (New York: Farrar, Straus & Giroux, 1985), 227.

22. Merton to Ludovico Silva, 10 April 1965, in Thomas Merton, *The Courage for Truth: Letters to Writers*, selected and edited by Christine M. Bochen (New York: Farrar, Straus & Giroux, 1993), 225.

23. Thomas Merton, *The Wisdom of the Desert* (New York: New Directions, 1960), 23.

24. Merton to Leslie Dewart, 10 May 1963 and n.d. (between 10 May and 28 June 1963), *Witness to Freedom: Letters in Times of Crisis*, selected and edited by William H. Shannon (New York: Farrar, Straus & Giroux), 287–288, 291.

25. Merton to Daniel Berrigan, 25 June 1963, in Thomas Merton, *The Hidden Ground of Love: Letters on Religious Experience and Social Concerns*, selected and edited by William H. Shannon (New York: Farrar, Straus & Giroux), 78–79.

26. Thomas Merton, *Turning Toward the World: The Journals of Thomas Merton, Volume Four 1960–1963*, edited by Victor A. Kramer (New York: HarperCollins, 1996), 75.

27. Thomas Merton, *Dancing in the Water of Life: The Journals of Thomas Merton, Volume Five 1963–1965*, edited by Robert E. Daggy (New York: HarperCollins, 1997), 100–101.

28. Ibid., 297–298.

29. Ibid., 325–326.

30. *Thomas Merton and James Laughlin: Selected Letters*, 291.

31. John Howard Griffin, *Follow the Ecstasy: Thomas Merton, The Hermitage Years, 1965–1968* (Fort Worth: JHG Editions/Latitudes Press, 1983), 81–82.

32. Mott, *The Seven Mountains of Thomas Merton*, 454.

33. Thomas Merton, *The Asian Journal of Thomas Merton*, edited by Naomi Burton Stone, Patrick Hart, ocso, and James Laughlin (New York: New Directions, 1973), 286.

34. Merton to Rosemary Radford Ruether, 5 May 1967, in Thomas Merton, *At Home in the World: The Letters of Thomas Merton & Rosemary Radford Ruether*, edited by Mary Tardiff, op (Maryknoll: Orbis, 1995), 65–66.

35. *The Asian Journal of Thomas Merton*, 236.

36. Thomas Merton, *Woods, Shore, Desert — A Notebook, May 1968*, introduction and notes by Joel Weishaus (Santa Fe: Museum of New Mexico Press, 1982), 55.

37. Merton to Sister J.M., 17 June 1968, *The School of Charity*, 385.

CHAPTER 2 / THARMAS: THE REBEL

1. Thomas Merton, *The Literary Essays of Thomas Merton*, edited by Patrick Hart, ocso (New York: New Directions, 1981), 451.

2. Ibid., 6.

3. Peter Ackroyd, *Blake* (London: Minerva, 1996), 89.

4. Ibid., 200.

5. Ibid., 337.

6. *Literary Essays*, 6.

7. Ibid., 425–426.

8. Ibid., 8.

9. Ibid., 9.

10. Thomas Merton, *Seven Storey Mountain* (New York: Harcourt Brace, 1948), 190.

11. *Literary Essays*, 7.

12. Michael Mott, *Seven Mountains of Thomas Merton* (Boston: Houghton Mifflin, 1984), 37.

13. *Seven Storey Mountain*, 51.

14. *Seven Mountains of Thomas Merton*, 40.

15. Andrew Sinclair, *Dylan Thomas: No Man More Magical* (New York: Holt, Rinehart and Winston, 1975), 229.

16. Thomas Merton, *The Secular Journal of Thomas Merton* (New York: Farrar, Straus & Cudahy, 1959), 28.

17. Thomas Merton, *My Argument with the Gestapo* (New York: Doubleday, 1969), 160–161.

18. Ibid., 127.

19. Ibid., 128.

20. Thomas Merton, "Monastic Peace," in *The Monastic Journey*, edited by Patrick Hart, ocso (Kansas City: Sheed Andrews and McMeel, 1977), 62.

21. Ibid., 43.

22. Raimundo Panikkar, *Blessed Simplicity: The Monk as Universal Archetype* (New York: Seabury Press, 1982), 11.

23. Francis Thompson, "The Hound of Heaven," in *A Little Treasury of Modern Poetry*, edited by Oscar Williams (New York: Charles Scribner's Sons, 1952), 602.

24. Thomas Merton, *The Sign of Jonas* (New York: Doubleday/ Image, 1956), 199–200.

25. Northrop Frye, *Fearful Symmetry: A Study of William Blake* (Princeton: Princeton University Press, 1947), 195.

26. Thomas Merton, *The Silent Life* (New York: Farrar, Straus & Giroux, 1957), xiii.

27. Thomas Merton, *Run to the Mountain: The Journals of Thomas Merton, Volume One 1939–1941*, edited by Patrick Hart, ocso (New York: HarperCollins, 1995), 223.

28. Thomas Merton, *Entering the Silence: The Journals of Thomas Merton, Volume Two 1941–1952*, edited by Jonathan Montaldo (New York: HarperCollins, 1996), 174.

29. Merton to Dom Jean Leclercq, 3 June 1955, in Thomas Merton, *The School of Charity: Letters on Religious Renewal and Spiritual Direction*, selected and edited by Patrick Hart, OCSO (New York: Farrar, Straus & Giroux, 1990), 86.

30. Thomas Merton, *A Search for Solitude: The Journals of Thomas Merton, Volume Three 1952–1960*, edited by Lawrence S. Cunningham (New York: HarperCollins, 1996), 202.

31. Thomas Merton, *Turning Toward the World: The Journals of Thomas Merton, Volume Four 1960–1963*, edited by Victor A. Kramer (New York: HarperCollins, 1996), 64–65.

32. Merton to Wilbur Ferry, 18 September 1961, in Thomas Merton, *The Hidden Ground of Love: Letters on Religious Experience and Social Concerns*, selected and edited by William H. Shannon (New York: Farrar, Straus & Giroux, 1985), 203.

33. Ibid., Merton to James Forest, 29 April (Low Sunday) 1962.

34. *Turning Toward the World*, 250.

35. Thomas Merton, *Dancing in the Water of Life: The Journals of Thomas Merton, Volume Five 1963–1965*, edited by Robert E. Daggy (New York: HarperCollins, 1997), 46.

36. Ibid., 79.

37. Merton to Jean Leclercq, 22 October 1964, in *The School of Charity*, 247.

38. Merton to Jim Forest, 9 December 1964, in *The Hidden Ground of Love*, 283.

39. Ibid., Merton to Dom Francis Decroix, 21 August 1967, 158.

40. Ibid., Merton to June J. Yungblut, 29 March 1968, 643–644.

41. *Literary Essays*, 7.

42. *A Search for Solitude*, 351.

43. *Dancing in the Water of Life*, 289.

CHAPTER 3 / URIZEN: THE MARGINAL CRITIC

1. Thomas Merton, *Turning Toward the World: The Journals of Thomas Merton, Volume Four 1960–1963*, edited by Victor A. Kramer (New York: HarperCollins, 1996), 320.

2. David Bindman, *William Blake: His Art and Times* (Toronto: Yale Center for British Art, Art Gallery of Ontario, 1982), 17.

3. Thomas Merton, *The Literary Essays of Thomas Merton*, edited by Patrick Hart, OCSO (New York: New Directions, 1981), 427–428.

4. Merton to Leslie Dewart, n.d., between 10 May and 23 June 1963, in *Witness to Freedom: Letters in Times of Crisis*, selected and edited by William H. Shannon (New York: Farrar, Straus & Giroux, 1994), 291.

5. Ibid., Merton to Dewart, n.d., but between 10 May and 28 June 1963, 292–293.

6. Thomas Merton, *A Search for Solitude: The Journals of Thomas Merton, Volume Three 1952–1960*, edited by Lawrence S. Cunningham (New York: HarperCollins, 1996), 316.

7. *Literary Essays*, 409.

8. Northrop Frye, *Fearful Symmetry: A Study of William Blake* (Princeton: Princeton University Press, 1947), 114.

9. *Literary Essays*, 426, 427.

10. Ibid., 391.

11. Ibid., 444–445.

12. Jacques Maritain, *Creative Intuition in Art and Poetry* (New York: World Publishing Company, 1965), 90.

13. William Blake, *Blake: Complete Writings*, edited by Geoffrey Keynes (London: Oxford University Press, 1969), 794.

14. *Literary Essays*, 443.

15. *Fearful Symmetry*, 206.

16. Thomas Merton, *The Secular Journal of Thomas Merton* (New York: Farrar, Straus & Cudahy, 1959), 24.

17. *Literary Essays*, 436.

18. Mark Van Doren, introduction to *Selected Poems of Thomas Merton* (New York: New Directions, 1967), xii.

19. Norman O. Brown, *Love's Body* (New York: Vintage Books, 1966), 183.

20. Archibald MacLeish, *The Fall of the City* (New York: Farrar & Rinehart, 1937), 23.

21. Carl Gustav Jung, *The Undiscovered Self* (New York: Mentor Books, 1958), 88–89.

22. Thomas Merton, quoted in Edward Rice, *The Man in the Sycamore Tree: The Good Times and Hard Life of Thomas Merton* (New York: Image Books, 1972), 149.

23. Thomas Merton, "Cargo Cults of the South Pacific," *Love and Living*, edited by Naomi Burton Stone and Patrick Hart, ocso (New York: Farrar, Straus & Giroux, 1979), 87.

24. W.H. Auden, *Forewords and Afterwords* (New York: Vintage Books, 1974), 78.

25. Thomas Merton, *Conjectures of a Guilty Bystander* (New York: Doubleday/Image, 1968), 349.

26. Thomas Merton, *Raids on the Unspeakable* (New York: New Directions, 1966), 160.

27. Ibid., 161.

28. Ibid., 159.

29. Ibid.

30. Merton to Rosita and Ludovico Silva, 10 April 1965, in *The Courage for Truth: Letters to Writers*, selected and edited by Christine M. Bochen (New York: Farrar, Straus & Giroux, 1993), 225.

31. *Raids on the Unspeakable*, 173.

32. Ibid., 106.

33. Thomas Merton, *A Vow of Conversation: Journals 1964–1965* (New York: Farrar, Straus & Giroux, 1988), 99.

34. *Conjectures*, 76–77.

35. George Steiner, *In Bluebeard's Castle: Some Notes Towards the Re-definition of Culture* (London: Faber & Faber, 1971), 53–54.

36. Merton to Sister M. Emmanuel, 9 August 1961, in Thomas Merton, *The Hidden Ground of Love: Letters on Religious Experience and Social Concerns*, selected and edited by William H. Shannon (New York: Farrar, Straus & Giroux, 1985), 185.

37. *Conjectures*, 288.

38. *Raids on the Unspeakable*, 46–47.

39. *Conjectures*, 241.

40. Thomas Merton, *Seeds of Destruction* (New York: Farrar, Straus & Giroux, 1964), 297.

41. *Turning Toward the World*, 317–318.

42. Thomas Merton, *Dancing in the Water of Life: The Journals of Thomas Merton, Volume Five 1963–1965*, edited by Robert E. Daggy (New York: HarperCollins, 1997), 15–16.

43. Thomas Merton, *The Seven Storey Mountain* (New York: Harcourt Brace, 1948), 345–346.

44. Thomas Merton, quoted in the Canadian Broadcasting Corporation's *Ideas* series, "Thomas Merton: Extraordinary Man," originally aired in December 1978, during the tenth anniversary week of Thomas Merton's death. This excerpt is from Program Three: "Marginal Man/Social Critic."

45. *Turning Toward the World*, 300.

46. *Seeds of Destruction*, 44.

47. Merton to Robert Lawrence Williams, 16 July 1968, in *The Hidden Ground of Love*, 605.

48. Merton to Cid Corman, 5 September 1966, in *The Courage for Truth*, 248–249.

49. Thomas Merton, *The Way of Chuang Tzu* (New York: New Directions, 1969), 30.

50. Thomas Merton, "Final Integration — Toward a 'Monastic Therapy,'" in *Contemplation in a World of Action* (New York: Doubleday/Image, 1973), 225–226.

51. Thomas Merton, *The Asian Journal of Thomas Merton*, edited by Naomi Burton Stone, Patrick Hart, ocso, and James Laughlin (New York: New Directions, 1973), 118.

52. Thomas Merton, "'Baptism in the Forest': Wisdom and Initiation in William Faulkner," in *Mansions of the Spirit: Essays in Literature and*

Religion, edited by George A. Panichas (New York: Hawthorn Books, 1967), 26–27.

53. Thomas Merton, "The Pasternak Affair," in *Disputed Questions* (New York: Farrar, Straus & Giroux, 1960), 31.

CHAPTER 4 / LUVAH: THE LOVER

1. Merton to Clayton Eshelman, 18 October 1966, in Thomas Merton, *The Courage for Truth: Letters to Writers,* selected and edited by Christine M. Bochen (New York: Farrar, Straus & Giroux, 1993), 263.

2. Thomas Merton, *Learning to Love: The Journals of Thomas Merton, Volume Six 1966–1967,* edited by Christine M. Bochen (New York: Harper-Collins, 1997), 79.

3. John Howard Griffin, quoted in *Ideas,* "Thomas Merton: Extraordinary Man," Program One: "Introduction to the Man."

4. Thomas Merton, *The Seven Storey Mountain* (New York: Harcourt Brace, 1948), 403.

5. Mark Van Doren, introduction to *Selected Poems of Thomas Merton* (New York: New Directions, 1967), xvii.

6. James Fox, "The Spiritual Son," in *Thomas Merton, Monk,* edited by Patrick Hart, OCSO (New York: Sheed and Ward, 1974), 143.

7. Thomas Merton, *Entering the Silence: The Journals of Thomas Merton, Volume Two 1941–1952,* edited by Jonathan Montaldo (New York: Harper-Collins, 1996), 261.

8. Ibid., 224.

9. Thomas Merton, *A Search for Solitude: The Journals of Thomas Merton, Volume Three 1952–1960,* edited by Lawrence S. Cunningham (New York: HarperCollins, 1996), 60.

10. Merton to Boris Pasternak, 23 October 1958, in *The Courage for Truth,* 90.

11. *A Search for Solitude,* 241.

12. Ibid., 326.

13. Thomas Merton, *Turning Toward the World: The Journals of Thomas Merton, Volume Four 1960–1963,* edited by Victor A. Kramer (New York: HarperCollins, 1996), 151–152.

14. Thomas Merton, *Dancing in the Water of Life: The Journals of Thomas Merton, Volume Five 1963–1965,* edited by Robert E. Daggy (New York: HarperCollins, 1997), 198.

15. Ibid., 259.

16. Ibid., 281.

17. Ibid., 327–328.

18. *Learning to Love,* 44.

19. Ibid., 52.

20. Ibid., 54.
21. Ibid., 66–67.
22. Ibid., 71.
23. Ibid., 75.
24. Ibid., 77.
25. Ibid., 312.
26. Ibid., 328–329.
27. Ibid., 330.
28. Ibid., 94.
29. Ibid., 108.
30. Ibid., 162.
31. Ibid., 234.
32. Ibid., 87.

CHAPTER 5 / URTHONA: THE WISE ONE

1. T.F. Rigelhof, *A Blue Boy in a Black Dress* (Ottawa: Oberon, 1995), 64.
2. Thomas Merton, *Conjectures of a Guilty Bystander* (New York: Doubleday/Image, 1968), 131–132.
3. Thomas Merton, *Turning Toward the World: The Journals of Thomas Merton, Volume Four 1960–1963*, edited by Victor A. Kramer (New York: HarperCollins, 1996), 17.
4. *Conjectures*, 158.
5. George Steiner, *Language and Silence: Essays on Language, Literature and the Inhuman* (New York: Atheneum, 1976), 49–51, 54.
6. Thomas Merton, *Contemplation in a World of Action* (New York: Doubleday/Image, 1973), 210.
7. Thomas Merton, *The Monastic Journey*, edited by Patrick Hart, ocso (Kansas City: Sheed Andrews and McMeel, 1977), 153–154.
8. *Contemplation*, 176.
9. Thomas Merton, *Raids on the Unspeakable* (New York: New Directions, 1966), 182.
10. *Contemplation*, 386.
11. Gabriel Marcel, *Man Against Mass Society* (Chicago: Henry Regnery, 1962), 65.
12. Thomas Merton, *The Asian Journal of Thomas Merton*, edited by Naomi Burton Stone, Patrick Hart, ocso and James Laughlin (New York: New Directions, 1973), 333.
13. R. Murray Schafer, *The Tuning of the World* (Toronto: McClelland and Stewart, 1977), 258.
14. Thomas Merton, *Zen and the Birds of Appetite* (New York: New Directions, 1968), 48–49.
15. *Conjectures*, 284–285.

16. Ibid., 285.

17. *Zen and the Birds of Appetite*, 140–141.

18. *Conjectures*, 144.

19. Thomas Merton, *The Sign of Jonas* (New York: Doubleday/ Image, 1956), 313.

20. Thomas Merton, *A Search for Solitude: The Journals of Thomas Merton, Volume Three 1952–1960*, edited by Lawrence S. Cunningham (New York: HarperCollins, 1996), 168–169.

21. Thomas Merton, *The Courage for Truth: Letters to Writers*, selected and edited by Christine M. Bochen (New York: Farrar, Straus & Giroux, 1993), 141.

22. George Woodcock, *Thomas Merton: Monk and Poet* (Vancouver: Douglas & McIntyre, 1978), 181.

23. Daniel Berrigan, *Cross Currents*, 27, no. 4 (Winter 1977–78), 390.

24. Thomas Merton, *Ishi Means Man* (Greensboro: Unicorn Press, 1976), 20.

25. Ibid., 58–59.

26. Ibid., 65.

27. Ibid., 11.

28. *Asian Journal*, 101.

29. The Dalai Lama, in *Merton By Those Who Knew Him Best*, edited by Paul Wilkes (New York: Harper & Row, 1984), 147.

30. *Asian Journal*, 233–236.

31. This excerpt is from "Pilgrim to the East," in the CBC *Ideas* series, "Thomas Merton: Extraordinary Man," subsequently published as an epilogue to *Thomas Merton: Pilgrim in Process* by Donald Grayston and Michael W. Higgins (Toronto: Griffin House, 1983).

List of Interviews

(Unreferenced quotations derived
from the following interviews)

Bamberger, John Eudes, ocso: interviewed at the Abbey of the Genesee, New York, on January 31, 1998.

Berrigan, Daniel, sj: interviewed at New York on July 25, 1992, and on August 9, 1997.

Bochen, Christine: interviewed at Rochester, New York, on January 30, 1998.

Forest, Jim: interviewed at Alkmaar, Netherlands, on February 20, 1997.

Giroux, Robert: interviewed at the Abbey of Gethsemani, Kentucky, on October 9, 1997.

Grayston, Donald: interviewed at Vancouver, British Columbia, on March 19, 1998.

Goulet, Jacques: interviewed at Mobile, Alabama, on June 13, 1997.

Hart, Patrick, ocso: interviewed at the Abbey of Gethsemani on October 12, 1997.

Kelly, Timothy, ocso: interviewed at the Abbey of Gethsemani on October 9, 1997.

Labrie, Ross: interviewed at Mobile, Alabama, on June 13, 1997.

Mott, Michael: interviewed at Williamsburg, Virginia, on February 11 and 12, 1998.

Padovano, Anthony: interviewed at Mobile, Alabama, on June 12, 1997.

Quenon, Paul, ocso: interviewed at the Abbey of Gethsemani on October 9, 1997.

Rigelhof, T.F.: interviewed at Montreal, Quebec, on December 11, 1996.

Shannon, William: interviewed at Rochester, New York, on January 30, 1998.

Seitz, Ron: interviewed at Mesa, Arizona, on January 27, 1998.

Zahn, Gordon: interviewed at Vancouver, British Columbia, on May 10, 1978.

Sources Cited

Ackroyd, Peter. *Blake.* London: Minerva, 1996.

Auden, W.H. *Forewords and Afterwords.* New York: Vintage Books, 1974.

Berrigan, Daniel. "The Seventy Times Seventy Seven Storey Mountain," *Cross Currents*, 27, No. 4 (Winter 1977–78).

Bindman, David. *William Blake: His Art and Times.* Toronto: Yale Center for British Art, Art Gallery of Ontario, 1982.

Blake, William. *Blake: The Complete Writings.* Ed. Geoffrey Keynes. London: Oxford University Press, 1969.

Brown, Norman O. *Love's Body.* New York: Vintage Books, 1966.

Clapp, Suzannah. "The Life and Early Death of Bruce Chatwin," *The New Yorker*, December 23 and 30, 1996.

Cooper, David D., ed. *Thomas Merton and James Laughlin: Selected Essays.* New York: W.W. Norton, 1997.

Fox, James. "The Spiritual Son," in *Thomas Merton, Monk.* Ed. Patrick Hart, ocso. New York: Sheed and Ward, 1974.

Frye, Northrop. *Fearful Symmetry: A Study of William Blake.* Princeton: Princeton University Press, 1947.

Griffin, John Howard. *Follow the Ecstasy: Thomas Merton, The Hermitage Years, 1965–1968.* Fort Worth: JHG Editions/Latitude Press, 1983.

Hart, Patrick, ocso, ed. *Thomas Merton, Monk.* New York: Sheed and Ward, 1974.

Jung, Carl Gustav. *The Undiscovered Self.* New York: Mentor Books, 1958.

MacLeish, Archibald. *The Fall of the City.* New York: Farrar & Rinehart, 1937.

Marcel, Gabriel. *Man Against Mass Society.* Chicago: Henry Regnery, 1962.

Maritain, Jacques. *Creative Intuition in Art and Poetry.* New York: World Publishing Company, 1965.

Merton, Thomas. *A Search for Solitude: The Journals of Thomas Merton, Volume Three 1952–1960.* Ed. Lawrence S. Cunningham. New York: HarperCollins, 1996.

_____. *The Asian Journal of Thomas Merton.* Ed. Naomi Burton Stone, Patrick Hart, OCSO, and James Laughlin. New York: New Directions, 1973.

_____. *At Home in the World: The Letters of Thomas Merton & Rosemary Radford Ruether.* Ed. Mary Tardiff, OP. Maryknoll: Orbis, 1995.

_____. *A Vow of Conversation: Journals 1964–1965.* New York: Farrar, Straus & Giroux, 1988.

_____. *Collected Poems of Thomas Merton.* New York: New Directions, 1977.

_____. *Conjectures of a Guilty Bystander.* New York: Doubleday/Image, 1968.

_____. *Contemplation in a World of Action.* New York: Doubleday/Image, 1973.

_____. *The Courage for Truth: Letters to Writers.* Selected and edited by Christine M. Bochen. New York: Farrar, Straus & Giroux, 1993.

_____. *Dancing in the Water of Life: The Journals of Thomas Merton, Volume Five 1963–1965.* Ed. Robert E. Daggy. New York: HarperCollins, 1997.

_____. *Disputed Questions.* New York: Farrar, Straus & Giroux, 1960.

_____. *Entering the Silence: The Journals of Thomas Merton, Volume Two 1941–1952.* Ed. Jonathan Montaldo. New York: HarperCollins, 1996.

_____. *The Hidden Ground of Love: Letters on Religious Experience and Social Concerns.* Selected and edited by William H. Shannon. New York: Farrar, Straus & Giroux, 1985.

_____. *Introductions East & West: The Foreign Prefaces of Thomas Merton.* Ed. Robert E. Daggy. Greensboro: Unicorn Press, 1981.

_____. *Ishi Means Man.* Greensboro: Unicorn Press, 1976.

_____. *Learning to Love: The Journals of Thomas Merton, Volume Six 1966–1967.* Ed. Christine M. Bochen. New York: HarperCollins, 1997.

_____. *The Literary Essays of Thomas Merton.* Ed. Patrick Hart, OCSO. New York: New Directions, 1981.

_____. *Love and Living.* Ed. Naomi Burton Stone and Patrick Hart, OCSO. New York: Farrar, Straus & Giroux, 1979.

_____. *The Monastic Journey.* Ed. Patrick Hart, OCSO. Kansas City: Sheed Andrews and McMeel, 1977.

_____. *My Argument with the Gestapo.* New York: Doubleday, 1969.

_____. *Raids on the Unspeakable.* New York: New Directions, 1966.

_____. *The Road to Joy: Letters to New and Old Friends.* Selected and edited by Robert E. Daggy. New York: Farrar, Straus & Giroux, 1989.

_____. *Run to the Mountain: The Journals of Thomas Merton, Volume One 1939–1941.* Ed. Patrick Hart, OCSO. New York: HarperCollins, 1995.

_____. *The School of Charity: Letters on Religious Renewal and Spiritual*

Direction. Selected and edited by Patrick Hart, OCSO. New York: Farrar, Straus & Giroux, 1990.

_____ . *The Secular Journal of Thomas Merton*. New York: Farrar, Straus & Cudahy, 1959.

_____ . *Seeds of Destruction*. New York: Farrar, Straus & Giroux, 1964.

_____ . *Selected Poems of Thomas Merton*. New York: New Directions, 1967.

_____ . *The Seven Storey Mountain*. New York: Harcourt Brace, 1948.

_____ . *The Sign of Jonas*. New York: Doubleday/Image, 1956.

_____ . *The Silent Life*. New York: Farrar, Straus & Giroux, 1957.

_____ . *Turning Toward the World: The Journals of Thomas Merton, Volume Four 1960–1963*. Ed. Victor A. Kramer. New York: HarperCollins, 1996.

_____ . *The Way of Chuang Tzu*. New York: New Directions, 1969.

_____ . *The Wisdom of the Desert*. New York: New Directions, 1960.

_____ . *Witness to Freedom: Letters in Times of Crisis*. Selected and edited by William H. Shannon. New York: Farrar, Straus & Giroux, 1994.

_____ . *Woods, Shore, Desert — A Notebook, May 1968*. Introduction and notes by Joel Weishaus. Santa Fe: Museum of New Mexico Press, 1982.

_____ . *Zen and the Birds of Appetite*. New York: New Directions, 1968.

Mott, Michael. *The Seven Mountains of Thomas Merton*. Boston: Houghton Mifflin, 1984.

Panichas, George A., ed. *Mansions of the Spirit: Essays in Literature and Religion*. New York: Hawthorn Books, 1967.

Panikkar, Raimundo. *Blessed Simplicity: The Monk as Universal Archetype*. New York: Seabury Press, 1982.

Porter, J.S. "Silent Lamp: The Lives of Thomas Merton," *Brick: A Literary Journal*, no. 55, Fall 1996.

Rice, Edward. *The Man in the Sycamore Tree: The Good Times and Hard Life of Thomas Merton*. New York: Image Books, 1972.

Rigelhof, T.F. *A Blue Boy in a Black Dress*. Ottawa: Oberon, 1995.

Schafer, R. Murray. *The Tuning of the World*. Toronto: McClelland and Stewart, 1977.

Sinclair, Andrew. *Dylan Thomas: No Man More Magical*. New York: Holt, Rinehart and Winston, 1975.

Steiner, George. *Extraterritoriality*. New York: Atheneum, 1971.

_____ . *In Bluebeard's Castle: Some Notes Toward the Re-definition of Culture*. London: Faber & Faber, 1971.

_____ . *Language and Silence: Essays on Language, Literature and the Inhuman*. New York: Atheneum, 1976.

Van Doren, Mark. Introduction to *Selected Poems of Thomas Merton*. New York: New Directions, 1967.

Wilkes, Paul, ed. *Merton By Those Who Knew Him Best*. New York: Harper & Row, 1984.

Williams, Oscar, ed. *A Little Treasury of Modern Poetry*. New York: Charles
    Scribner's Sons, 1952.
Woodcock, George. *Thomas Merton: Monk and Poet*. Vancouver: Douglas &
    McIntyre, 1978.

Additional Sources on and by Thomas Merton

Adams, Daniel J. *Thomas Merton's Shared Contemplation: A Protestant Perspective.* Kalamazoo, Michigan: Cistercian Publications, 1979.

Bailey, Raymond. *Thomas Merton on Mysticism.* Garden City, NY: Doubleday, 1975.

Baker, James Thomas. *Thomas Merton, Social Critic: A Study.* Lexington: University Press of Kentucky, 1971.

Carr, Anne E. *A Search for Wisdom and Spirit: Thomas Merton's Theology of the Self.* Notre Dame: University of Notre Dame Press, 1988.

Cashen, Richard Anthony. *Solitude in the Thought of Thomas Merton.* Kalamazoo, Michigan: Cistercian Publications, 1981.

Cooper, David D. *Thomas Merton's Art of Denial: The Evolution of a Radical Humanist.* Athens: University of Georgia Press, 1989.

De Waal, Esther. *A Seven Day Journey with Thomas Merton.* Ann Arbor, Michigan: Servant Publications, 1992.

Del Prete, Thomas. *Thomas Merton and the Education of the Whole Person.* Birmingham, Ala: Religious Education Press, 1990.

Forest, James H. *Thomas Merton: A Pictorial Biography.* New York: Paulist Press, 1980.

Furlong, Monica. *Merton: A Biography.* New York: Harper & Row, 1980.

Grayston, Donald. *Thomas Merton, the Development of a Spiritual Theologian.* New York: E. Mellen Press, 1985.

Griffin, John Howard. *A Hidden Wholeness: The Visual World of Thomas Merton.* Boston: Houghton Mifflin, 1970.

_____. *The Hermitage Journals: A Diary Kept While Working on the Biography of Thomas Merton.* Garden City, NY: Image Books, 1983.

Higgins, John J. *Thomas Merton on Prayer.* Garden City, NY: Image Books, 1975.

Higgins, Michael W. and Grayston, Donald. *Thomas Merton: Pilgrim in Process.* Toronto: Griffin House, 1983.

Kelly, Frederic Joseph. *Man before God: Thomas Merton on Social Responsibility.* Garden City, NY: Doubleday, 1974.

Kilcourse, George. *Ace of Freedoms: Thomas Merton's Christ.* Notre Dame: University of Notre Dame Press, 1993.

King, Thomas Mulvihill. *Merton: Mystic at the Center of America.* Collegeville, Minnesota: Liturgical Press, 1992.

Kountz, Peter. *Thomas Merton as Writer and Monk: A Cultural Study, 1915–1951.* Brooklyn, NY: Carlson Publishing, 1991.

Kramer, Victor A. *Thomas Merton: Monk and Artist.* Kalamazoo, Michigan: Cistercian Publications, 1987.

Labrie, Ross. *The Art of Thomas Merton.* Fort Worth: Texas Christian University Press, 1979.

Lentfoehr, Therese. *Words and Silence: On the Poetry of Thomas Merton.* New York: New Directions, 1979.

Malits, Elena. *The Solitary Explorer: Thomas Merton's Transforming Journey.* San Francisco: Harper & Row, 1980.

McInerny, Dennis Q. *Thomas Merton: The Man and His Work.* Spencer, Mass: Cistercian Publications, 1974.

Meatyard, Ralph Eugene. *Father Louie: Photographs of Thomas Merton.* New York: Timken Publishers, 1991.

Merton, Thomas. *A Catch of Anti-Letters.* Kansas City, Kansas: Sheed Andrews and McMeel, 1978.

_____. *The Ascent to Truth.* New York: Harcourt Brace Jovanovich, 1981.

_____. *Contemplative Prayer.* New York: Image Books, 1992.

_____. *Eighteen Poems.* New York: New Directions, 1985.

_____. *Faith and Violence: Christian Teaching and Christian Practice.* Notre Dame: University of Notre Dame Press, 1968.

_____. *Letters from Tom: a Selection of Letters from Father Thomas Merton, monk of Gethsemani, to W.H. Ferry, 1961–1968.* Scarsdale, NY: Fort Hill Press, 1983.

_____. *Life and Holiness.* New York: Doubleday, 1990.

_____. *The Living Bread.* New York: Farrar, Straus & Giroux, 1980.

_____. *Mystics and Zen Masters.* New York: Farrar, Straus & Giroux, 1967.

_____. *No Man Is an Island.* New York: Phoenix Press, 1986.

_____. *The Nonviolent Alternative.* New York: Farrar, Straus & Giroux, 1980.

_____. *Spiritual Direction and Meditation.* Collegeville, Minn: Liturgical Press, 1960.

_____. *Thomas Merton in Alaska.* New York: New Directions, 1989.

_____. *Thomas Merton on Saint Bernard.* Kalamazoo, Michigan: Cistercian Publications, 1980.

_____ . *Thomas Merton on the Psalms*. London: Sheldon Press, 1977.

_____ . *The Waters of Siloe*. New York: Harcourt Brace Jovanovich, 1979.

Nouwen, Henri J.M. *Thomas Merton: A Contemplative Critic*. Notre Dame: Fides Publishers, 1972.

Padovano, Anthony T. *The Human Journey: Thomas Merton, Symbol of a Century*. Garden City, NY: Doubleday, 1982.

Pennington, M. Basil. *Thomas Merton, Brother Monk: The Quest for True Freedom*. San Francisco: Harper & Row, 1987.

Rice, Edward. *The Man in the Sycamore Tree: The Good Times and Hard Life of Thomas Merton: an Entertainment with Photographs*. San Diego: Harcourt Brace Jovanovich, 1985.

Seitz, Ron. *Song for Nobody: A Memory Vision of Thomas Merton*. Liguori, Missouri: Triumph Books, 1993.

Shannon, William Henry. *Silent Lamp: The Thomas Merton Story*. New York: Crossroad, 1992.

_____ . *Thomas Merton's Dark Path: The Inner Experience of a Contemplative*. New York: Farrar, Straus & Giroux, 1981.

Sussman, Cornelia. *Thomas Merton: The Daring Young Man on the Flying Belltower*. New York: Macmillan, 1976.

Index

Copyright
Acknowledgements